Neon Genesis
Evangelion and
Philosophy

Pop Culture and Philosophy®

General Editor: George A. Reisch

For full details of all Pop Culture and Philosophy® books, and all Open Universe® books, visit www.carusbooks.com.

Pop Culture and Philosophy®

Neon Genesis Evangelion and Philosophy

That Syncing Feeling

Edited by
CHRISTIAN COTTON AND
ANDREW M. WINTERS

OPEN UNIVERSE
Chicago

Volume 2 in the series, Pop Culture and Philosophy®, edited by George A. Reisch

To find out more about Open Universe and Carus Books, visit our website at www.carusbooks.com.

Neon Genesis Evangelion *and Philosophy: That Syncing Feeling*

ISBN: 978-1-63770-004-4

This book is also available as an e-book (978-1-63770-005-1).

Library of Congress Control Number: 2021941785

AMW: For Shawn and my
students who convinced me to watch
Neon Genesis Evangelion.

CC: To all the
Neon Genesis Evangelion *fans,*
freaks, and philosophers,
past, present.

Contents

Thanks

Thank you to George Reisch and David Ramsay Steele for taking on this project. A heartfelt 'thank you' to all the authors who have been patient with the editing process as we watched the world go through the transformation in 2020 and 2021. You can (not) return to what is normal. Last, a big thank you to both the fans of *Neon Genesis Evangelion* and the fans of philosophy who inspired this project.

The Consolations of Anime

ANDREW M. WINTERS

Imagine all things have gone dark. You do not know who or where you are. Your lungs feel as though they're filled with liquid. You panic, thinking that you will drown. But with each gasp for air, you realize that you are not suffocating. You begin to relax. Soon you're able to breathe more normally.

Where am I? You struggle to open your eyes, realizing that they are firmly squeezed shut. As amber-colored light penetrates your eyelids, you slowly begin to open them. A control panel is before you. Its glowing buttons and knobs invite you to go on a journey. *Where will I go?* You are connected to something that is not yourself, but oddly you are in sync with it. Each of your movements corresponds to a movement of this thing that is larger than yourself. Or have its movements caused you to move? You are somehow one with this thing that is not you. Yet, you still do not know who this you *is. Who am I?*

From the depths of your mind you hear a soft voice singing. *Zankokunatenshi no yō ni (Like a cruel angel).* Who is this cruel angel? *Shō nen'yo shinwa ni nare (Boy, become a legend).* Who is this boy? What is the legend to be fulfilled?

Who is singing these words? They do not provide comfort. Yet, they encourage you to discover where you are, where you will go, and who you are. Only through your persistence will you realize that you are the pilot of something greater than yourself. Only through your willingness to discover who you are will your life have meaning. Waking to realize that you are the pilot of an EVA is similar to the experience of realizing that you are alive. Only when answering the call of a cruel angel will you have the chance to shine like a legend. Each of us has been confronted with the challenge of discovering who we are and who we wish to be. Yet, we must first recognize where we are to reasonably expect who we can be.

Many of those who came before us found solace in philosophy while grappling with similar existential quandaries. For example, the Roman statesman Boethius (around 477–524) looked to the muses for answers to similar questions while imprisoned awaiting his own execution.

I who once wrote songs with joyful zeal
Am driven by grief to enter weeping mode.
See the Muses, cheeks all torn, dictate,
And wet my face with elegiac verse.

It was when Philosophy greeted him with her "awe-inspiring appearance" that he was able to better understand his fate. With the aid of song, she guided Boethius to realize that his pursuance of Fortune led him down the path of despair. Instead of focusing on the larger truths provided by Philosophy, he had committed himself to a life of pride and success. But Fortune does not care how success is gained and to become prideful is to take on the unreflective values of others. Philosophy helped him see how pursuing Fortune is to give away his life. The extent to which he had given away his life was made even more clear as he awaited his own execution. But Philosophy did more than reveal to Boethius how he had ended up in chains. She showed him how in his final moments he could regain his freedom; he could still die a free man.

Boethius is not the only one to have been comforted by philosophy. As Alain de Botton (still alive) discusses in his *Consolations of Philosophy*, historical figures such as Socrates (around 470–399 B.C.E.), Epicurus (341–270 B.C.E.), Montaigne (1533–1592), Seneca (around 4 B.C.E.–65 C.E.), Schopenhauer (1788–1860), and Nietzsche (1844–1900) looked to the muses and philosophy to overcome the obstacles of existence and find meaning in their lives, regardless of their situations. Socrates faced his own death sentence with equanimity. Epicurus learned to find pleasure in the company of close friends without the burdens of material goods. Montaigne took on the challenges of encountering different cultural practices. Seneca modeled his own death sentence after Socrates's. Schopenhauer (who coined the *hedgehog dilemma*) found consolation in philosophy while overcoming the pain of heartache when dealing with others. Nietzsche found his ambition and inspiration from philosophy in his attempts to overcome banality and live a courageous life.

Socrates, Seneca, and Boethius, like Shinji, did not ask to be imprisoned as they faced the inevitability of their own deaths. Yet, with the aid of philosophy and deep reflection they were able to accept their fates (*amor fati*). Like us, Shinji and the aforementioned thinkers did not ask to be born, yet our deaths are inevitable. With the aid of philosophy, we can learn to become more tranquil and courageous, learning that many of our own fears, anxieties, and frustrations are the results of ill-guided perceptions and not the situations themselves.

Whereas Shinji discovered himself by answering the call of cruel Angels, Boethius and the others found themselves consoled by the words of philosophy. Where might we find solace given that many of us do not have the kinds of leisurely lives necessary for deep philosophical reflection? The authors in this book offer some consolation for the precariousness of life by drawing connections between the anime *Neon Genesis Evangelion* and philosophy. Why anime, though?

When most people think of anime, they think of large-eyed adolescents fighting fearsome monsters (*kaiju*). This was certainly the case for many anime from the 1990s that made their way from Japan to American television sets. These earlier anime, however, gave Westerners the impression that Japanese exports would only highlight battle scenes involving mecha and overly enthusiastic high schoolers who always donned their school uniforms and possessed supernatural abilities.

Anime as a stylized form has much more to offer than mere flashy entertainment and fan service. Even when shows like *Dragon Ball Z, Sailor Moon, Gundam Wing, Cowboy Bebop,* and *Detective Conan* were becoming popular outside Japan, a wide range of anime shows and movies were pushing artistic, emotional, and intellectual boundaries. The seemingly light Ghibli Studios production *Spirited Away* incorporates key aspects of Shintoism to highlight how humans can have a better relationship with nature by respecting *kami. Grave of the Fireflies* explores the human cost of war. *Akira* explores themes dealing with human experimentation and governmental control. *Ghost in the Shell* considers the nature of personal identity and the relationship between humans and technology. The nature of the self and religion in light of technological advancements are explored in *Ergo Proxy.*

And then there's *Neon Genesis Evangelion.* Utilizing the common tropes of large-eyed adolescents wearing skintight uniforms and using oversized mecha to fight *kaiju,* the show appears to be an anime designed by and for geeks (*otaku*) and hermits (*hikikomori*). While this is partly the case for *Neon*

Genesis Evangelion, that is only a surface understanding of the show. Beyond the fearsome monsters and Evangelions, the show explores the depths of the psyches of the adolescents when they become the very weapons needed to destroy the onslaught of Angels. Unfortunately, in the process of defending Tokyo-3 from a Third Impact, the three main characters, Shinji Ikari, Rei Ayanami, and Asuaka Langley Soryu, run the risk of destroying themselves.

The emotional complexities of the show could be attributed to its creator, Hideaki Anno. In a 1995 interview, he explains how the show was his own emotional catharsis.

> I tried to include everything of myself in *Neon Genesis Evangelion*—myself, a broken man who could do nothing for four years. A man who ran away for four years, one who was simply not dead. Then one thought, "You can't run away," came to me, and I restarted this production. It is a production where my only thought was to burn my feelings into film.

Understanding the intentions behind Hideaki Anno having created *Neon Genesis*, the show deserves deeper consideration of the sort required by more cerebral anime in line with those mentioned above. That is what the current collection of essays accomplishes—to show how we can mutually satisfy our more juvenile inclinations while also leading us to reflect on ourselves (calling upon us to fulfill the Delphic command *know thyself*).

The experiences the young adolescents face and the amount of secrecy that large organizations maintain makes *Neon Genesis Evangelion* an emotional and intellectually challenging anime to watch. Fortunately, many of us do not undergo as extreme of experiences facing Shinji, Rei, and Asuka. But many of us *do* face tragedies that prompt us to ask questions about our own existence, how to live, and how to relate to others. These are questions that are explored in philosophy. Yet, many of us do not have resources or the freedom to indepthly pursue philosophy. Instead, we may seek out more readily available resources in the forms of books, television, film, and, in this case, anime to give us deeper insight to the human condition.

The range of topics the authors, or pilots, explore include the meaning of life. How do we know when we have found meaning? How do we know who we are? Does the meaning of our life change once we are no longer an adolescent? Do we require other people to have meaning? What determines our meaning?

In Part II, the authors discuss the different phases of life. Can we choose who we become? Can we become better people as we age? What do we owe children? What choices can adolescents reasonably make? Part III addresses many existential and metaphysical dilemmas. How do we understand reality when we're alone? Can we bring about revolutions without the aid of others? Where is the mind when we are connected to others? Part IV further builds upon existential themes, but ties them to ethical concerns. How do we continue to exist when we realize our existence is absurd? How should we best communicate our ideals to others? Are we really free to make moral decisions? In the final Part V, the authors consider how we should think about the audience's reception and influence on the show; how to approach the show from a philosophical perspective; and the significance of the occult and religious symbols interlaced within the episodes.

May you explore with your fellow pilots the wide range of philosophical topics found within *Neon Genesis Evangelion*. Like *Neon Genesis*, they will challenge and encourage you to reflect on who you are and how to live with others. Yet, they do so from a position of care in a very similar way to how Misato cares for and challenges Shinji to discover who he is. May the chapters you read challenge you so that you, like Shinji, will "shine like a legend."

I

Finding
Meaning
in
Instrumentality

1
The Desperate Search for Meaning in Life

HEATHER BROWNING AND WALTER VEIT

Reason for existing, raison d'être. The reason why we're allowed to be here.

—Episode 25, "Do You Love Me?"

Why do we exist? What's our purpose in life? These are some of the oldest questions in philosophy and also form the heart of Hideaki Anno's *Neon Genesis Evangelion*.

While on the surface *Neon Genesis Evangelion* may seem to be just another story of epic giant robot battles, fans know that there's much more to it. The focus is actually the personal struggles of the young EVA pilots and those around them, looking to find meaning in their lives. Here we see echoes of Albert Camus, who famously wrote on what he labeled the *only really serious philosophical problem*: suicide.

Camus argued that "Deciding whether or not life is worth living is to answer the fundamental question in philosophy. All other questions follow from that" (*The Myth of Sisyphus*). Like any typical teenagers, the three main characters question their own reasons for existence and attempt to find their own identities. It's this deeper exploration of the search for meaning that has led to the show's lasting cult status. Come for the robots, stay for the existentialism.

Duty, Meaning, Loneliness

All of the three main characters initially try to answer these questions through their identity as EVA pilots, drawing their purpose, their meaning, and their identity from piloting the

EVAs. Shinji takes on the task of piloting an EVA with a sense of duty. He does so mechanically, and it's clearly difficult for him. Though he starts by claiming that he pilots for the sake of others, he comes to realize that his motivations are more self-ish. When piloting the EVA, he gains praise and attention from others, particularly his father, and this makes him feel valu-able. Without his task he feels worthless, unable to accept that the people around him might like him for any other reason than his role as an EVA pilot.

Though, in the beginning, it's clear that he doesn't enjoy piloting the EVA, over time Shinji increasingly accepts this role. After his father overrides him and uses his EVA to destroy Unit 03, putting Toji at risk, Shinji decides not to pilot the EVA again. But when he sees his friends defeated, he realizes he must step up and returns to NERV, begging to be allowed to pilot, gathering his courage and for the first time owning this as his identity: "I'm the pilot of Evangelion Unit 01. I'm Shinji Ikari!"

Rei takes a similarly dutiful attitude towards piloting her EVA. Quiet and unassuming, she follows orders as she is given them. Yet we also see that it's through piloting the EVA that she feels connected with others, telling Shinji that it's "her link" to everyone and that she "doesn't have anything else." She places little value on her own worth or safety, as shown when she steps up to shield Shinji from the attack of the fifth Angel, risking her own life in the process. At Asuka's goading, she even admits that she would give up her life if ordered to by Commander Ikari. It's through piloting her EVA that Rei feels connected to the world, as though she has some worth. It's all she has.

Asuka also finds meaning in piloting an EVA, but for differ-ent reasons. For her, it's about succeeding and being the best. This desire to prove herself often leads to her rushing into bat-tles unprepared and ending up defeated. Her insecurity is fur-ther evident in her ongoing rivalry with Shinji. Asuka's sense of purpose is derived from the recognition of others. Her child-like need for attention shows itself in the way that she con-stantly performs, calling others, especially Shinji and Kaji, to watch her as she acts. Her response to Shinji's question about why she pilots an EVA is "Why else? To show the whole world how talented I am!" When Shinji enquires "To let them know you exist?" she replies "Yeah. Something like that."

She also tries to find her connection to others through pilot-ing the EVAs. After losing against several Angels and finding it increasingly difficult to block the memories of her traumatic past, Asuka is no longer able to sync with her EVA and must be withdrawn from battle. She falls into a deep depression, feeling the loss of her identity. Without the validation she receives from piloting the EVA, she no longer feels like her life is worthwhile.

Suicide is a recurring theme throughout the show, considered by several characters as a means to escape the apparent worthlessness of their lives. For Asuka this is perhaps most striking, since her mother hanged herself, an image that still haunts her. For Camus, suicide wasn't an acceptable response to the meaninglessness of existence. Many existentialists, such as Jean-Paul Sartre, thought that we can face this by creating our own meaning. Camus argued instead that we need to revolt in the face of a life without purpose and enjoy it anyway. *Neon Genesis Evangelion* follows the journeys of the characters as they similarly discover their own ways of finding meaning in their lives.

Although these characters are seemingly finding their meaning in their work, it's evident that what really matters to them is trying to find attention from, and connection to, others. The work they do is only instrumental in pursuing this goal. For them, true meaning is found in these human connections; however, they struggle to ever get what they need from others. This is an example of the Hedgehog's Dilemma.

The Hedgehog's Dilemma

The Hedgehog's Dilemma arises from the writings of Arthur Schopenhauer (though he talks about porcupines, animals not closely related to hedgehogs), and forms the title of the fourth episode of the series. Schopenhauer tells of porcupines, coming together for warmth but driven apart again by the pain of each other's spines, drawing a parallel with the human condition of creating distance between ourselves because of our desire to avoid harm. Though we crave connection, we aren't ever able to fully satisfy this desire. He writes:

> A number of porcupines huddled together for warmth on a cold day in winter; but, as they began to prick one another with their quills, they were obliged to disperse. However the cold drove them together again, when just the same thing happened. At last, after many turns of huddling and dispersing, they discovered that they would be best off by remaining at a little distance from one another. In the same way the need of society drives the human porcupines together, only to be mutually repelled by the many prickly and disagreeable qualities of their nature. The moderate distance which

they at last discover to be the only tolerable condition of intercourse, is the code of politeness and fine manners; and those who transgress it are roughly told—in the English phrase—to keep their distance. By this arrangement the mutual need of warmth is only very moderately satisfied; but then people do not get pricked. A man who has some heat in himself prefers to remain outside, where he will neither prick other people nor get pricked himself. (*Parerga and Paralipomena*, Volume 2, pp. 651–52)

This pattern is repeated throughout the series. The characters all feel lost, and alienated, because of a lack of strong connections to parent figures or peers. They have experienced pain and losses that make them wary of growing close to others, and they employ defensive mechanisms to try to protect themselves from further pain.

Shinji has never really belonged anywhere, his life a series of "unfamiliar ceilings." He was abandoned by his father after the death of his mother, and his father remains cold and distant, only reaching out when he needs Shinji for something. To avoid further rejection and abandonment, Shinji has become obedient, trying to follow orders and please others by piloting the EVA or playing the cello at the advice of his teachers. He's also defensive, unwilling to allow anyone to get really close.

Shinji deals with his fear of hurt and rejection by running away, leading to his repeated mantra throughout the series: "I mustn't run away." He runs away not just literally, by leaving when things get hard, but also figuratively, by avoiding things that are difficult. The very act of hating himself, of feeling like he doesn't matter, is itself a form of running away, of avoiding having to engage with life, or with others.

Rei has similar issues with Gendo, who acts as a father figure to her. Although he shows some attachment to and protectiveness toward her, this is a result of her link to his late wife, Yui, as well as his need for her as part of his Instrumentality Project. Rei is well aware of the reason for his attention and though she craves it, she understands the reality behind it. Rei also suffers from a feeling of disconnection and a struggle with self-identity, as she is a clone and thus doesn't feel entirely human. In response to this, Rei is an isolated and almost robotic character who separates herself from others. She doesn't seem to know how to interact with them but passively does as she is told and accepts what happens to her without complaint, strikingly illustrated by a scene of her lying naked, impassive, below Shinji, after he accidentally falls on her. She then gets dressed and leaves without saying a word.

Asuka also suffers from childhood abandonment, with her father absent, focused on his work, and her mother first having a breakdown that leads to her taking a small doll as her child in Asuka's place, and finally committing suicide. When Asuka overhears her new stepmother telling her father that she could stop being a mother if she chose, this terrifies the young girl. She develops a steely determination to be strong, living without relying on others. She protects herself through her loud and aggressive behavior and as her struggles intensify through the series, she begins to express hatred towards everyone, including herself.

These traumas, rejections, and abandonments in the characters' pasts lead them to be afraid of future harms, building up defenses to protect themselves. All classic examples of the Hedgehog's Dilemma. In fact, the idea is introduced directly in the series. In Episode 3 ("A Transfer"), Ritsuko tells Misato about it, in an attempt to help her understand Shinji, explaining that he may be scared of taking risks with others because he could be hurt again:

> RITSUKO: Shinji might be the kind of person who can't make friends easily. Have you ever heard of the Hedgehog's Dilemma?
>
> MISATO: Hedgehog? Those spiky animals?
>
> RITSUKO: Hedgehogs have a hard time sharing warmth with other hedgehogs. The closer they get, the more they hurt each other with their quills. People are also like that. I think some part of Shinji is afraid to take that risk because he's afraid of being hurt.
>
> MISATO: He'll figure it out eventually. Part of growing up is trying again and again using trial and error to work out the right distance to avoid hurting each other.

This dialogue is poignantly delivered over scenes of Shinji walking and sitting quietly alone amongst his chattering classmates. Because of Shinji's past hurts, he now feels unable to get close to others, scared of being hurt again, and simultaneously hurting others in return.

Episode 4 tackles this parable head-on, and we get a glimpse at its possible resolution. After fighting with Misato, Shinji runs away. Misato realizes that both Shinji and she are scared of lashing out at one another, leading to further hurt and withdrawal: "The Hedgehog's Dilemma, huh? The closer they get, the more they hurt each other. I get it now. He talks like that because he doesn't know how else to express his feelings." The visuals of this scene, Shinji's speaking face fading into Misato's, further emphasizes the similarity between them.

This leads her to race to the train station to try to stop him from leaving, only to find that, remembering her words, he has decided to stay. They have both made an effort to overcome their tendency to hurt or withdraw, in order to benefit from the warmth that comes from connection.

The Human Instrumentality Project

That's how everyone's Instrumentality began. Parts they were missing, hearts they had lost, that emptiness in their hearts was filled. The Instrumentality of the heart, the soul, begins. Everyone's Instrumentality begins, returning everything to nothingness.

—Episode 25, "Do You Love Me?"

I'm tired of being . . . alone.

SHINJI, Episode 16, "Splitting of the Breast"

The early episodes on the Hedgehog's Dilemma are a teaser of what's to come. Hideaki Anno uses the small-scale story between the characters in the beginning to later reveal and connect the plans of the secret organization SEELE and their Human Instrumentality Project.

The isolation we have seen in the characters, the prior hurt and abandonment that leaves them damaged and scared to connect, while they crave the love and acceptance of others, is exactly what SEELE plans to overcome using Instrumentality. Throughout the series, the Angels are able to generate AT fields that cannot be penetrated by any conventional weaponry. This is why the EVAs are a necessary weapon, themselves able to manifest these shields and penetrate those of the Angels. Close to the ending of the series, however, it's revealed that the AT fields actually arise from possession of a soul. They hold together the ego, or sense of self, protecting against others. These are physical manifestations of the psychological barriers between individuals.

Here, the plot converges: SEELE (the German word for "soul") aims to destroy these barriers that separate humans from one another, solving the Hedgehog's Dilemma by merging all souls and overcoming the problems of alienation and loneliness by making everyone whole. Instrumentality is the dissolution of the self into the collective, the loss of boundary. In this, there are echoes of Heidegger, who saw the self as having an authentic form of being (which he called *Dasein*) that involved identification of the self as separate from but interacting with the world of others; whereas the inauthentic being would choose to lose themselves in the world of others, the They. Instrumentality is thus a form of losing the self and giving into the They. The motivation for this project is to bring everyone together, a single soul, filling all the empty spaces in the hearts and minds of people. A world in which there is no authenticity.

Shinji is shown a world of complete freedom, a world in which there are no others. However, he's disturbed by the emptiness of this world and realizes that it's the presence of others in the world that provides the boundaries by which he can define himself: "If nothing exists outside of yourself, you can't determine your own shape . . . You visualize your own shape by seeing the wall between 'self' and 'other'. You can't see yourself unless others are with you."

Although he has his own self, it's only meaningful through contrast with others. This idea is raised in the work of some of the post-Kantian German idealists, such as Johann Gottlieb Fichte and Georg Wilhelm Friedrich Hegel. They explored the idea that the awareness of the self could only be fully realized through the presence of others. It is only in contrasting yourself with those around you that you can recognize your own identity. It is the interaction between self and other that is crucial for human awareness and experience. Although the otherness removes some freedom, without it, the self cannot exist.

Instrumentality erases these barriers and thus the self along with it, a consequence which leads to losing what it is that makes a person human in the first place. This is an outcome that Shinji is unwilling to accept. He fears that by joining with others, he will lose himself and realizes that although he has internalized the rejection of others and started to hate himself, thus building the protective walls that keep others out, he could learn to like (or love) himself, and that he wants to continue to exist. As he draws these realizations, the manufactured world around him shatters. He breaks through once more to the world containing others and he finds himself surrounded by congratulatory friends and family. Although aware that separation from others will re-create the barriers and allow the fear and loneliness to return, he accepts this as a necessary cost of the potential joy that can be achieved in relationships with others and chooses to return to the world, thus making the same choice possible for others. In the end, it's Shinji's will to live, and will to be a self, his desire to retain his identity through his separation from others, that allows him to break free from Instrumentality and create a new world.

The failure of Instrumentality is driven by this unwillingness to accept the loss of self. The conclusion we're led to is that connection with others can only be made meaningful through the separation of individuals, despite the pain of isolation that this entails. The story suggests that the meaning the characters seek can only be found through human connection, their relationships with one another, but while also maintaining some distance.

During Instrumentality, Rei defends the idea that she has an identity found through her interactions with others. She gains a sense of self, independently of her clones, through these connections: "I am the real me. I became myself over the time that I've existed and through the connections that I've formed with others. The person I am is shaped by my interactions with others. Interactions with others and the passage of time will change the shape of my heart . . . Those are what created the person that I have been, the object called Rei Ayanami. They will create the person I will be."

The value of connections with others is emphasised throughout the show. Although the characters struggle with their fears and hurts, we also see that they're able to strengthen and grow through the connections they make with one another. This is particularly true of Shinji, and it's the relationships he forms, and the ways in which they change him, that ultimately decide the fate of humanity through Instrumentality.

Misato acts as a parent figure, helping him feel accepted and at home and in the end it's she who pushes Shinji to meet his destiny, challenging him to grow up, and start making decisions for himself. He also develops bonds with his fellow pilots, Asuka and Rei. These relationships are conflicted and ambiguous. Like typical teenagers, they are navigating the complicated strands of friendship, family, and romance. However, it's obvious that they truly care for one another. In the end, this is what causes Rei to put her faith in Shinji, rather than Gendo, determining the entire outcome for Instrumentality. And, in *The End of Evangelion* when Shinji breaks free from Instrumentality, it's Asuka whom he finds at his side back on Earth. The relationship which Shinji builds with Kaworu, the Fifth Child, and seventeenth Angel, is a key defining one for him. Their relationship is ambiguous, sitting between friendship and romance, and they quickly become close. Kaworu encourages Shinji to think about himself and his place in the world and tells Shinji that he loves him, the first time that Shinji has ever heard those words. In the end, when Shinji is fearful of Rei/Lilith as she tries to take him and Unit 01 into her hands, it's when Kaworu's form emerges that he joyously accepts the union.

Through these relationships, Shinji builds more confidence, becoming stronger and more assertive. Instead of simply trying to follow orders and please others all the time, he begins to stand up for what he wants and make decisions for himself. Eventually, it is his connections with others that help Shinji find himself and save humanity. The meaning that he has sought for himself is discovered in defining his identity through his relationships with those around him. He accepts that it is better to continue to exist, with all the pain that it may entail, than to lose himself in the formless safety promised by Instrumentality.

We may remain hedgehogs, unable to ever completely shed our spikes, but we should never stop trying to seek that warmth, the human connection that defines us.

2

How Do We Know Who We Are?

NATHAN VISSER AND ADAM BARKMAN

How do we know who we are? *Neon Genesis Evangelion* wrestles with this question through the eyes of troubled teenagers.

The main protagonist, Shinji Ikari, is the most prominent example of the human struggle with the self. After his mother died at an early age, Shinji's father, Gendo Ikari abandoned him, leaving him feeling alone in the world. Eleven years later, Gendo summons him to the futuristic city of Tokyo-3. When Shinji arrives, his cold-hearted parent shows him no support or remorse, blatantly stating that he only called on Shinji for use as a fighter pilot against the powerful monsters known as Angels.

Despite initial refusal, Shinji eventually decides to pilot the giant bio-mecha known as the Evangelion (EVA) and shows surprising promise in his first battle, where he defeats the first Angel in a stunning upset. However, piloting an EVA comes at a great cost to Shinji. Piloting the EVA doesn't mean merely remote control—it means connecting the EVA to the very neurons of his brain. It's a very difficult and dangerous thing to do; every time the EVA sustains damage, Shinji feels the impact directly. Due to this pain and stress, he's constantly asked why he continues to pilot, both by himself and others.

While Shinji struggles with piloting the EVA, he states many times that he has no choice and is being forced to do so. Others reject this and stoutly remind him that he's always free to make his own decisions. He can walk away any time he chooses. Often Shinji does walk away, only to return when another Angel threatens to destroy the planet.

Does Shinji really have a choice? Does he truly have the free will everyone claims he does?

Absolute Control

The first theory *Evangelion* presents is that humans have total control over their own will, and whatever they will to happen *will* happen. This view is physically represented in the character of Asuka, the confident and colorful girl who pilots EVA-02 with attitude. She takes it upon herself to prove that anyone can do anything alone, as long as they try hard enough. Asuka's "by myself and for myself" attitude exists in stark contrast to Shinji's quiet complacency, and yet over time we are shown just how similar these characters are. Their relationship is used to present the tension with another implicit philosophy known as Structuralism. This is the theory that ideas and beliefs are formed through comparison and contrast to other ideas and beliefs. As Shinji is repeatedly told to "think for himself," he protests on the basis that he doesn't know who or what "himself" is, as he has had nobody in his life to show him who he is. How can he decide what he wants when he has no idea who he is? How can Shinji come to know who he is?

This question isn't answered until the anime's explosive finale, when Shinji is given the choice to accept or reject the "Human Instrumentality Project," a phenomenon that would make all humans into one single entity. Although initially drawn to Instrumentality by the fact that it would take away pain, suffering, and conflict from everyone, Shinji then rejects Instrumentality on the basis that these emotions, although problematic, are exactly what makes him who he is.

Shinji concludes that humans can only form their identity based on their differences and relationships with other human beings. We determine who we are based on what we are not. This ideology conflicts with the existentialist claim that we can create an identity by ourselves, yet is ultimately what prompts Shinji to reject the "Human Instrumentality Project" and remain his own separate entity, as he knows that to be his true self. He will still live in pain, sorrow, and strife with others, but he's certain that his feelings towards others are real, and that's the one thing he can know to be true.

You Do (Not) Have a Choice

Throughout the show, much of Shinji's character is revealed through his relationship with his father. Shinji is escorted into

Tokyo-3 by Misato Katsuragi, a character who's both his mentor and his supervisor. Katsuragi brings Shinji into the secret headquarters of the government-funded defense organization run by his father, known as NERV. After having not spoken to him for three years, Shinji's father simply orders him to pilot this large, strange, mecha monstrosity introduced as Evangelion Unit 1 (EVA-01). Shinji's totally taken aback by this. Not only did Ikari not even bother to greet Shinji by name, but he expects him to be capable of piloting something he's never even heard of.

When Shinji angrily refuses, Ikari firmly lays out an ultimatum: Pilot the EVA or leave. Shinji persists in his refusal, so Ikari declares him "unusable" and orders in another pilot, Rei Ayanami. Rei emerges in a critically wounded state, making it obvious to everyone why Ikari brought Shinji in to take her place. Shinji looks on with horror as this bandaged young girl, unable even to walk on her own, painfully struggles to board the EVA. After watching this in turmoil, Shinji changes his mind and announces he will be an EVA pilot.

What brings Shinji to this decision? The answer is twofold: The most obvious factor is the pity that he feels for Rei, which morphs into guilt from the knowledge that he's partially responsible for bringing such distress upon her by refusing to pilot the EVA. The second factor is more subtle. Ikari's ability to bring out another pilot confirms what Shinji fears, that he isn't needed. Even though he despises his father for abandoning him at such a young age, he still desires Ikari's approval. He needs to be needed. Such reasons bring Shinji to make this fateful choice. However, this raises the question: Is it really a *choice*? How can anyone act against a combination of satisfying desire and avoiding guilt?

Infamous psychologist Sigmund Freud (1856–1939), who has had a profound influence on *Neon Genesis Evangelion*, proposes an answer with what he calls the "pleasure principle." According to this theory, everything a person does they do from a desire to seek pleasure and avoid pain. In situations where there's pain on both sides, people will choose whichever option they believe will offer them the least pain. However, each of us derives pleasure and pain in different ways and from different sources. So, what determines how we derive pleasure and pain? Freud claims the determination is set by the individual *id*, the deepest part of our unconscious mind that controls our needs and urges. In *The Ego and the Id*, Freud argues that the *id* is also the only part of the unconscious mind that exists from birth, which suggests that many of our needs and desires are predetermined.

An important part of Shinji's unconscious mind is revealed in Episode 18 ("Life and Death Decisions"/"Ambivalence"), where he's told to fight against the thirteenth Angel, Bardiel. However, there's a catch: Bardiel has taken control of another EVA. This EVA has a real human pilot inside, but it's become corrupted and is now attacking NERV and the other EVA units. When Shinji realizes this, he's horrified. Bardiel lunges and begins to strangle Shinji inside EVA-01, and Gendo orders Shinji to fight back and destroy it. Shinji refuses, quickly stating that he would rather die than risk harming another human being. Ikari then activates the experimental "dummy plug" system, which allows him to take full control of EVA-01 remotely. EVA-01 proceeds to free itself and destroy the corrupted EVA in a barbaric manner. Shinji's trapped inside, helpless, as he watches his own EVA brutally slaughter another EVA, going so far as to extract the unit's entry plug (where the pilot is seated) and crush it with one hand. Shinji's utter devastation is met with a glimpse of relief when he's told the pilot is miraculously still alive, but he's quickly defeated by the realization that the severely injured pilot is one of his best friends, Toji. This gives us a brief glimpse into Shinji's true character. At no point in the altercation did Shinji attempt to attack the corrupted EVA. One could argue that this was hesitation brought about by panic or uncertainty, but Episode 18 is the most certain we have seen Shinji thus far.

Even when directly ordered by his father to attack, he firmly refuses, and immediately asserts that he would rather die. There's no way he would risk harming another human, even if that meant losing his life. This shows just how powerfully the *id* influences Shinji's choice. He knows that hurting others causes him more pain than anything else, so much so that he's willing to endure the intense physical pain of strangulation even to the point of death. This also points to how little Shinji values his own life.

All Shinji has gotten from life is pain and confusion. Although his subconscious mind directs him to avoid the most painful of endeavors, it's his conscious mind that needs to figure out what brings him pleasure. But, because his conscious mind hasn't yet grasped what it is that brings him pleasure, Shinji feels that life is about nothing more than avoiding the worst pain, and if death offers that avoidance, death will be chosen over life.

You Can (Not) Do It Alone

Not knowing what brings him pleasure also leads Shinji to behave in an exceedingly compliant manner. Throughout the series, Shinji is shown to be a very quiet, submissive, docile person who does what others tell him to do. In Episode 8 ("Asuka Arrives in Japan"/"Asuka Strikes!"), these traits are emphasized by the antagonistic arrival of Asuka Langley Soryu, pilot of Evangelion Unit 2.

In polar opposition to Shinji, Asuka overflows with confidence and assertiveness. She demands attention with her impressive performance and colorful attitude. Her relationship with Shinji has many volatile moments as these two contrasting characters live and work together for the survival of the world. Both directly and indirectly, Asuka challenges Shinji on his complacent attitude. For example, Episode 16 ("The Sickness Unto Death, and then . . ."/ "Splitting of the Breast") begins with Asuka berating Shinji for constantly apologizing. She expresses disgust at Shinji's acceptance of anything and angrily insists he should stand up for himself. Asuka believes that if you want something, all you need to do is work hard enough to get it. She adamantly asserts that she's her own person and needs no one else to tell her who she is or what she should do. Asuka exists as a physical representation of the surface-level philosophy behind the series: existentialism.

Contrary to Freud, existentialism is famous—through perhaps its most prominent proponent, Jean-Paul Sartre—for asserting that no part of a human exists prior to consciousness. Existentialism argues that if perception occurs, there must be a consciousness doing the perceiving. If the consciousness perceives everything, then the only thing that could perceive the self would be the self. Therefore, the task of the consciousness is to perceive the self, and this must be done, as Sartre argues in his most important work, *Being and Nothingness*, "in itself and for itself."

Asuka takes this task head-on, subjecting herself to hard work and dedication so that she can prove her ability to do things all on her own. In Episode 9 ("Mind, Matching, Moment"/"Both of You, Dance Like You Want to Win!"), Asuka complains that her task to sync with Shinji is impossible. Katsuragi responds by offering a replacement, who quickly does much better. This rapidly motivates Asuka to try much harder, as she says to Shinji, "It's a matter of honor now, can't you understand that?" Asuka defines herself according to her own success. This mentality leads her to reject offers of help from others and berate Shinji for his reliance on other people's help. In doing this, she appears to succeed in being truly independent. However, this confidence often turns to arrogance, and often leads her to reject orders during battle and attempt to enact her own strategy. This almost always results in Asuka needing to be rescued by Shinji, which deals powerful blows to her self-reliant ego.

Asuka's identity is ultimately put to the test in Episode 22 ("Staying Human"/"Don't Be"), where Asuka encounters the fifteenth Angel, Arael. Defying orders and straying from her position, Asuka attempts to engage Arael head-on, only to be caught in a special beam of light protruding from the distant Angel. However, this beam is no mere physical attack, but a psychological weapon that forcibly invades Asuka's mind. She screams in pain and violently convulses as Arael commandeers her mind and begins to pull up traumatic memories. Here, we're given a glimpse into Asuka's tragic past, where it's revealed that her father abandoned his family and her mother killed herself while Asuka was very young.

Such events are revealed as the cause of Asuka's hardened demeanor, fashioned from suppressing the pain by telling herself she didn't need a mother or a father to love her. She didn't need anyone to tell her who she was. She didn't need anyone; she could be her own person. Episode 22 then spirals into a sequence of psychological torture via these painful memories, as Arael forces Asuka to realize that the idea of total independence is merely a facade. Despite Asuka's outward assertions, it's revealed that what Asuka truly desires is to be noticed by someone, cared for by others, and to be loved by those she loves, proving that she's always been reliant on others.

You Are (Not) Your Own

When she's finally rescued from Arael by Rei, the damage has already been done. The traumatic invasion of her mind, combined with yet another humiliating loss on her part, deals the final blow to her fragile sense of self-worth. This raises the question: Did she fail the existentialist's task of defining herself? Asuka tied her entire sense of identity and value to her skills as a pilot. When she failed at that, she failed altogether. One could argue that she failed the existentialist's task by relying on something other than herself.

However, this example raises an inherent contradiction within Existentialism: How can we truly define ourselves with nothing but ourselves? How do we form our identity without the ability to define what it is? The philosophy is forced to admit that consciousness is about something and so is always defined in relation to something else. At this point, the mask of Existentialism is torn off to reveal the real philosophy Evangelion is supporting: Structuralism. This philosophy argues that all things are defined according to their relationship with other things. But, if we're defining consciousness by its relation to other things, how do we form a unique, individual identity? How do we know who we are?

This is the question that has crippled both Shinji and Asuka by the time we reach the series finale, *The End of Evangelion.* All Shinji knows is pain; all Asuka knows is failure. Both see their own existence as nothing more than that, and therefore no longer see the value of living. Thus, when the final battle takes place, both are very reluctant to participate, even though they're the last chance Earth has. At this point it's revealed that the ultimate goal of the Angel attacks is to initiate what is labeled the "Human Instrumentality Project." This project is supported by the members of the secret organization SEELE, who were controlling, and who ultimately betray, NERV in order to advance their agenda.

The goal of the "Human Instrumentality Project" is to merge all human beings in the world into one, single, unified entity. Doing so would ascend humanity into the next major evolutionary stage. Only through destruction of every individual body and assimilation of every individual soul would this jump be possible, and so this is accomplished through the initiation of the Third Impacct. After SEELE defeats Asuka in EVA-02, and captures Shinji in EVA-01, the Third Impact is initiated and the world's souls are collected and assimilated. Due to the complex yet crucial nature of EVA-01 and Shinji's relationship with it, Shinji is now given a choice to accept or reject Instrumentality. If he accepts, there will no longer be different persons; all will be one single being, perfectly unified without division or separation. Complete removal of separation would thereby eliminate all pain, strife, disparity, conflict, and difference from the world. If he rejects Instrumentality, the world will return to what it was before, with different people living separate lives. What should Shinji choose?

Initially, Shinji is drawn to the idea of Instrumentality through the idea that it will eliminate his pain. He will finally be connected with people, no longer feeling so alone all the time. If everybody is one, there can be no such thing as loneliness, no such thing as separation. Episode 26 ("The Beast that Shouted 'I' at the Heart of the World"/"Take Care of Yourself") visualizes Shinji's thought process as he contemplates the idea of combining everyone into a single entity. The question is once again asked: How do you know who you are? Shinji visualizes a world of "total freedom." In this world nothing exists but himself, and he can create anything by merely thinking of it.

The problem is that Shinji doesn't know what to think. Shinji doesn't know what he wants. He doesn't know what he wants because he still doesn't know who he is. He realizes that he can't know who he is unless there's something to tell him who he is. That something has to be separate from him, something that he can base himself off of, something that shows him what he is and what he isn't. Therefore, if he's all that exists, there can be no difference between him and nothing. How can this be called existence? If Shinji accepts Instru-mentality, he would be accepting the destruction of everything that makes Shinji, Shinji. He would no longer have a self. But what is self? What is it that makes Shinji who he is? To answer that question, Shinji looks again at what Instrumentality would take away. It takes away pain, loneliness, and conflict. It takes away sadness, isolation, and disagreement. It takes away all difference. If this is what gets taken away in Instrumentali-ty, and Instrumentality takes away the very essence of humanity, Shinji infers that the essence of humanity is in fact difference.

This is the conclusion Shinji finally reaches. Every individual is unique. Every individual is a different person. How do we know this? We know this because we can compare each person to another. We can compare ourselves to each other. Shinji knows that he's not Asuka because he's like her in some ways and unlike her in others. Shinji knows he's a pilot because he controls EVA-01. Shinji knows he's skilled at piloting based on what other people tell him and how his piloting affects others. Shinji may not fully understand who he is, but what he does know he learns by what he's not. In the same way, our sense of self is based on our differences from (and inter-actions with) others. We learn who we are based on what we're not.

We're all separate individuals, constantly shaping each other in an ever-changing world. Although we're separate, we desire to become close to each other. We desire unity. There's a part of us all that desires Instrumentality. However, because we're separate beings defined by our differences, achieving that total unity isn't possible. The closer we are, the easier it is to hurt each other. This is why we have strife, disparity, and pain. The desire to become united as individuals simultaneously brings us together and pulls us apart. This tension is what causes Shinji so much pain, so much confusion, and so much anger.

But, after getting a glimpse of what Instrumentality looks like, Shinji realizes what it is that makes him who he is. All his life Shinji has been running from pain. He's been trying to hide from it, trying to rid himself of it. By doing this he runs away from everyone who loves him, closing himself off from those who want to be close to him. He hides himself from others so that he won't risk getting hurt, and more importantly not risk hurting them. Closing himself off from all others brings Shinji to a point where he no longer sees the purpose of life, as all life seems to offer is pain and confusion. Now Shinji realizes that pain and confusion are exactly what life is. These are the only things that Shinji truly feels, and therefore the only things he can actually know to be real. Knowing these are real is how he can know he's real, and knowing what makes him real finally shows him who he really is. Such realizations ultimately bring Shinji to reject the Human Instrumentality Project, eventually restoring the world to the state it once was, where everyone exists as their own individual person.

Neon Genesis Evangelion presents a profound story about the human struggle with identity. Through the person of Shinji Ikari, the series asks deep, thought-provoking questions about how we comes to know ourselves. We follow Shinji as he struggles with the question of free will, asking if he really has the freedom to choose like everyone says he does, and how he can choose what he wants when he doesn't know who he is. This question is tackled by the confident character of Asuka, who boldly claims we can create our own identity by ourselves and for ourselves.

However, after a crushing defeat from Arael, her crimson color scheme is finally revealed to represent a philosophical red herring, as her strong Existentialist worldview is revealed to be an implicit Structuralism all along. This philosophy is then thoroughly analyzed by Shinji during his Instrumentality decision, as he must decide whether to bring all people together as one single being, or let them continue to live separate lives of pain and strife. Shinji realizes that the difference between people that creates this pain and strife is precisely what makes them who they are.

All things are defined by their similarities and differences from other things. Since humans have an innate desire for companionship and fear being alone, this division causes pain. However, Shinji ultimately concludes that this exact pain, his feelings towards others, desires for what he may never be able to obtain, and disparity among those closest to him are the only things he knows to be real. If that's the realest thing to him, then that must be exactly what makes him who he is.

3
A Teenage Existence

SANO YASUYUKI

Tsunehiro Uno, a Japanese subculture critic, wrote in his 2008 book that *"Neon Genesis Evangelion* is in every way a symbol of old imagination."* He adds that we who live in the twenty-first century must "bury" this imagination because it's out of date.

What Uno is criticizing as "old imagination" is called *sekai-kei*, a genre of Japanese otaku fiction that was fashionable from the mid-1990s to the early 2000s. Its literal translation is "world-type." However, in this case, the word *sekai* has a specific meaning.

A Kind of Mary Sue Syndrome?

Sekai is written in *katakana*, a Japanese syllabary mainly used for foreign words and onomatopoeia. This notation has a slightly mocking tone. Generally, *sekai-kei* stories are composed of two plots: a minor narrative of the protagonists' everyday life (usually the school life of an average boy with a "beautiful fighting girl") and a grand narrative of global apocalyptic events, such as an extraterrestrial invasion.

Common sense suggests no causal link exists between these two plots. However, in *sekai-kei*, the ups and downs of the minor narrative immediately influence the grand narrative. That's why people write *sekai* in *katakana*; *sekai-kei* stories seem to express the narrow view and adolescent megalomania of those who tend to identify their individual existential anxiety with worldwide catastrophe.

Why did Uno say that *Evangelion* is a symbol of *sekai-kei*? He said so probably because of its historical position as an origin. In the world of *Evangelion*, there are armies, governments, and the United Nations, similar to the real world. However, they cannot maintain the world: it's only the EVA and its pilot that can annihilate the Angels to save the world. Hence, the minor narrative has a crucial influence on the grand narrative in *Evangelion*.

However, this characteristic is insufficient to explain *Evangelion's* originality, or more importantly, the particular personality of the central character, Shinji Ikari. As is well known, Japanese classic mecha anime, such as *Mazinger Z* and *Mobile Suit Gundam,* describe mecha as a means of social self-actualization, a representation of the adult body. Their protagonist is usually a young but talented man who fights bravely against enemies with mecha, and thus is finally recognized by others. It is a type of coming-of-age story.

Conversely, Shinji is far from that character: he hesitates to pilot the EVA; even when he chooses to pilot it, he does not feel responsible for his choice. Through the eyes of those familiar with classic mecha anime, Shinji appears too childish, lacking autonomy as a responsible individual. Furthermore, Shinji never overcomes his childishness. At the end of the television series, Shinji decides to escape from reality by withdrawing into his inner world instead of facing his trauma and other people. This huge gap between the incurable immaturity of Shinji and the enormousness of the responsibility he takes on characterizes *Evangelion* as the origin of *sekai-kei*.

Some feel sympathy for Shinji's ordinariness, unsuitable for a mecha anime protagonist, while others are disgusted at his indecisive and extrapunitive character. Uno is one of the most scathing and influential critics of *Evangelion*. He criticized Shinji's attitude as a mere "mullygrub and withdrawal" against the opacity of society and appreciated other characters who are more active and ambitious—Light Yagami (in *Death Note*) or Lelouch (in *Code Geass: Lelouch of the Rebellion*). He considers them products of a "contemporary imagination" that has bloomed since the beginning of the 21st century. However, even if Shinji is a childish character, it doesn't follow that creating a character like Shinji is a childish attempt. What does *Evangelion* present through Shinji's attitude?

The Power to Add "Not"

To help illustrate *Evangelion's* objective, we summon famous French philosopher Jean-Paul Sartre. *Evangelion* seems to be based on the Sartrean conception of human reality. In *Being and Nothingness*, one of the most influential philosophical works of the twentieth century, Sartre states that human reality has a dualistic ontological structure. On the one hand, human reality *is what it is*: it has a unique existence defined by physiological, psychological, social, and historical qualities— beautiful or ugly, male or female, abled or disabled, brave or coward, rich or poor, to name a few. Sartre called such qualities that form our existence *facticity*.

On the other hand, human reality *is not what it is* or *is what it is not*: it's never causally or deductively determined by its existence. According to Sartre, what determines the most profound structure of human reality is not its facticity but the manner of dealing with it. There are various ways of assuming our facticity—some authentic and responsible, others inauthentic and irresponsible. While we cannot choose our facticity, the tools we use to address it depend on our freedom; in some situations, we can radically change our way of being.

Notably, Sartre thought that this dualism is based on the power to bring "negativity" or "nothingness" into the world, into the absolute positivity of being; that is, human reality has the power to add "not." This "not" provides us freedom but also conveys a fundamental split between what we are and what we are *not*. This split presents various conflicts and suffering. Naoko Akagi's conduct in Episode 21 is a good example: when she was called a "hag" by little Rei, she was incensed to the point of madness.

Some may believe that her reaction reflected her belief that she was *not* old. However, if that was true, how could Rei's remark hurt her so badly? Perhaps it would be more correct to say that her reaction reflected the dismay that she felt herself getting old, although she believed she was *not*. The tragedy's origin is this split between the fact that she is old and the belief that she is *not*. An animal would not suffer from such distinction, only us humans; we always feel that we exist beyond the qualities imposed on ourselves and thus could refuse them at any time. To borrow Paul Valéry's phrase, the structure of human reality provides us with the possibility of "an indefinite refusal to be anything whatsoever."

An Indefinite Refusal to Be Anything Whatsoever

Refusal is a central theme in *Evangelion*. Shinji repeatedly refuses to pilot the EVA throughout the story: he refuses to accept the blame by Toji for injuring his little sister in Episode 3; he repeatedly refuses to decide to pilot EVA by his own initiative in Episode 4; he repeatedly refuses to communicate with others at the end of the television series; and be absorbed in the unity of humankind in the old theatrical edition, *The End of Evangelion*.

The notion of the AT Field is also meaningful. Kaworu calls it "the internal barrier that we all possess." Sartre would say it's the power of negation. The AT Field refuses all exterior attacks as if to say "I'm *not* this knife," or "I'm *not* that bomb." It thus represents the theme of refusal.

However, the conclusions of the television series and *The End of Evangelion* seem to take a negative view of this theme. In Episode 26, Shinji is congratulated by others around him after a long and unequivocal self-negation. As many critics point out, this is a parody of cult programming represented by Aum Shinrikyo, which shocked Japan with the Tokyo subway sarin attack in 1995. Moreover, in the last scene of *The End of Evangelion*, Shinji himself is refused by Asuka with a striking word: "Disgusting . . ."

Why did *Evangelion* come to such a bad ending? There appears to be a message that the effort to gain complete freedom by refusing every restriction, like Shinji, makes us anxious and empty rather than happy. Simone de Beauvoir, Sartre's partner and also a famous French philosopher, made this point better than Sartre. *Pyrrhus and Cineas*, Beauvoir's first philosophical essay describes two inauthentic attitudes denying our facticity. For one, we attempt to deny our facticity by refusal. We suffer from our circumstances because we resist them: if we did nothing, we wouldn't be injured or betrayed by reality. This is the attitude that Shinji takes in *The End of Evangelion*. He protests throughout the story, saying "All I do is hurt people. So it's better if I don't do anything!"

For the other, we attempt to efface our facticity by identifying ourselves with the universal. For instance, Beauvoir shows a fictional conversation between a boy and his parents. The boy is saddened to hear that a concierge's child died. His parents become impatient with his crying and say, "That small boy wasn't your brother," continuing, "don't keep crying all your life. Every day, thousands of children die all over the world." This is a trick denying our facticity. Beauvoir says that if we refused our particular ties with others and things, our world would become empty; if people across the world were our brothers or sisters, then we wouldn't have any brothers and sisters.

According to Beauvoir, it's nothing more than another way to do nothing, allowing us to escape from doing something under the pretext that we cannot do everything. However, even if we cannot mourn children worldwide, can we not mourn *this* child right before us? Even if we cannot do everything, can we not do something? Our preference for the universal conceals these questions.

A dialog about "a world of freedom" in Episode 26 seems to describe such an attitude. It's a world where nothing restrains us. However, it makes Shinji anxious rather than relieved because it's completely empty and gives him no direction. A short animation follows this scene, where "another possible world" suddenly begins. In that world, there's neither the Evangelion nor the Angels, and Shinji lives an ordinary school life with his friends. At its end, Shinji says, "The me that I am now isn't the entirety of what I am. Different versions of me may exist. Oh, right! There could even be a me that isn't an EVA pilot!" Thus, he thinks he can be everything. However, this is merely a way to escape from the world that he faces. By presenting such a "solution" as if it were a result of cult programming, the end of the television series indicates that it's nothing more than Shinji's self-deception.

Hence, both the television series and *The End of Evangelion* present Shinji's way of being as an inaction that derives from negation of his facticity. However, is it the only way to handle our facticity? Probably not. Our facticity is an ensemble of things that restrain us. Simultaneously, it's the ensemble of motivations and means that enables us to realize ourselves in the world. Therefore, the negation of facticity means the abandonment of self-actualization. According to Sartre, we can approach our facticity from three aspects: past, body, and others. Our facticity comprises our past and our body and is deepened by others. Let us examine Shinji's attitude toward these aspects and compare the television series and *The End* with the new theatrical edition: *Rebuild of Evangelion*, presenting some interesting changes.

The Past: Motivation for Our Actions

Throughout the story, Shinji's previous life is steeped in mystery, except for a brief mention of his father. Although he tells Kaworu that he used to stay with "*Sensei*" and "days there were quiet and uneventful," this is more an indication of the blankness of his past than a revelation. According to Sartre, our past is not only a restriction that we cannot choose or modify but also our motivation, without which we cannot do anything. We can explain Shinji's inactivity from this viewpoint. His only vivid recollection was being abandoned by his father. The desire to be recognized by his father inspired him to pilot the

EVA, and when he felt betrayed by his father in episode 18, he lost his motivation.

Episodes 19 and 20 provide turning points for him. Although EVA piloting was tormenting, he decides to pilot it again. His impressive declaration, "I . . . I'm the pilot of Evangelion Unit 01! I'm Ikari Shinji!" indicates that he's trying to assume facticity as an EVA pilot. The internal dialog with Misato after the battle also indicates such a trial. Shinji says, "I promised myself that I wouldn't get into the EVA again," and Misato answers, "but you *did* get into it. Shinji, you're here right now because you got into the EVA. You're the person you are now because you piloted the EVA. You can't reject your past or who you were." It's this internal voice that brings him back to the world. Thus, the theme of these scenes is the assumption of the past.

Nevertheless, Shinji couldn't completely assume his past. He finally refused facticity. Why could he not do it? To answer this question, we must examine his attitude toward his body, which is another aspect of his facticity.

Body: The Means of Our Actions

The ontological dualistic structure of human reality is exemplified by the relationship between mind and body. There's a significant tension between them. For the most part, our body appears as a restriction to our mind: we can perceive the world only from *here*, where our body is located. Our body's condition—fatigue, illness, or incapacity—prevents us from conducting our plans. Thus, our body is the central part of our facticity.

According to Sartre, there are many ways to deal with the body, one of them being *abandonment*. If our body was an insuperable obstacle, how best should we address it? We must abandon ourselves entirely to it, without resistance. If we do not try to control our body, obstacles cease to exist. Sartre provides examples such as to give way to fatigue or warmth, to fall back upon a chair or a bed with sensual pleasure, or to get drunk.

We can understand Shinji's way of existing in his body from this perspective. Both the television series and *The End of Evangelion* repeatedly highlight the EVA's uncontrollability. It often becomes berserk, and its battery tends to drain at critical times. Although there are some exceptional episodes, such as Episode 9 where Shinji and Asuka beautifully pilot the EVA, the EVA's actions are generally distinct from Shinji's own will.

Episode 3 shows this separation impressively. In the middle of a training to pilot the EVA, Shinji parrots Ritsuko's order, "Center the target, pull the trigger." His eyes are leaden as if he was playing a video game. To Shinji, the EVA is nothing more than a video game whose system is controlled by another mysterious will, which is why he finally succumbed to inaction. Following the formula of classic mecha anime, the EVA should become Shinji's extended body. However, he cannot control this "body" adequately. The best way to mix with the EVA is to *abandon* himself to it in the Sartrean sense.

Yet our body isn't only an obstacle to our will but also a means to realizing it. Although we may not perfectly control our body, we have to use it to influence the world. A comparison with *Rebuild of Evangelion* shows us another way of existing in our body. I'd like to focus on Operation Yashima. In the television series, both shots of the positron rifle were controlled by the machine. Conversely, in *Rebuild of Evangelion*, there's an added scene before the second shot, where Maya Ibuki switches the final firing system from automatic to manual. This change is slight but important because it returns responsibility to Shinji. Shinji is no longer a puppet of the EVA and the mysterious will behind it. The results of the shot depend on him. Of course, Shinji's body might betray him by missing, but he's responsible for all his actions, including failure. *Rebuild of Evangelion* thus attempts to describe Shinji as an individual who's more responsible than in the old edition, highlighting the role of the EVA as an organ of Shinji's will.

Others: Our Hell, Our Salvation

According to Sartre, the existence of others isn't an immanent structure of our being, but an attempt to assume our facticity is complicated by others. Almost all our activities can be characterized socially. Even those that appear to have nothing to do with others can be construed as a refusal of communication because they exist in a world shared with others. Hence, our attempt to assume our facticity is evaluated not only by ourselves but also by others. If we want to assume our facticity, we must achieve recognition. Otherwise, our assumption becomes self-satisfaction.

We are all more or less aware of this. This is exemplified by the fact that we desire contact with others. Shinji suffers from it. He's afraid to communicate with others, but he cannot cease from desiring to touch others. He wants to be recognized by his father and has sexual interests in the female body. This leads him to the state that Ritsuko called "Hedgehog's Dilemma."

In *Being and Nothingness*, Sartre considers this dilemma a split between our "being-for-others" and our "being-for-itself." The former means our being as seen by others and the latter by ourselves. Various social definitions such as "lackey," "coward," or "bureaucrat" are imposed on us from the outside, whereas we can internally refuse these qualities and be anything we want.

However, being able to be anything is just being nothing. Moreover, we can never completely deny these qualities. Let's recall Naoko's case. While she internally refused to get old, she was aware that she was actually getting old. This split led her to kill little Rei. Our being-for-others is thus not something like clothes that we can put on or take off whenever we like. It's a crucial problem in our lives. In his play *No Exit*, Sartre expressed such inevitability of others with the famous phrase, "Hell is other people."

In Episode 16, Shinji notes this problem. Absorbed in the shadow of Leliel, he's talked to by another Shinji within him, who describes "the self that is seen by others, and the self that observes that act. There are even multiples of the individual named Shinji Ikari. Each is a different Shinji Ikari, and yet they're all the real Shinji Ikari. You're afraid of the Shinji Ikaris that are inside others."

These others are as ambiguous as in our past and our bodies. While it is others that transform us, like Medusa, into a thing we don't want to be, it's also others who recognize and justify our attempt to assume our facticity. A philosopher friend of Sartre's, Maurice Merleau-Ponty, says, "'Hell is other people' doesn't mean 'Heaven is me.' If others are instruments of our torture, that's because they are first indispensable to our salvation." Therefore, the only solution to the hedgehog's dilemma is to try to connect with others by moving through the fear of hurting and being hurt.

From this viewpoint, let's look again at Operation Yashima in *Rebuild of Evangelion*. Seeing Shinji unable to recover from Ramiel's attack, Gendo commands his dismissal. However, Misato objects that Gendo should trust his son. The faith shown by Misato isn't found in the old edition. Although she showed a parental attachment to him, she seldom expressed such faith. In the old edition, Shinji wasn't an autonomous subject and wasn't recognized as such by others. Conversely, Shinji's assumption of facticity is supported by others around him in *Rebuild of Evangelion*. Thus, others are not only the possibility of our hell but also our salvation.

An Existential Phenomenology of Adolescence

The old edition described Shinji's way of being as an indefinite refusal of his facticity. This consisted of two attitudes: the attempt not to do anything and the attempt to be everything. As Beauvoir pointed out, these are two sides of the same coin.

We can thus examine the final question: What does *Evangelion* present through such an attitude? To answer it, I'd like to focus on the most embarrassing and problematic scene in *The End*. There, the movie suddenly displays the auditorium of the theater after the lines, "You want to be one with me, don't you?" "But not me with you. I'd rather die!" Critics have noted that we can consider this scene to be a criticism of those who love anime like *Evangelion*. Displaying in anime the real world's landscape, the anime characters' lives are superimposed on our own, meaning Shinji is a caricature of us. *Evangelion* thus reveals its function—to let us see our own existence.

What kind of existence does *Evangelion* describe? I'd like to call it *an adolescent existence,* whose characteristics are represented by Shinji's way of being. Although these characteristics are usually found in adolescents, adolescence is not identical to their existence; there are adults whose way of being is adolescent. We may become adolescents in certain situations that demand complex existential decisions, such as love, politics, or artistic creation. In such situations, we can easily slip into an attitude like Shinji's. For instance, in love, we might attempt not to do anything for fear of being dumped. In politics, we might give up on helping the oppressed under the pretext that we cannot help everyone.

It's such an attitude that *sekai-kei* represents; the dimension that *sekai-kei* seems to lack is the weight of our past, the (in)voluntary relationship with our body, and the adventure of achieving recognition by others, which we saw in *Rebuild of Evangelion*. If we lose these moments, indispensable to the self-cultivation of our existence, our being becomes empty and starts to shuttle between inaction and mere contemplation of the universal, which is another name for inaction. The link between the minor and grand narratives in *sekai-kei* represents such a back-and-forth. Therefore, we can call *sekai-kei* an existential phenomenology of adolescence; as such, it will never be "old."

4

My Life Is Worth Living Here!

JAKE POTTER

The first time anyone watches *Neon Genesis Evangelion*, they almost all have the same reaction: something along the lines of "What the actual heck did I just watch?!" But in order to fully understand and appreciate what *Evangelion* is doing, especially in the last few episodes, you have to understand how Evangelion is applying Søren Kierkegaard's *The Sickness unto Death*.

The Sickness unto Death has influenced *Neon Genesis Evangelion* at a fundamental level, reaching core aspects of the show such as character archetypes, themes, and even narrative. Particularly, Kierkegaard's assertion that the human condition is despair, a misrelation of the self to itself (or rather, an existential crisis), has influenced all of *Evangelion*'s main cast of characters, seen especially clearly in the show's controversial final two episodes, the second half of its theatrical conclusion, and Episode 16, which director Kazuya Tsurumaki said in *The End of Evangelion Theatrical Film Program* that he considered to be the turning point of the entire series.

The Sickness unto Death (subtitled *A Christian Psychological Exposition for Upbuilding and Awakening*) stands as a staple of existential philosophy, which is a philosophical approach that focuses on the existence of the individual person. But at the same time, it is just as concerned with being a theological work. *Evangelion*'s use of Kierkegaard's work is similar in that while it's highly existential, addressing questions like the nature of the self, it's just as concerned with addressing a theological problem: the problem of the human heart. The program that was released with *The End of Evangelion*'s theatrical release had some fascinating commentary on this:

A major theme in *Evangelion* is the problems of "people's hearts," and this is one of the attractions of the series which could not be found in other anime. Relationships with others, the meaning of one's existence, what is the self. . . . *Evangelion* started as a semi-realistic science-fiction mecha-action anime, and at first it was thought that the "people's hearts" of the characters were merely added as dramatic flavoring. However, as the series progressed, the issue of "people's hearts" grew in importance until it ultimately outstripped the other elements of mecha-action or solutions to the various mysteries. (*The End of Evangelion* Theatrical Program Book, translation by evaotaku.com)

What Is the Sickness unto Death?

The "sickness unto death," besides being a book title and the title of Episode 16, is actually another one of *Evangelion*'s many biblical references. In John 11, Jesus got word that Lazarus was sick. Jesus's response was that "the sickness is not unto death." But as Kierkegaard oh so acutely observes, Lazarus still died. To Kierkegaard, the sickness unto death was deeper than any physical sickness, even death itself, not because Jesus raises Lazarus to life, but because Jesus *exists*. This is why he introduces his book with such a bold statement:

Humanly speaking, death is the last of all, and, humanly speaking, there is hope only as long as there is life. Christianly understood, however, death is by no means the last of all; in fact, it is only a minor event within that which is all, an eternal life, and, Christianly understood, there is infinitely much more hope in death than there is in life. (*The Sickness unto Death*, p. 7)

This outlook is shared by many characters in *Evangelion*, particularly the members of SEELE, who make their hope for humanity clear in *The End of Evangelion* when they discuss the Human Instrumentality Project: "The fate of destruction is also the joy of rebirth. Through the sacrament of death, God, humanity, and all living beings will be reunited and reborn as one."

To Kierkegaard, the sickness unto death is despair, which he defines as a misrelation of the self to itself, which is in and of itself a synthesis that relates itself to itself. Confused yet? That's understandable. And yes, that's how Kierkegaard writes for his entire book. He died at forty-two!

Kierkegaard goes on to say that this sickness can take three forms: despair in not being conscious of having a self; despair in not willing to be oneself; and despair in willing to be oneself, all of which are illustrated clearly by a particular main character who just won't get in the robot! The task of the self is then to become itself, but due to the sheer depth of despair that all human beings have, this task is simply impossible. This is in essence the human condition—that because humanity is broken and unable to repair itself, we will never become our true selves. Kierkegaard's response to this problem is that the self can only become itself through the power of imagination, which he acknowledges is the means of the self's reflection. But ultimately he asserts that the self can only become itself through the relationship to God:

> What is decisive is that with God everything is possible . . . but the critical decision does not come until a person is brought to his extremity, when, humanly speaking, there is no possibility. Then the question is whether he will believe that for God everything is possible, that is, whether he will believe . . . At this point, then, salvation is, humanly speaking, utterly impossible; but for God everything is possible! This is the battle of faith, battling, madly, if you will, for possibility, because possibility is the only salvation.

This existentialist work may seem a lot like a Sunday school lesson, but then again, so can *Evangelion*. (Except, you know, with giant robots fighting *kaiju*. Sick!) This is because *The Sickness unto Death* and *Neon Genesis Evangelion* both have a unique philosophical framework, a kind of *theological existentialism,* an existential philosophy that only works in relationship with God. At Evangelion's cinematic conclusion, eternity has opened up and the beginning and the end of the world are both on full display. But at the climax of *The End of Evangelion*, it comes down to Shinji and the problems of his heart. Rather than explain all of the crazy symbolism or give answers to the mysteries of the series, everything boils down to whether or not Shinji thinks existing is worth it. Kierkegaard once again has written about this exact scenario:

> And when the hourglass has run out, the hourglass of temporality, when the noise of secular life has grown silent and its restless or ineffectual activism has come to an end, when everything around you is still, as it is in eternity, then . . . eternity asks you and every individual in these millions and millions about only one thing: whether you have lived in despair or not, whether you have despaired in such a way that you did not realize that you were in despair, or in such a way that you covertly carried this sickness inside of you as your gnawing secret, as a fruit of sinful love under your heart, or in such a way that you, a terror to others, raged in despair. And if so, if you have lived in despair,

then, regardless of whatever else you won or lost, everything is lost for you, eternity does not acknowledge you, it never knew you—or, still more terrible, it knows you as you are known and it binds you to yourself in despair. (p. 28)

Throughout the entirety of *The Sickness unto Death*, Kierkegaard's existentialism is intimately related to his theology, and vice versa. God's existence informs and shapes his existence. While Evangelion may or may not share the same worldview as Kierkegaard (though it's certainly up for debate), what's important is that *Evangelion* also addresses these existential themes in light of an overall framework of God's relationship with humanity. Regardless of the nature of this relationship, it's by nature a uniquely theological existentialism.

EVA Characters or Kierkegaard's Metaphors? You Decide.

But this theological existentialism isn't just examined by naming an episode after *The Sickness unto Death* or drawing inspiration from its themes. The theme of the problem of the human heart is examined by fleshing out characters that directly reflect content found in *The Sickness unto Death*. Some of these examples are so eerily similar to each other, that one can imagine Hideaki Anno working on the show with a copy of *The Sickness unto Death* open at his side.

Let's start with Misato. In his letter with the first volume of the manga, Anno describes Misato as "a 29-year-old woman who lives life so lightly as to barely allow the possibility of a human touch. She protects herself by having surface level relationships, and running away" (Sadamoto, p. 170). Throughout the series we see Misato fully fleshed out: We see how she dealt with her parent's relationship problems, and how this fractured her identity. We see how she dealt with the death of her father, the man whom she hated who died saving her life. We see how she threw herself into a co-dependent relationship with Kaji and how his death compounded her past traumas and emotionally broke her.

Ultimately in Episode 25 we see inside her heart. When the Human Instrumentality Project has been enacted, and Misato is able to see her life from the outside, she at first defends herself saying that she is happy. However she then turns from this, acknowledging that she isn't truly happy, and that the self that she wants everyone to see isn't her true self, screaming "This isn't the real me!" Thinking about everything we know of

Misato, look at this example of despair that Kierkegaard gives early in his book:

> A young girl despairs of love, that is, she despairs over the loss of her beloved, over his death or his unfaithfulness to her. This is not declared despair; no, she despairs over herself. This self of hers, which she would have been rid of or would have lost in the most bliss-ful manner had it become 'his' beloved, this self becomes a torment to her if it has to be a self without 'him'. This self, which would have become her treasure (although, in another sense, it would have been just as despairing), has now become to her a nauseating reminder that she has been deceived. Just try it, say to such a girl, 'You are consuming yourself,' and you will hear her answer, 'Oh, but the tor-ment is simply that I cannot do that.' (p. 20)

Misato is a perfect example of Kierkegaard's definition of despair because she represents the idea that even though she has experienced deep pain, it's not the loss of Kaji or the con-flict and loss of her father that's the true problem—the true problem is that her self is broken. Finding someone to spend her life with, or even excelling at her job to get revenge on the Angels for the death of her father are all temporary fixes that won't give her what she needs, because they aren't addressing the real problem of her brokenness.

Now let's look at Shinji. Anno described Shinji as a four-teen-year-old boy who

> shrinks from human contact. And he tries to live in a closed world where his behavior dooms him, and he has abandoned the attempt to understand himself. A cowardly young man who feels that his father has abandoned him, and so he has convinced himself that he is a completely unnecessary person, so much so that he cannot even commit suicide. (Sadamoto, p. 170)

Harsh. But Shinji has been abandoned by his father, though Shinji was also the one who ran away. And so he continues to run away. From everything. But just as Shinji feels abandoned by Gendo, Shinji has abandoned his true self and chooses to live in despair. This is again eerily similar to an example from Kierkegaard:

> Nevertheless, this despair is classified under the form: in despair not to will to be oneself. Like a father who disinherits a son, the self does not want to acknowledge itself after having been so weak. In despair it cannot forget this weakness; it hates itself in a way, will not in faith humble itself under its weakness in order thereby to recover itself—

no, in despair it does not wish, so to speak, to hear anything about itself, does not itself know anything to say. (p. 62)

Shinji is also a perfect example of despair because he exemplifies all three forms of despair that Kierkegaard proposes at different times. When we first meet Shinji, he acts as if his existence is unnecessary, as if there's no point to his being alive. This is what Kierkegaard describes as "in despair not to be conscious of having a self."

But then later in the series, Shinji acknowledges things he has done and things about himself, but he doesn't like those things, and wants to become a person who lives for the praise of others in order to mask his own inadequacy with himself. This is what Kierkegaard describes as "in despair not to will to be oneself."

Then finally in the later part of the series, Shinji does want to be himself, but struggles until the very end of Episode 26, resulting in some of his deepest despair. He has developed his sense of self, but sinks to a level of despair where his sense of self is consumed by despair, and is seen in a near-catatonic state in *The End of Evangelion*. This is what Kierkegaard describes as "in despair to will to be oneself."

Sad Boy Shinji Is . . . Our Example?

But Shinji, though in despair for ninety-nine percent of the series, is also a hopeful example for the audience to follow. In *The Sickness unto Death*, Kierkegaard sets out a dichotomy of sin and faith that all people must choose between: "Sin is: before God, or with the conception of God, in despair not to will to be oneself, or in despair to will to be oneself . . . Faith is: that the self in being itself and in willing to be itself rests transparently in God" (pp. 77–82). For most of the series, Shinji is fighting messengers of God (Angels or Apostles depending on whether you watch in English or Japanese) while living in despair. But when he encounters an Angel who looks like him and cares for him in Kaworu, Shinji not only questions who the enemy really is, but also questions his attempt at trying to forge his self while in despair.

But it's in the climax of the entire series where Shinji finds himself in a reality where "God, humanity, and all living beings are united." It's in the scientifically engineered Human Instrumentality Project that Shinji has his miraculous turning point. The Shinji who was depressed and ran away from reality because of the pain he felt around other people is given the world that he's always wanted. Rei describes it as "a world where you cannot tell where you end and others begin. A world where you exist everywhere and yet you exist nowhere all at once." Shinji asks if this is death, to which Rei replies, "Not quite. This is the world where we are all one. This is the world you wished for. Your world." This mirrors what Kierkegaard wrote about in *The Sickness unto Death* where the ultimate end of the self's despair is the equation of self to God and the creation of one's own universe:

> For even if this self does not go so far into despair that it becomes an imaginatively constructed god—no derived self can give itself more than it is in itself by paying attention to itself—it remains itself from first to last; in its self-redoubling it becomes neither more nor less than itself. In so far as the self in its despairing striving to be itself works itself into the very opposite, it really becomes no self. (pp. 68–69)

As Rei is talking to Shinji, he examines Misato's cross necklace, no doubt remembering her sacrifice for him. Upon seeing the cross, he responds that this world he wished for where no one else exists but himself is wrong. He acknowledges that even in the world that he escaped to where no one else existed, he still felt pain. "I thought it was alright to run away, but there was nothing good in the place I escaped to."

As Shinji and humanity are reborn and the world is being restored, a reflection is made by Rei, Kaworu, and Shinji. Rei says they are "the hope that one day people will be able to understand one another." Kaworu says they are "the words, 'I love you'." Shinji's response still struggles to accept that the hope and love Rei and Kaworu spoke about are real: "But that's just a pretense. A selfish belief. Like some kind of prayer. It can't possibly last forever." And yet Shinji does accept this.

These three characters each coincide with a theme. Rei represents hope. Kaworu represents love. But Shinji represents the action Kierkegaard calls us to: faith, or more specifically, faith to be yourself and rest in God. This scene, subtly referencing 1 Corinthians 13:13, shows that in the light of eternity, the three things which remain are faith, hope, and love. But our job first and foremost, as we stand in Shinji's place, is to have faith to be who we truly are and rest in God. Perhaps then it is no mere coincidence that the word "shinji" can also be the command form of the Japanese verb for "Believe!" or "Have faith!"

It's when Shinji decides to be himself that Human Instrumentality ends. The souls of humanity emerge as crosses of light ascend. As the world is being reborn, a dialogue unfolds:

> Reality exists in a place unknown, and dreams exist within reality. And truth lies in your heart. The contents of a person's heart shape their appearance, and new images will change their hearts and their form as well. The power of imagination is the ability to create your own future and your own flow of time. But if people don't act of their own free will, then nothing will change at all. So, you must regain your own lost form by your own volition . . . Anyone can return to human form, as long as they are able to imagine themselves within their own heart . . . All living creatures have the power to be brought back to life and the will to go on living. Anywhere can be paradise, as long as you have the will to live. (*The End of Evangelion*)

This dialogue is also laced with the theology of Kierkegaard. Like Kierkegaard's emphasis on the self's necessity of first imagining the possibility that God can save us, then imagination giving birth to faith, and ultimate emphasis in choosing to believe in Christianity and thus be reborn with correct identity and purpose, *Evangelion* establishes that hope for resurrection must first be born in the imagination, then evolve into reality when the person chooses to live with hope in community with others.

This is why in the final episode, "Take Care of Yourself," Shinji makes a miraculous realization: "I hate myself. But—but maybe—maybe I could love myself. Maybe my life could have a greater value. That's right, I am no more and no less than myself. I am me. I want to be myself. I want to continue existing in this world! My life is worth living here!" (Episode 26, "Take Care of Yourself"). At this, the veneer of the show drops. There are no more robots to pilot, no more science-fiction jargon, no more end of the world. Shinji is seen standing upon a newly formed Earth with blue skies, as the rest of the cast cheers and claps for him, congratulating him on his miraculous epiphany.

Shinji Is Hideaki Anno and Shinji Could Also Be the Audience

Neon Genesis Evangelion is the heart and soul of creator Hideaki Anno burned into animation. Through the lens of a science-fiction, giant robot, end of the world story, Anno sorted out his grappling with depression and poured all of himself and his thoughts into it. By referencing *The Sickness unto Death* throughout Evangelion, he didn't simply create a philosophical or a theological work, but a personal work that fluidly incorporates both.

He made Shinji his image in the animation and used *Evangelion* to explore his deepest questions. Through wrestling with issues of God, human identity, and the sickness of the human heart, Anno seems to have found an answer: life is worth living, and even though we are weak and we fail, we can be born again and move forward.

Søren Kierkegaard's theological existentialism is mirrored in *Neon Genesis Evangelion*'s theme and narrative, though perhaps with a more ambiguous approach than Kierkegaard's that could only be accomplished in the medium of animation. In this manner, *Neon Genesis Evangelion* can be viewed as a Japanese reflection and response to Kierkegaard's theological existentialism.

And although Anno doesn't give a Sunday morning gospel presentation, he presents his journey in animation as a template for others to follow and ask the questions he asked, giving them opportunity to find answers for themselves. In the live-action scene of *The End of Evangelion*, he even breaks the fourth wall, forcing the audience literally to look at themselves and ask if they are truly happy. Perhaps it's Bach's "Jesu, Joy of Man's Desiring" playing or the cross in the empty theater seats that truly makes this moment feel like a response after the preacher finishes his Sunday sermon. At its core, *Evangelion* is an invitation to let go of the escapism offered by science fiction and anime, and to be reborn and live life as it was meant to be lived. Perhaps intentionally, *Evangelion* shares that invitation in common with its namesake. It is, after all, Hideaki Anno's Gospel of a new beginning—his good news that life is still worth living.

5
The Meaning of You

Jonas Faria Costa

Man fears the darkness, and so he scrapes away at the edges of it with fire.

—Rei Ayanami

"What is man? Something created by God? Man is something created by man? All I have is my life, my heart. Entry plug, the vessel of the heart. The seat of the soul. Who is this? This is me. Who am I? What am I? What am I? I am myself. This object is myself. The shape that forms my self. This is the me that can be seen. But I sense that I am not me. It's very strange. I feel my body melting away. I no longer recognize myself. My form is fading away. I sense someone who is not me. Is somebody there, beyond here?"

These are the thoughts of Rei Ayanami when she tests the Unit 01, the EVA piloted by Shinji.

What am I? And why am I doing what I'm doing? *Neon Genesis Evangelion* has amazing fighting scenes, but this anime is so much more than just fights. I was young when I first watched *Evangelion*. I remember I was playing a massive multiplayer online (MMO) game with a lot of player vs. player (PvP) action. I remember feeling bad. Why was I defeating other players? I felt bad when I lost, but winning would mean I was making another person feel bad. What's the point of playing, anyway? It is just a game. Virtual. Have you ever felt like this? The feeling that things seem pointless. It all gets lost in the end. Deleted. Aside from when he had to fight Toji Suzuhara's possessed EVA, Shinji was not fighting other people. Yet, he felt emptiness in his efforts, and he felt both hurt by others and hurting others. Shinji keeps fighting. "And then what?" asks Rei in Shinji's mind. What's the point of fighting? Nothing seems to have meaning.

Though philosophy isn't traditionally known for giving answers, it at least helps us better understand the complexities of the topic we're dealing with. This understanding allows us to not be content with just any old answer. For these reasons, philosophy assists us better understand the complexities of *Evangelion*. When I watched *Evangelion*, I witnessed Shinji share in many of the same fears I felt. Well, maybe not the same fears, but I felt that his level of existential dread was on a similar level of the kind that I've experienced. Now, years after having watched *Evangelion* for the first time, after having read what others have written about the meaning of life, I revisited *Evangelion* with a bit more clarity in my mind. I would like to share this tiny bit of clarity with you, and to invite you to revisit *Evangelion* with me. Many of the reflective and dream sequences in *Evangelion* take place on a train. This makes sense. *Evangelion* takes you to many places. From contemplations about what is the divine to reflections about depression. The journey I'm inviting you on is just one tiny part of the bigger journey. Let's together (re)think, with Shinji, Rei, and Asuka about the meaning of life, who we are, and who you are.

What Am I?

Philosophy aims to make things clearer. One way to make things clearer is by better understanding the questions we're posing in the first place by employing the *Socratic Method*. This typically involves two steps, first getting clear on the thing we're investigating and then asking what could count as evidence in support of our beliefs about that thing.

The way we structure a question will impact how we'll answer it. The question "What am I?" already implies that *I* exist. And, yet, it seems that first we should answer "What am I?" so that we can answer "Why do I exist?" But when Shinji tries to see what he is, what he really is, he sees nothing. When Shinji loses his body, when it somehow fuses with the Unit 01, Shinji is only his conscience. But when he's only his conscience, he's nothing. Many times, the characters in *Evangelion* reflect about what they are, and they barely grasp anything.

This is no easy question. And it's up to each one of us to find an answer. Reflecting on what others have answered might help each one of us on our quest for an answer. When Shinji gets swallowed by Leliel, the Angel with a black hole-like shadow, he starts reflecting about what he is. Shinji realizes that there's more than one Shinji. "The self that is seen by others, and the self that observes that act," Shinji thinks. When you direct your awareness towards yourself, you're making yourself the object of your attention. So, there's you who is aware of object, and there's you as the object. Your awareness must fully detach from yourself to recognize yourself. But what is doing the recognizing? The same way you can be conscious of yourself, others are also aware of you. "There are even multiples of the individual named Shinji Ikari: The other Shinji Ikari, that's in your own heart. The Shinji in Misato Katsuragi's heart. The Shinji in Asula Soryu's heart. . . . Each is a different Shinji Ikari, and yet they're all the real Shinji Ikari."

One Shinji, No Shinji, a Hundred Thousand Shinjis

Each person has a different perception of Shinji. Is each perception of Shinji as real as any other perception? If so, then there are thousands of Shinjis. But there's also Shinji's conscience. Where is that when only Shinji can perceive that part of himself? When Shinji is aware of himself, he's aware of the Shinji to himself. But what is Shinji when he's aware of himself? If you become detached from your own self when you become aware of yourself, then what are you when you are observing yourself? Who are you? When Rei Ayanami reflected about who she was when she was inside Unit 01, she senses something that she feels it wasn't her. It's as if she was alien to herself, a stranger to herself. "A stranger inseparable from me." "Who was I? I was nothing." While these could be words from Shinji, Rei or Asuka, but they're words from the author Luigi Pirandello, in his book *One, None, and a Hundred Thousand.*

In Pirandello's book, the protagonist Moscarda starts his existential crisis when his wife points out to him that the right side of his nose is a little lower than the left side. Moscarda realizes that the image he had of himself was different from the image his wife had of him, which was as real as his own conception of himself. Shinji's in Rei's heart is as real as Shinji's in Asuka's heart, or in Shinji's own heart. There are a hundred thousand Shinjis, as there are a hundred thousand Reis as well.

When Rei thinks about what she is, she finds nothing, just like Moscarda in Pirandello's story. This active state of being conscious of your own self is the *one*, but it's a *one* that amounts to nothing. An eye sees the world, but it doesn't sees itself. The eyes you see in the mirror are strange to you. Moscarda can reflect about what he is. When Moscarda does that, he becomes the object of his conscience. This object is a Moscarda as a body in the world. "This object is myself. The shape that forms my self. This is the me that can be seen. But I sense that I am not me. . . . I sense someone who is not me"—Rei's thoughts.

Existence Is Absurd

The world is strange. When Shinji sees the flesh of his EVA, when he sees her eyes, he gets terrified. The world is strange to him. It's as if he doesn't belong to this world, as it does not make sense to him. When you perceive your own body as a thing in the world, this body becomes a stranger too. The philosopher Albert Camus said that this is the feeling of the absurd. It's absurd that we're alive and that we're going to die. When Shinji is swallowed by Leliel, just before he starts his reflections, he feels the smell of blood. It's the feeling of mortality. Death is absurd. For this reason, life is absurd.

Life is absurd because it results in death. No matter what we do, one day we'll die. If we'll die, then does anything matter? If the Angels will eventually destroy the world, why do we even try to save it? Why do we pilot EVAs? Death is the certainty of the limit of our existence, but it isn't the only limit. We're finite creatures, and we're very limited in what we can and can't do. The world is also absurd because it's beyond us and it too will end. We never see its true face, and when a part of it reveals itself to us in a glimpse, it's a desolating and terrifying view, as much as when Shinji looked upon the eyes of Unit 01 looking at him.

It seems existence has no meaning if we are to look for it beyond ourselves. Even if there was a meaning out there, it's beyond us, so we cannot recognize it for ourselves in a similar way to how we cannot recognize ourselves. Thus, we have to live without fully understanding our own meaning. But how can we live without knowing what it means to live a meaningful life?

I Don't Feel at Home in This World Anymore

"What am I?" quickly becomes "Why do I exist?" Shinji's own reflections on his existence lead him to be confused about the meaning of his life. Shinji is both a stranger to himself and the world. The world is strange when we don't feel we belong to it. This is the feeling experienced by both Shinji and Moscarda. The world is also strange when we fail to see any meaning. This is the feeling experienced by both Rei and Camus. There seems to be a connection between the feelings of not belonging and lacking meaning. Meaning and belonging go hand in hand.

Shinji tried many times to escape from his individual circumstances. Is it possible to escape from the feeling of desperation, though? Is it possible to go back to a world that we were deluded into believing made sense? This may be when you let yourself go into the hands of the divine. Things don't make sense, as we aren't supposed to make sense of them. We let the divine take care of it for us. This may be when you say that meaning is not in the divine, but in the material world, more precisely, in society. We can escape from that feeling of absurdity by letting our own identity dilute into the identity of the crowd, of the social class. This, however, may be the path of Instrumentality.

This may be when you become stubborn, refusing everything including life itself. Camus, however, thinks that we can live without escaping. He argues that a lucid person is someone who is constantly aware of the absurd, who is constantly aware of the limits in life but who doesn't give in, who doesn't try to escape. Life might have no meaning, but I'll try to get most of what I can. However, this is not what happens to Shinji.

No Escape from This World

Shinji doesn't escape because he's concerned about others. Shinji fails to conceive a meaning for what he does. Shinji doesn't grasp a *meaning* for his life—meaning in the sense of a *reason to exist*. Remember that there is the feeling of absurdity deriving from the lack of meaning, and also from the lack of belonging.

Sometimes, we feel alone, we feel empty. Sometimes, it seems impossible to reach other people. These feelings were expressed by all of the characters in *Evangelion*. They all feel very isolated. At one point, Asuka thinks she's useless, and nobody would ever connect with her, nobody would ever be kind to her. She hates everybody. In hating everybody, she hates herself most. Something very similar happens to Shinji. He feels alone, forgotten by the world. He hates himself, but he doesn't hate other people. He wants to be kind to others, but the world forces cruelty on him and around him.

It's hard to sustain values when the world falls apart. When the world is cruel and unkind to you and others, how can you still believe in kindness? How can you believe that what you're doing is worth anything? When no connection seems possible with other people, when the abyss between you and the others seems impossible to cross, the world loses value. And when the world loses value, the value of your *self* is also lost. As Shinji ends up realizing, the self is nothing but the relations built with others.

It's Okay for Me to Be Here!

In the end of *Evangelion* (I'm talking about the last episode of the series, not the movie), Shinji finds his resolution to this feeling of being a stranger in a strange world. Nothing makes sense. He doesn't know who he is or why he does the things that he does (even when he repulses himself). Above all, he fears being alone. He despairs when he feels alone. Using Pirandello's words, you feel most solitude when you feel you're a strange to yourself. In the end, Shinji finds a way out of this solitude.

> I get it, this is another possible world. A possibility that's inside me. The me that I am now isn't the entirety of what I am. Different versions of me might exist. Oh, right! There could even be a me that isn't an EVA pilot! If you think of it that way, this real world isn't such a bad place. The real world might not be so bad. . . . It's okay for me to be here!

Shinji finally feels he belongs to the world when he feels in his own heart that he's never alone. The others are always with him and they accept him. Shinji doesn't know what the meaning of life is, but it does make sense for him to fight for his friends. By reflecting about what's in his heart, which is a reflection about "What am I?", Shinji fulfils the answer to the other question, "Why do I exist?" It's okay to exist with so many limits because some of these limits are the frontiers between you and others. These are as much frontiers as they are connections. There can only be a *connection* between things that are not the one and same thing. You don't overcome solitude by diluting yourself into a crowd, but by making connections, making bridges. Maybe the meaning of life isn't something to be understood, but to be felt.

"Right, . . . I'm me. But at the same time, it's true that *other people make up parts of my heart*! That's right, Shinji Ikari.

II

After (Re)Birth and Before Death

6

When Heroes Can (Not) Choose to Become Themselves

ANDREW M. WINTERS

"This is humanity's very last trump card." Ritsuko Akagi's words strike Shinji Ikari as he takes in the gravity of the situation he must face. The white eyes of EVA Unit 01's purple-domed head stare at Shinji, awaiting his decision to become a pilot. Having been brought to the underground layer of NERV, Shinji is confronted with the decision to save humanity by piloting the giant EVA or return to the daily humdrum of adolescence.

By agreeing to become a pilot Shinji creates the opportunity to discover whether he is the hero that everyone hopes he is, but at the potential cost of his mental and physical well-being. To choose to not become a pilot he secures his fate as a coward and estranged son from his father at the potential cost of humanity. In the very first episode of *Neon Genesis Evangelion* ("Angel Attack"), Shinji is presented with choices that are not of his own design.

Shinji is not alone, though, in being forced to confront unsavory options. Both Asuka Soryu and Rei Ayanami must also make decisions to become pilots. None of the adolescents can make adequate preparations to take on the mental and physical turmoil that awaits them as they sync with mecha beasts to battle with Angels set on destroying all of humanity. Like all adolescents, Asuka, Rei, and Shinji must recognize that it is not up to them to become something else as they transform into adults. Instead, it is a matter of how they will undergo that change.

In becoming adults, Asuka, Rei, and Shinji must undergo a transformative process. By becoming pilots, they are to undergo a rite of initiation to ensure that they become the adults they are meant to be. As Mircea Eliade states in *Rites of Symbols of Initiation*, "Initiation represents one of the most significant spiritual phenomena in the history of humanity." It is by going through initiations that a person becomes what they should be. Many of the initiations we go through are to assist us undergo the passages of life we must go through regardless of our choosing to do so. These passages include being born, obtaining sexual maturity, and dying, all of which we go through without giving consent.

While Shinji and the others could certainly choose not to become pilots, they cannot choose not to become adults. Furthermore, the consequences of not being initiated among the EVA pilots leave the burgeoning teens with little choice. Asuka's personal sense of self and confidence would be shattered (as evinced by her reactions to no longer being able to sync with her own EVA in Episode 23 "Tears"). Rei's ability to fulfill the duties for which she was cloned, including protecting Shinji, would be diminished. Shinji would become even more alienated from his father. In addition to their personal consequences, all three of them would carry the burden of contributing to the demise of humanity.

The severity of their respective consequences indicates that the three characters are not presented with the authentic decision to become pilots. Instead, they are susceptible to coercion. The option to become adults is even more of an illusion. To choose not to become an adult would require them choosing their own deaths. Whereas Asuka, Rei, and Shinji are coerced (and deceived) by NERV and SEELE into becoming pilots, we are all coerced by Nature to go through the processes of life.

To Sync or Not to Sync

While becoming an EVA pilot might be a rite of initiation for becoming an adult (which I hope is the case for only a select few), becoming a pilot and becoming an adult are both transformative experiences. Transformative experiences alter our core values and shape our future decisions. They fundamentally change who we are and how we see ourselves. In her *Transformative Experiences*, L.A. Paul (still alive) appeals to the hypothetical transformative experience of becoming a vampire or the potentially real decision to become a parent to illustrate how we cannot *rationally* decide to become either. Traditional views of rational decision-making involve appealing to evidence to which we have access and is relevant to the kind of decisions we are considering.

There are some problems, though, with the traditional view when it comes to making decisions that will result in a change to the very values we use to determine what evidence is relevant. First, when considering becoming a pilot Shinji only takes into consideration his relationship with his father and his personal sense of shame if he lets everyone else down. As he becomes more comfortable piloting Unit 01, we see him become more single-minded. "Target in the center, pull the switch" (Episode 3, "The Phone that Never Rings"). It's no longer a matter of maintaining relationships, but it is a matter of survival that keeps Shinji in the pilot seat. What is more relevant to choosing to become a pilot? Pride? Relationships? Survival? As Shinji goes through the change of becoming a pilot, so do his preferences for determining why he should continue to be a pilot.

Second, Shinji cannot know what it's like for him to be a pilot until he is a pilot. Before attempting to sync with Unit 01 Shinji can ask Rei what it is like to be a pilot while she is laid out on the stretcher recovering from her wounds incurred during her battle with Sachiel. Her testimony, however, would only be reliable for what it was like for her to be a pilot. Shinji could watch videos, read manuals, and study everything there is to know about piloting EVAs. Still, he would not know what it is like for him to pilot the EVA, which is his concern in making the decision to pilot or not.

Instead of attempting to make the decision to become a pilot on the basis of evidence Shinji believes will help him understand what it is like to be a pilot, without becoming a pilot, Paul recommends that we should be more concerned with discovering who we will be after having undergone a transformative experience. So, instead of Shinji being concerned with what it is like to be a pilot before deciding to be one, he should be interested in discovering who he will become once he begins piloting. Does he wish to discover whether he will be a hero?

A Call to Action

Shinji quickly syncs with Unit 01 (it houses the soul of his mother, Yui Ikari, after all). As he transforms after undergoing each training session and battle, so does the EVA. Unit 01 does things that no other EVA has done. Unit 01 operates without a pilot in the entry plug. It (she?) functions without being tethered to a power source. More importantly, Unit 01 goes berserk. When going berserk, Unit 01 seems to awaken. But, Unit 01 isn't the only thing to awaken when going berserk. Something inside Shinji also awakens. For him it is the call to become a hero. A call to become himself.

Joseph Campbell outlines in his *Hero with a Thousand Faces* three stages a hero must undergo. A hero must go through a separation, an initiation, and a return. While it is likely that we can imagine the ways that both Asuka and Rei go through these stages, it is clearer as to how Shinji goes through the hero's journey as told in the series. Let's follow him on this journey.

The first stage of separation requires that the would-be hero becomes aware of information that calls for them to go on a quest. At the very outset of the series Shinji is presented with the calling to save humanity. Misato bringing him to NERV, Ritsuko telling him of the importance of the task, and his father, Gendo, demanding of him to make a decision. Shinji's self-doubt leads him to feel even more useless as he realizes that his own father would not have called him had Shinji not been of any use. All of these factors shape his understanding of what is being demanded of him, even though he cannot have a complete understanding of what it is like for himself to fulfill those demands.

It would seem that Shinji fails to be a hero at his first opportunity, but, on Campbell's model, the hero refuses the initial call. Shinji is overwhelmed by information and makes excuses as he crumbles at the very thought of piloting the massive EVA. Even those who instruct him to overcome his fear feel some level of sympathy. Misato tells Ritsuko, "It seems cruel, making him bear the burden of mankind's destiny." The hero cannot be forced into taking on the heroic tasks, but has to fully commit to the quest. It is not enough to follow orders to become a hero.

Once Shinji commits to fighting the Angels, even if he doesn't like it, he is provided with a special weapon or power that will make his task that much easier. He clearly has the EVA at his disposal, but Unit 01's abilities to function without power and to go berserk are unique tools that will assist Shinji in his journey. The connection he has with his EVA allows him to further commit to destroying Angels.

Yet, Shinji's quest is not just about defeating Angels and saving humanity. His quest is ultimately about discovering himself. By fully committing to his quest of figuring out who he is, proving himself to others, and saving humanity, Shinji is able to cross the threshold and embark on the journey. This is when he is able make the final separation from his home (the seemingly trite world of music, reading, and school) so that he can successfully embark on the quest.

Initiation

Once Shinji has fully separated from his past, he must go through a sequence of initiations. The first of these is the road of trials. Campbell outlines this as being a series of tests and trials. The hero is not always successful, though, but even uses failures to proceed down the path of becoming a hero. Shinji certainly undergoes a set of trials, including combating Angels, his father, and himself. The Angels' abilities to adapt to their environments means that Shinji must quickly adapt and change if he is to be successful with each one. For example, the seventh Angel, Israfel, is able to split into two twins, which requires that Shinji learn how to fight in sync with Asuka (Episode 9, "Both of You, Dance Like You Want to Win!").

In addition to going through numerous trials, the hero must have a meeting with The Goddess, during which the hero experiences a love that has the power and significance to that of a mother. Shinji's connection with his EVA is likely due to the connection he had with his mother, Yui, whom he had witnessed dying during the Unit 01 Contact Experiment when he was only three years old. In the fifteenth episode ("Those Women Longed for the Touch of Others' Lips, and Thus Invited Their Kisses"), Shinji visits Yui's grave along with his father.

While Shinji does not directly interact with Yui, the grave plot facilitates a conversation between Shinji and Gendo that aids Shinji in developing a better understanding of their relationship. This understanding further assists Shinji in learning why he has been tasked with fighting the Angels in the first place. Shinji is honest about why he's been afraid to visit the grave site in over three years. Gendo shares that there is no body buried at the plot, but that the headstone is merely decorative—a way of remembering. Yet, Gendo also acknowledges that humans survive by forgetting. Shinji uses this conversation to find some level of comfort with the loss that he's experienced.

While parental figures play a significant role in helping the hero advance in their journey, others can be deterrents. Temptations arise on the journey in the form of attractive bodies. Campbell labels this phase as the recognition of the woman as temptress, but it can be any kind of body that tempts the hero to abandon the journey for the sake of material or personal gain. We see both Asuka and Misato play this role by arousing Shinji's sexual desires.

In the first episode, Shinji ogles Misato's photo of her bent over revealing cleavage while donning short denim shorts. She later uses her sexual charms to motivate and tempt Shinji when she kisses him and says, "We'll do the rest later" (*End of Evangelion*). In the tenth episode ("Magma Diver"), Asuka casually flirts with Shinji as he attempts to study, drawing attention to her breasts as examples of thermal expansion. Despite Asuka's unsuccessful attempts to get Shinji's (and Ryoji Kaji's) attention, Shinji is tempted by her and only able to act when he's not being watched. Their dynamic culminates in the infamous sequence in *The End of Evangelion*.

Even though Shinji regularly grapples with his sexual identity and the temptations that surround him, he is able to pursue his heroic journey. The next part of the initiatory phase is to obtain atonement with the father. Shinji must confront and be initiated by whomever holds the ultimate power in his life. Unsurprisingly, this is Gendo. Shinji is frequently seen confronting the feelings he has for his own father and it is when he gets small glimmers of approval that Shinji lights up. We do things for praise, since it is through the acknowledgement from others that we know that we exist. Shinji must confront these beliefs when being interrogated by the Angel Leliel (Episode 16, "Splitting of the Breast").

It is through the recognition of a father who has deserted that leads us to feel deserted, yet we survive by deceiving ourselves. In order to continue we must believe that we can change ourselves. This is a particularly difficult stage for the hero since the atonement that is sought does not mean that the father atones, but instead that the hero finds peace with the relationship—not that the peace is given. This stage also requires recognizing the amount of suffering that exists within the world, the suffering that exists within ourselves. As Shinji says in response to Leliel's inquiry, "This world is filled with too much pain and suffering to continue." It is only when Shinji comes to accept these truths and his relationship with his father that he can continue on his quest.

Once peace is obtained, the hero must undergo *apotheosis*—a spiritual death and rebirth. Not only is Shinji's quest a battle with the Angels, but he must also undergo a radical transformation to recognize his own identity—his own meaning. In many ways Shinji's transformation is analogous to the transformation that humanity must undergo if it is to survive. As Rei states towards the end of Episode 11 ("In the Still Darkness"),

> Man has always feared the darkness so he scrapes away at its edges with fire. He creates life by diminishing the darkness.

It is this very process that allows humanity to be reborn. We observe Shinji also go through this process in his discussions with Leliel when he exhibits the duality of the self: a self that is observed by the observing self. Through this awareness that there is a self that exists in the perception of one's own self and in the perception of others Shinji is able to emerge from Leliel. Both Shinji and Unit 01 are born anew.

Shinji's newfound understanding is not the victory, though. It is a necessary step to the ultimate boon of him recognizing that he is worth living. In Episode 17 ("The Fourth Child"), Shinji becomes more sympathetic to the idea that people don't understand themselves, which allows him to accept people's flaws, including his own. This, however, is not enough to prevent him from running away again when he decides that he will not pilot his EVA again (Episode 19, "A Man's Battle"). When Shinji does return, though, both Shinji and Unit 01 are unbound. They have completed their spiritual transformation.

We Must Change to Succeed

In a similar way, this is what it is to become an adult. By recognizing that we are made in our parents' images, we take on a large amount of suffering. It is through the transformation, though, that we become independent and not defined by our parents. In order to get to this stage, we must relax our souls while not denying our pasts. We must recognize that we decide our futures. As Shinji overhears his mother say,

> Anywhere can be paradise as long as you have the will to live. After all, you are alive, so you will always have the chance to be happy. As long as the Sun, the Moon, and Earth exist, everything will be all right." (Episode 20, "Shape of Heart, Shape of Human")

How Do We Find Paradise?

The members of SEELE have set themselves on a similar task of breaking free from their maker, while at the same time knowing that they cannot create gods. Instead, they attempt to bring about a "new genesis for mankind" through the Human Instrumentality Project. Instead of creating gods, they strive to create dolls because they are alone. The fifth child and seventeenth Angel, Kaworu Nagisa reflects on the plight of humans to find comfort as they overcome themselves to become something new, "Man can never make loneliness disappear because man is alone, but many can forget. So man can find the will to live" (Episode 24, "The Final Messenger"). How do we find ourselves?

Rei's own ruminations further highlight the complexity of discovering where the will to live resides.

> Who are you? I am neither false nor fake. I am simply me. Are you an object pretending to be human? I became myself through the instrumentality of the links and my relationships with others. I am formed by interactions with others. They create me as I create them. These relationships and interactions serve to shape the patterns of my mind.

Instrumentality serves as a return to the beginning through the mechanizations devised by SEELE. The human will is a product of the hope of filling the void and the fear that it produces. The darkness will never vanish as long as humanity is merely human. Yet, through Instrumentality humanity must go through destruction and death to return to nothingness. This may appear to be Shinji's wish when he no longer sees himself as having anything to contribute. He believes that we attempt to become one with others because we recognize a deficiency in ourselves. He believes that we cannot survive alone.

He does not stop here, though. Like a good philosopher, Shinji recognizes how each question's meaning is dependent upon some other deeper question. Through Episodes 24, 25, and 26 (including the complementary endings), Shinji visits questions dealing with his self-worth, self-identity, and our hatred towards others. He identifies his desire to be worth something and comes to understand that we have to find our own values for ourselves. How, then, can we do this if we exist because we are defined by others? Again, what is the self? We change, but how can we do this freely when the self is restrained by the boundaries with others. "By recognizing the differences between yourself and others you establish your identity as yourself." In other words, where does the self end and others begin? "I am worth living here!" wherever that boundary with others happens to be. That is the victory. Shinji and the other characters understand that Shinji has succeed in his quest when they congratulate him, allowing him to reject Instrumentality.

Victory Is Only Part of the Journey

Shinji is inclined to bask in his newfound bliss. Campbell identifies this as the hero's refusal to return to his previous life and share his lessons with others. For Shinji, the return to his previous life and move away from Instrumentality is to expose himself to the feelings of doubt, fear, and shame that he had left behind. We see him lose his deep understanding of the self in *The End of Evangelion*. Even though he is self-aware, "I'm so fucked up," he is unable to fully control his desires while in the presence of Asuka's unconscious naked body.

While the hero's victory must be done on his own, Shinji could not have advanced along the path without the aid of Unit 01 (his mother), Rei, Asuka, Misato, Ritsuko, Ryoji, and even Gendo. It shouldn't be surprising, then, that the third stage of returning is itself a daring escape from the blissful state of having succeeded. For Shinji, the return is to leave the space where wisdom and peace were obtained. Those who had helped him along the path are also responsible for ensuring that he can safely return to somewhat a normal life.

Shinji is unlikely to return to being a boring insecure adolescent once he has confronted both internal and external threats in a similar way to how we cannot return to being adolescents after having gone through the pains of becoming an adult. Once we have found the ability to return to the world, we have a responsibility to aid others so that their own transformations may go more smoothly. This is Shinji's responsibility to protect and support others as humanity continues to sustain its existence. Doing so requires maintaining a balance of two worlds.

One of those worlds is where the self is defined by others as part of Instrumentality and the other is the world where each person establishes her own values. With others, but not too close. By learning to master these two worlds, Shinji is free from regrets of the past and worries of the future. He is able to focus on the present. That's what it is for him to be a hero. Yet, not all heroes come home. Not all heroes have a home to which they can return. So, why become a hero? In many ways, we cannot choose to be what we are. Sometimes we must answer a call to discover who we are—even if doing so may require going through stages of suffering. Maybe we should turn on some anime and listen: "Like an angel without mercy, rise young boy to the heavens as a legend."[1]

---

[1] For Fionnuala.

7

The Young, the Old, The Monstrous

HANS-GEORG EILENBERGER

If you ignore the post-apocalyptic setting, the bizarre creatures, and the mishmash of Christian themes, *Neon Genesis Evangelion* is essentially a coming-of-age story.

It features the fourteen-year-old antihero Ikari Shinji who joins humanity's battle against the mysterious Angels. Unexpectedly, Shinji finds himself in the no-man's-land between childlike sensitivities and an unforgiving adult world. His situation is paradoxical: while Shinji greatly differs from his adult peers, he is destined to become one of them.

How can two very different beings eventually become the same? How is it that the passage of time turns children into adults? Is this an automatic process or does it matter how time is "spent"? Such are the questions raised by the paradox of growing up.

We get a glimpse of the paradox by looking at a conversation between Shinji and Kaji (Episode 18, "Ambivalence"). Shinji asks for details about his father's life, saying that he has already learned quite a few things about Gendo. Kaji, however, denies this:

KAJI: You're wrong there. You only believe that you've learned. People can't understand others completely. Who knows if you can even understand yourself? Understanding each other one hundred percent is impossible. Of course, that's why we spend so much time trying to understand ourselves and others. That's what makes life so interesting.

SHINJI: Is that also true for you and Miss Misato?

KAJI: The word we use for "she" literally means "the woman far away." To us, women will always be on the distant shore. Basically, there's a river dividing men and women, deeper and wider than the ocean.

SHINJI: I don't understand adults.

Kaji's cryptic remarks give Shinji pause. It almost seems as if Kaji is holding something back and tries to deflect from the actual issue. Shinji's conclusion is striking: he doesn't say "I don't understand what you're saying, Kaji" but rather "I don't understand adults." What could he mean by this? Perhaps Shinji interprets Kaji's way of communicating as secretiveness or game-playing—something he has seen in Misato, Ritsuko, and Gendo as well. He doesn't understand why adults would talk like that. Why wouldn't you just openly admit your feelings and intentions?

If it's impossible to understand others completely, as Kaji claims, children and adults are struggling to have even an incomplete understanding of each other. They are separated by their different bodies, emotions, and attitudes. And yet, if they want to inhabit a common world, they need to reach out to each other, which is "what makes life so interesting."

Children can anticipate the roles and conflicts of adult life; adults, in turn, can recall their own childhoods. As life progresses, children move even further to the position of the adult. Growing up means to eventually cross the experiential divide between the two "tribes." One day, Shinji may be able to put himself in Kaji's shoes, to understand his allusions and the motives for using them.

Like the conversation of Shinji and Kaji, growing up is complex and multi-layered. It clearly deserves the attention of great thinkers, such as the French philosopher Maurice Merleau-Ponty (1908–1961). Merleau-Ponty was greatly interested in the child psychology of his time, studying the ways in which children experience themselves, how they relate to adults, and how they deal with growing up. Through the lens of his philosophy, we get a better grasp of what is at stake in Shinji's coming-of-age story. In turn, the lively details of Shinji's experience help to illuminate the less accessible parts of Merleau-Ponty's thinking.

Shinji's situation

Neon Genesis Evangelion starts with a bang, introducing most of the show's major themes. In the first episode ("Angel Attack"), Shinji finds himself in an unfamiliar city with nothing but a saucy postcard from his guardian to-be, is dragooned into mortal combat with the Angel Sachiel (also known as the Third Angel—the Fourth Angel in *Rebuild of Evangelion*), and has two near-death experiences. Throughout his career as an Evangelion pilot, Shinji has similar encounters with sexuality, power, and violence. They are the great external forces that shape Shinji's life, the power of circumstance beyond his control. It's through Shinji's grappling with these forces that his story unfolds.

Following Merleau-Ponty, we can describe sexuality, power, and violence as major elements of Shinji's *situation*. If Shinji's situation were a kaleidoscope through which he looked at his surroundings, the three forces would be shards of glass inside of it. A situation is thus a unique standpoint or perspective that allows us to move through the world. There are no truly impartial observers, according to Merleau-Ponty, since we are essentially situated beings. As such, we always find ourselves in particular circumstances, bodies, families, nations, and stories that condition what we can see, feel, or think.

Shinji's situation resembles typical adolescence in a number of ways. In adolescence, virtually all children face great developmental tasks. They need to integrate into the adult world, governed by obscure rules and powerful institutions. It's a place where facts and objectivity rule supreme, to the point of brutality. As she grows up, the child's very body becomes foreign, a site of unsuspected growth and disturbing new sensations. All of these elements are present in Shinji's situation as well, but to an extreme degree. Shinji experiences terrible violence at the hands of the Angels and is straitjacketed by NERV's regime. His situation leans more toward typical adolescence in the area of sexuality, where Misato, Asuka, and arguably Kaworu prompt a gust of erotic curiosity.

Shinji cannot control the sexual, institutional, and violent forces that intervene in his life. They are the unaccountable torrents that shape his situation. This does not mean, however, that these forces impose rigid limits on his actions. While Shinji cannot will away his sexual feelings, NERV's influence, or the Angel threat, he can respond to them in creative ways. This is consistent with Merleau-Ponty's understanding of situation not as rigid confinement, but as the background for action.

Merleau-Ponty develops the notion of the background in his discussion of human perception. Whenever we focus on an object, we perceive it as a *Gestalt*, that is, a figure or shape, that stands out against a background. While the background is not as such the object of our perception, it is vaguely present and by this presence "supports" the appearance of the object. Imagine, for instance, the difficulty of spotting the Angel Leliel (also known as the Twelfth Angel—doesn't appear in the *Rebuild* series)—or rather, its shadow—in a herd of giant zebras. Its black and white stripes would merge with the fur pattern of the animals, making it all but invisible. Against the clear blue sky of Tokyo-3, by contrast, the zebra print of Leliel's shadow stands out marvelously. In this way, different backgrounds support different figures, making some features leap out while obscuring others.

Used in a figurative sense, the notion of background helps us to clarify the working of situation. As the mainstays of Shinji's situation, sexuality, power, and violence form the background of his actions. In the above example, it would be strange to say that the blue sky "determines" the appearance of Leliel, and the same is true for the forces that shape Shinji's situation. Violence, power, and sexuality do not produce Shinji's actions like a cause brings forth an effect. Rather, they provide a context to which Shinji reacts and renders his actions meaningful.

By looking at the situations of people, we can also make sense of their attitudes toward life. Take the striking difference between Shinji and his father Gendo: raised in relative seclusion, Shinji's main concern is with the wellbeing of the people around him. This is why he finds it so hard to adapt to the mindset of NERV with its global outlook and calculating logic. Gendo, by contrast, has lived through the Second Impact and the loss of his wife. This situation afforded him very different possibilities for acting and feeling, doubtlessly contributing to his emotional hardening.

The Deficit View

The relation between children and adults is far from equal. In most societies, adults have authority over children, who are expected to be respectful and compliant. Children embody the promise of the future, but it's only by fulfilling this promise— that is, by becoming adults—that they are taken seriously.

Clearly, the Evangelion pilots are indispensable for the operation of NERV (and the survival of humanity). *As children* with particular ideas, abilities, and needs, however, they have little value. Gendo, for one, has no patience with the caprices of a child who refuses the adult mindset. Against Shinji's vehement protests, he allows the butchering of the Angel-infested Evangelion Unit 03 (Episode 18, "Ambivalence"). Even Misato, who is genuinely concerned about Shinji's wellbeing, undervalues the boy's childlike self. Neglecting what Shinji already knows, she focuses on all the things he still needs to learn: to open up to others, make his own decisions, and face up to his father. In the eyes of Gendo and Misato, the boy Shinji has value only in relation to the adult he will become. *As a child*, he is imperfect, irrational, whiny, and weak. We may call this view the "deficit view" of the child.

Merleau-Ponty rejected the deficit view, which dominated the child psychology of his time. In criticizing the child psychologists, he developed his own, more positive reading of the child's capacities and experience. According to Merleau-Ponty, the adult isn't better or more advanced than the child—their bodies and psyches are merely different. Take the example of perception: If we adopt the child's point of view, we realize that her way of viewing things actually makes a lot of sense. A small child may draw a cube not in perspective (that is, with only three sides visible), but with all its sides spread out. This flattened depiction allows the child to capture the cube in its entirety; it doesn't mean that she has failed at realistic drawing.

The deficit view is connected to the idea that growing-up is a one-way street of continuous improvement. Merleau-Ponty argues, by contrast, that development always comes with gains *and* losses. Many aspects of human minds and bodies deteriorate with age, such as curiosity, imagination, and brain plasticity. Depending on your perspective, you may consider Shinji's moral scruples an asset of his childlike mentality. His actions in the series show him capable of moral feelings that are lost in his adult peers. And isn't it striking that only children appear to be suitable Evangelion pilots?

The third episode "A Transfer" gives us a beautiful vision of the value in Shinji's childlike experience. It shows Shinji wandering around the countryside after running away from home. In one scene, Shinji is standing on a mist-shrouded ridge and gazes back at Tokyo-3. Through his eyes, we get to see the city in its broader context, embedded in a vast green landscape. NERV staffers are unlikely to indulge in such panoramic views. In their singlemindedness, they give absolute priority to the *technological questions* around humanity's survival. Shinji's childlike sensitivity, by contrast, opens our minds to the bigger picture: To the value of vulnerability, the importance of moral feelings, and the dignity of the natural world—things without which survival wouldn't be life, but only its dead, abandoned husk.

The Ambiguity of Growing Up

On his wanderings, Shinji comes across his classmate Kensuke playing war games in a meadow. The encounter of the two boys stages the clash of two opposing attitudes. On the one side, there is Shinji, who dreads fights and violence; on the other side, there is Kensuke, who is obsessed with the military and cannot wait to join the ranks of NERV. Both boys express their attitudes in childlike ways. While Shinji has run away, Kensuke is playing games. Yet, Shinji and Kensuke do not just show different attitudes toward the military; their encounter is also symbolic of the general ambivalence of the child who goes through adolescence. In the state of ambivalence, the child experiences contradictory emotions at the same time. She simultaneously dreads and anticipates adulthood.

The notions of ambivalence and ambiguity play a prominent role in the philosophy of Merleau-Ponty. Experience is ambiguous because it is bound to the body. When in sync with the EVA, Shinji launches at his enemies with effortless power. So firm is their connection that he doesn't notice any difference between his will and the EVA's movements. This unity of the EVA's body and Shinji's mind suddenly collapses when an accident stops the body in its tracks. Caught inside Leliel's belly, the EVA is no longer an extension of Shinji's will—it is a cage, a death trap.

What holds true between Shinji and the EVA also applies to the relation of mind and body more generally. In Merleau-Ponty's language, ambiguity arises from the fact that the body is at the same time a subject (a tool indistinct from the mind) and an object (an obstacle for the mind). This ambiguity is an essential characteristic of human existence. It plays a special role in the life of the child, where it gives rise to ambivalence.

Asuka is a showcase example of adolescent ambivalence. She brags about her sexual experience, plays erotic tricks on Shinji, and desperately tries to convince Kaji that she's no longer a child. On this account, Asuka eagerly anticipates the sexual role of the adult and embraces the bodily changes that put her on track toward adulthood. At the same time, however, Asuka clings to her childlike ways. When Misato denies that she is dating Kaji, Asuka berates the insincerity of adult relationships: "Sure, I've never been involved in an indecent adult relationship! And here you're acting like a proper guardian?! You hypocrite! You make me puke!" (Episode 16, "Splitting of the Breast").

Shinji discovers the infantile flipside of Asuka's confidence when he tries to kiss her in her sleep. Hearing her whisper "Mama," he stops his advance (Episode 9, "Both of You, Dance Like You Want to Win!").

Asuka's ambivalence is echoed by the anatomy of the Evangelions. Piloting their EVAs, the Children command the most powerful weapons humanity has ever dared to conceive—could there be anything more "grown up"? And yet, their presence inside the EVAs inadvertently enacts the most primordial infantile fantasy: re-entering the mother's womb. After all, the Evangelion are not only made of the flesh of Adam and Lilith, the progenitors of humans and Angels; they also contain the souls of their pilot's mothers (with the exception of EVA Unit 00).

Following Merleau-Ponty, we can interpret Asuka's ambivalence as an acting out of ambiguity. In puberty, Asuka's body undergoes profound changes that are beyond her control. In this way, her body becomes a kind of object, not only for her own mind, but also in the eyes of others. Asuka starts to feel unfamiliar sensations and notices the changing expectations of the people around her. Thus, she tastes the ambiguity of a body that is both subjective and objective. Together with her social environment, Asuka's body brings forth a situation that pulls the girl toward a future whose contours are only vaguely visible. This is both exciting and troubling. It is the coincidence of these contradictory feelings that makes up Asuka's ambivalence, her oscillation between anticipation and regression. Asuka wants to grow up, and yet she does not want to; she anticipates adulthood, and yet she regresses to childhood.

Freedom and Development

Like Asuka, Shinji moves hesitantly between the positions of the adult and the child. There are many examples of Shinji's ambivalence. Shinji quits the Evangelion program twice, but then re-joins it; he wants to be alone, yet he is lonely; he says he hates his father, but yearns for his attention. The Third Child has a hard time opening up to others and, as a result, is continuously wavering between emotional investment and retreat. His ambivalence echoes the Hedgehog's Dilemma mentioned in Episode 3 ("A Transfer").

In a conversation with Misato, Ritsuko likens Shinji to a hedgehog that avoids other hedgehogs because it is afraid of injury. To this, Misato replies that "growing up means finding a distance with other people where you can avoid hurting each other too much." Overcoming the hedgehog's dilemma is a task that many children face in one way or another. Leaving the cocoon of the family home, the child finds herself in an unfamiliar context filled with strange people and their inscrutable demands. In this radically changed situation, she needs to learn how to open up without sacrificing the integrity of her own self.

Though children in similar situations face similar developmental tasks, they experience and tackle these tasks in unique ways. In their roles as Evangelion pilots, Shinji is constantly looking into an abyss, Asuka first thrives and then breaks down, and Rei—is just being Rei. Merleau-Ponty helps us to appreciate such differences with his emphasis on individual freedom. As Merleau-Ponty points out, development is not an automatism. Bodily and social changes are general, anonymous forces that intervene in the life of the adolescent child. Yet, they do not *determine* the course of her development. It is still up to the child herself to *make sense* of the new situation. Making sense involves an act of freedom, where the child integrates the novelties of adolescence into her existing life projects.

We can interpret Shinji's story as a developmental puzzle. Living with his sensei, the boy's childhood was relatively sheltered and uneventful. Upon entering Tokyo-3, however, Shinji finds himself in an infinitely more challenging situation. Somehow he needs to make sense of the violence, power, and sexual cues around him. The demands on his personality are extreme. Shinji is told to man up, to open up emotionally, and once in a while to climb into a giant bioweapon and fight off alien invaders.

There is nothing like the threat of human extinction to catapult a child into adulthood. Yet, the pressure takes its toll on the sanity of the Evangelion pilots. While Asuka collapses completely, Shinji suffers in silence. Time and again he finds himself stuck between two alternatives. His ambivalence stifles his ability to act and choose—and yet, he is not paralyzed completely. In fact, Shinji shows surprising persistence as he navigates the stormy waters of an Angel-infested adolescence.

Ultimately, the series presents Shinji not as a victim of circumstance but as a human being in the making. He does not merely endure his situation but repeatedly takes an active stance toward it. Rather than retreating into himself, Shinji makes friends with Toji and Kensuke; rather than giving free reign to his resentment, he confronts his father at his mother's grave (Episode 15, "Those Women Longed for the Touch of Others' Lips, and Thus Invited Their Kisses."); rather than piloting the EVA for lack of alternatives, he *chooses* to save the lives of his friends. Sense-making takes place in these instances, small and large, when Shinji picks up his situation and turns anonymous forces into the stuff of his personal drama.

Development thus conceived is gradual. It isn't as if Shinji wakes up one morning and decides to be a grown-up. Rather, he makes many small choices along the way. Together, these choices shape the adult that Shinji will eventually become. So, while the realization of Human Instrumentality is the climax of the series, it is not necessarily the key moment of Shinji's development. Shinji doesn't grow up in one cosmic leap, but rather as the result of the repeated exercise of freedom.

What's the role of Instrumentality in Shinji's development? There is some debate about whether Shinji actually accepts or rejects Instrumentality in the series. For humanity, this makes kind of a difference. From a strictly developmental perspective, however, the point is not so much *what* Shinji chooses but *that* he chooses at all. Faced with the choice for or against Instrumentality, Shinji asserts his own truth and his own values. He makes his choice out of conviction, and not just to avoid the pain of existence. This sets him apart from the passive and insecure child that he used to be and demonstrates how much he has grown as a person.

Monstrous Futures

Ordinarily, children look at adulthood with ambivalence. But what about the ambivalence of adults toward children? Merleau-Ponty deals with this question in his discussion of parenthood. Despite the dominance of the deficit view, children have a positive public image. Few people openly despise them, let alone consider them a threat or a cause for fear. The emotional landscape is more uneven when your own offspring is concerned. Pregnant women, Merleau-Ponty points out, sometimes imagine their newborns as monsters. They fear the deformation of their bodies, the pains of birth, and the child's claims on their lives. Merleau-Ponty cites the philosopher Georg Hegel, who stated that "The birth of the child is the death of the parents." While the birth fulfills the parents' union, it also radically transforms their relationship, ending life as they knew it.

With the child, then, new life arrives. This life is not a simple copy of the past. It is open-ended, disruptive, and will continue beyond the intentions, actions, and very existence of those who produced it. We can now better understand Ritsuko's horror when EVA Unit 01 bursts out of Leliel's body (Episode 16, "Splitting of the Breast"). Trapped inside the Angel, Shinji is saved by the spirit of his mother, who lets the EVA go berserk. But this is not what Ritsuko sees. She doesn't see a mother raging to protect her son; she sees the birth of a new, savage being, born out of the evisceration of an Angel.

There are important parallels between the Evangelions and the children who pilot them: both are "created" by adults associated with NERV and SEELE; both are controlled and administered by these adults; both hold the promise for the future of humanity. While it's impossible to know what this future might look like, there is one safe bet: it will be unlike anything the adults have expected. As we are shown throughout the series, both EVAs and children have wills and desires of their own, impossible to curb by even the strongest restraints.

The EVAs repeatedly lash out against their creators, go berserk, or become the hosts of parasitic Angels. Such merging of lifeforms is not merely a malicious infestation; we could read it as yet another way in which the EVAs deviate from the plans of their creators. This open-endedness of their design is the ultimate mark of the EVAs' "monstrosity." If you want to know whether you've created a monster, you can ask the same question as Ritsuko: "Do they actually hate us?" Raising the question in the first place already gives you the answer.

Something is off with the children as well. Isn't there something monstrous about the fact that a fourteen-year-old boy gets to decide on the fate of humanity? Depending on your perspective, the freedom that fuels development appears as either liberating or destructive. Shinji's rejection of Instrumentality is SEELE's demise, just as the rebellion of the young spells the destruction of the old order. Their freedom is the power to destroy and reinvent; and yet, this power is never limitless.

Freedom can only materialize in a concrete situation, without which development would have no context, meaning, or direction. While Shinji transforms his situation, he is simultaneously conditioned by it. The imprint of his situation becomes visible in the last scene of *The End of Evangelion*. Shinji wakes up at the shore of a blood-red sea, the slain body of Lilith in the distance. What is the first thing that he does in this world that he has chosen? He grabs Asuka by the throat. The violence that was done to him becomes his own, his resentment boils over—and then he stops.

Why does he spare Asuka? We don't know. But it's a good way to begin anew.

8

What Do Children Find in the End?

Yuuki Namba

> Everybody finds love
> In the end.
>
> —Hikaru Utada

On February 17th, 2007, Hideaki Anno wrote a teaser campaign poster, EVANGELION: 1.0 YOU ARE (NOT) ALONE:

> "EVA" is a story of repetition.
> It is a story in which protagonists try to avenge the repeatedly horrible events they continue to suffer.
> It is a story about will; they move ahead, if only just a little.
> It is a story of resolution; they bear vague loneliness, fear reaching out to others, but still want to stay with others.

As Anno's statement reflects, the *Evangelion* series is full of repetitions: repetitions *in* the story and repetition *of* the story itself.

Neon Genesis Evangelion, originally broadcast as a twenty-six-episode television anime between October 1995 and March 1996, is full of violence, catastrophic events, and tragic stories, resonating ironically with its title (*evangelion* means "good news"). Its three protagonists are inexperienced fourteen-year-old children, Shinji Ikari, Asuka Langley Soryu, and Rei Ayanami, who continue to fight against the fifteen Angels which could end the world. Each child has the power to battle against Angels by piloting the All-Purpose Humanoid Decisive Battle Weapon Artificial Human Evangelion, or "EVA." If they lose, the human race will be destroyed.

In contrast to mecha anime in the past such as *Mobile Suit Gundam* (1979), EVA's damages are transmitted directly to the

71

pilot through a nerve cable (umbilical cable) as unbearable pain is imposed on them, which cannot be tolerated mentally or physically. They're tormented by past traumas, but repeatedly see faint hopes as they continue to be frustrated. Then, the story accelerates to a tragic end. *Neon Genesis Evangelion* is a work in which protagonists try to avenge the repeatedly horrible events they continue to suffer in the story. Moreover, the story of *Evangelion* is *itself* repetitive.

A year after the TV series *Neon Genesis Evangelion*, which sparked enthusiasm and controversy among audiences due to its endless violence, mysterious stories, characters fighting for their fate, and a shocking ending, a new movie, *Neon Genesis Evangelion: Death and Rebirth*, was released in March 1997, adding an edited version of the TV series and another story. In July the same year, the complete version of *Death and Rebirth: The End of Evangelion* was released in theaters.

Death and Rebirth and *The End of Evangelion* aren't sequels to the TV series. The newly produced shows, with twenty-five and twenty-six episodes, respectively, continued the story of the previous TV series, although there were contradictions with the TV series, leaving many mysteries unsolved.

After a long passage of time, another story repeats *itself*. A decade after *Death and Rebirth* and *The End of Evangelion* were released, Anno announced a new *Evangelion* series. In 2007, *Evangelion: 1.0 You Are (Not) Alone* was released. This new theatrical version reconstructs the story from the first episode of the TV series, but is more than just a reproduction of the story. It also foreshadows the development of different stories, such as differences in details of events, the appearance of new characters, Mari Makinami Illustrious, and more.

Two years later, in Evangelion: 2.0 You Can (Not) Advance, the story of *Neon Genesis Evangelion* was retold, but with drastic changes. The next film, *Evangelion: 3.0 You Can (Not) Redo* (2012), shared the world with *Neon Genesis Evangelion* and *The End of Evangelion* to a certain degree, but the story changed altogether, causing a controversy. The last part of *Evangelion*, *Evangelion: 3.0 + 1.0 Thrice Upon a Time* was released in August 2021 (hereafter, the three existing works and the works to be released are collectively called *Rebuild of Evangelion*).

Evangelion repeats. *Evangelion* shares the same characters and world, spanning three stories with at least two differing from each other. I was fascinated by this story as a teenager, like Shinji and the other EVA pilots, and after frequently watching *Death and Rebirth*, *The End of Evangelion*, and *Rebuild of Evangelion*, I observed how the meaning of this work had begun to change and various questions began to emerge. Why is *Evangelion* repeated? What do repetitions of stories mean? Why can't I take my eyes off the struggles of Shinji and the others fighting within their tragic fate? Moreover, what is the *Evangelion*?

Starting with Anno's word, "story of repetition" and using the three concepts of aesthetics—the *category*, the *tragedy*, and the *story*—as cues, I'm going to attempt to decipher the big message of the *Evangelion* series and the possibility of this work, which is yet to be comprehensively examined. Therefore, let's replay *Evangelion*.

Pattern Blue!

I propose that *Evangelion* is both "mecha anime" and "tragedy." It may be argued that whether we regard *Evangelion* as a tragedy or a comedy is simply a matter of labeling a genre, but I beg to differ. The genre from which we appreciate a work can drastically change the way we view that work and therefore how it's evaluated. Before I discuss whether *Evangelion* is a tragedy, I will clarify why it's important to consider *Evangelion* as a work of a particular genre, using some tools of analytic aesthetics.

Kendall Lewis Walton, who conducted many important studies in the aesthetics of the Anglo-American world in the twentieth century, presented the idea of there being categories of art in his 1970 paper, "Categories of Art." The experience of viewing a work can vary depending on the category from which it's viewed. In this context, what are categories? They refer to various genres of artistic expression. There are various categories of animation, for example, abstract animation, mecha anime, love comedy, and *Nichijou Kei* (slice of life, "cute girls doing cute things").

We watch *Evangelion* as animation belonging to more detailed categories such as subcategories of animation categories, therefore, this animation belongs to the genre of "mecha anime." If, instead, you view *Evangelion* as a fantasy, such as Hayao Miyazaki's *Nausicaä of the Valley of the Wind* (1984), or under the category of an animation where there's no magic or robots but instead, a serious mood, such as *The Wind Rises* (2013), you didn't view *Evangelion* as the producer intended. If people say *Evangelion* without the cute characters or magic isn't good fantasy or *Moe* anime, I say, "No, this is mecha anime, a genre that emerged in the history of animation with some particular features."

Perhaps you don't care to view a piece of work in any category or genre. You're free to appreciate animation in any category, but at least when an artist creates work that includes his or her intention as to how it will be viewed, it's common to view the work in accordance with that intention. A simple reason for this is that art is usually better appreciated in the category of the creator's intention than when viewed some other way. When initially watched without awareness of its history or genre of animation, *Evangelion* was dismal, filled with scenes of fighting, and too serious or violent to appreciate. However, if it's viewed as a tragedy, it's appropriate and enables viewers to understand the story's uniqueness.

It's important to identify the category of *Evangelion* and appreciate it in a particular genre in order to properly understand and enjoy it, just as the words "Pattern blue!" shouted by NERV operators will judge whether it's an angle and start the fight.

It All Returns to Nothing

Evangelion is a tragedy. Northrop Frye, an influential twentieth-century critic, in his *Anatomy of Criticism*, referred to the discussion of tragedy in Aristotle's *Poetics* which described tragedy in terms of the protagonist's behavior, characterizing him as "superior in degree to other men, but not to his natural environment." In *Evangelion*, innocent children face irreparable situations because of mistakes that should be allowed as failures of immature children. In the fierce battle with the ten Angels, it wasn't just their bodies, but also their minds, that were destroyed.

These three children don't receive legitimate protection and affection from their parents and the adults around them, even though they make their own way through harsh environments. The fourteen-year-olds were tasked with the mission to save mankind, which was too heavy for them. But, while *Evangelion* is a tragedy, it's not an ordinary tragedy. *Evangelion* is a *repeated* tragedy, and the repetition occurs on two levels. The first is repetition *in* the story, and the second is repetition *of* the story itself.

In *Neon Genesis Evangelion*, Shinji continues to swing between flight and determination. Shinji lost his mother when he was an infant, was neglected by his father Gendo, and wanted to live up to his father's expectations. He tried to escape from piloting the EVA in the first episode. However, when he saw Rei hurt, he said to himself:

Don't run away. Don't run away. Don't run away. Don't run away.
Don't run away.
—I'll do it. I'll pilot it.

Shinji isn't inherently weak-willed, but brave. However, in the fourth episode, "Rain, After the Escape," he runs away from home without getting used to the environment. He bitterly fights against the Angel and accidentally injures his classmate Toji Suzuhara's younger sister in a battle. Toji hits him. During the escape, he meets another classmate, Kensuke Aida, and decides to pilot it again. Furthermore, in the eighteenth episode "A Life Choice," Shinji is ordered by his father to kill Toji, but instead runs away again. In the nineteenth episode "A Man's Battle," when the Angel attacks the city, Shinji sees Asuka and Rei defeated and rushes to NERV and faces Gendo.

GENDO IKARI: Why are you here?

SHINJI IKARI: I . . . I'm the pilot of Evangelion Unit 01! I'm Shinji Ikari!

Shinji decides to risk his life and fight to protect those around him. However, he's betrayed by Kaworu Nagisa, whom he meets and confides in, learns that Kaworu is the Last Angel, and kills him. Then, Shinji is locked inside himself to introspective self-dialogue, and comes to a strange end.

The End of Evangelion tells a different story. Shinji refuses to take the EVA because he feels guilty about killing Kaworu. Shinji witnesses Asuka's struggles and defeat against creatures intended to cause the Third Impact (the end of mankind), and is persuaded by Misato Katsuragi to once again pilot the EVA. He's then forced to bring world salvation as if he's Jesus, finally awoken in the Red Sea with Asuka, and ultimately rejected by her.

Shinji fails many times and decides that determination is undermined by a more powerful and malicious environment. However, he's determined. The environment surrounding him isn't in agreement with him and makes him a tragic hero. In either case, *Neon Genesis Evangelion* or *The End of Evangelion*, Shinji comes to an end in a tragic story that seems absurd, mysterious, and hopeless.

Rei meets Shinji and fights with Asuka against the Angels, but gradually develops an interest in the outside world previously limited to Gendo as a surrogate parent. In Episode 16, Shinji escapes, and in order to fight against an Angel, Rei launches a suicide attack of her own volition. However, the attempt fails in its entirety. After the battle, Shinji returns to

Rei in her previously expressionless persona. Rei, who has not only lost her memory, lives with Shinji and Asuka never returns and has been replaced by a different soul of Rei's. Rei also repeats her determination and frustration in a vivid way.

Asuka prides herself on being an excellent EVA pilot. However, both her mind and body were devastated by repeated battles with the Angels, destroying her confidence. Asuka's mother had severe mental illness and eventually took her own life. Asuka then throws herself into being an EVA pilot because of her mother's suicide. But Asuka is rejected by the soul of the mother who was driving the EVA. Asuka will never again be relieved in the story of *Neon Genesis Evangelion*. On the other hand, in *The End of Evangelion*, she recovers her EVA sync rate, and fights bravely against the enemy. However, the enemies are so powerful that Asuka can't win alone, and she's badly defeated. Asuka also tries to overcome the setback of her mother's death by working as an EVA pilot, but fails. Amid the desolation, she still stands up again, but the attempt fails.

Evangelion isn't a simple *Bildungsroman* (a story dealing with a person's formative years), like any other mecha anime. The repeated failures of Shinji, Rei, and Asuka give us particular insight. This story is anti-*Bildungsroman*. If we're young like the three children, it's difficult for us to grow rapidly, correct mistakes of the past, and win in a harsh environment. We often hesitate and tend to go back, despite being only faintly hopeful. *Evangelion* correctly depicts our reality.

Evangelion is primarily viewed in the category of mecha anime. Additionally, as it has a very clear tragic structure of story and character features, the audience can focus on the structure of the story by viewing it in more detail as a tragedy and also a "repeated tragedy." The aesthetic significance of *Evangelion* lies in the presentation of our life's non-linear structure which is often ignored in a lot of ordinary stories and especially mecha anime. More so than a typical mecha anime, *Evangelion* portrays its characters as suffering, which makes it even more obvious that *Evangelion* has a certain critical attitude towards mecha anime. Watching *Evangelion* as a repeated tragedy leads us to rethink the values of the work. *Evangelion* is an animation that contemplates growth and failure by relentlessly repeated tragic events, showing the audience a preciousness of will and coldness of reality that is hard to confront with will alone. *Evangelion*, however, has another kind of repetition.

Rebirth, Rebuid, Replay

The story repeats in *Evangelion. Neon Genesis Evangelion* in 1994, *The End of Evangelion* from 1995 to 1997, and *Rebuild of Evangelion*, released between 2007 and 2012 (and hopefully in 2021), comprises three major stories.

The first, *Neon Genesis Evangelion*, spans twenty-six episodes and ends with Shinji's sudden self-affirmation. The second is *The End of Evangelion*. The story is set in the same world up to Episode 24 in *Neon Genesis Evangelion*, however, the world changes dramatically in Episodes 25 and 26, with the Human Instrumentality Project in which the artificial evolution of humanity with the Third Impact was completed, leaving Shinji and Asuka alone. Finally, the third story, *Rebuild of Evangelion*, is at first similar to *Neon Genesis Evangelion*, but instead a world where Asuka—not Toji Suzuhara—gets on an EVA tester; Shinji gets hurt; Rei is eaten by the fifth Angel; EVA wakes up; and the Third Impact occurs.

What does it mean that the three stories make up the works of *Evangelion?* In fact, *Evangelion* isn't a single story; if viewed as just one story, its potential is overlooked. In *Evangelion*, the story *repeats*. Just as repetition within a story leads to speculation about growth and frustration, the repetition of a work itself also incorporates the work's important messages. The fact that *Evangelion* is made up of several stories forces us to reconsider our ideas about it. Audiences can't forget *Evangelion* stories wherein they watch an *Evangelion* story. When you watch *Evangelion: 2.0 You Can (Not) Advance*, you remember *Neon Genesis Evangelion*, and cannot help comparing what is advanced or not.

We usually appreciate a story assigned to a work. For example, *Lord of the Rings* is a story of one world, although it's a combination of various histories. However, in *Evangelion*, multiple stories are told while sharing one world. This is understood via the contrast of *Evangelion* being a tragic work. *Evangelion* is a tragedy, and depicts the hero at the mercy of its fateful and irresistible narrative. Although Shinji tries to resist the environment, he encounters a sorrowful death. Notably, even in both of these already completed stories of *Neon Genesis Evangelion* and *The End of Evangelion*, Shinji and other children have repeatedly experienced setbacks and escapes, trying to move forward with renewed determination and will.

The tragedy of *Evangelion* repeats. The children dare to take on challenges and fail miserably. Failure is relentlessly repeated in the story, in various characters such as Rei and Asuka, as well as Shinji. Moreover, multiple stories and tragedies are also repeated.

Evangelion tells a horrible story, so it's not unreasonable to think that *Evangelion* conveys a gloomy worldview by portraying challenges of children in vain, amidst repeated tragedies within a story, and repeated tragedies among stories. Such an interpretation overlooks the messages of the work.

Evangelion has been replayed over and over again, initially it was broadcast in 1994 to 1995, the first movie released in 1996 and 1997, and then, it was filmed in 2007, 2009, 2012 (and in 2020)—it's clear that the message of *Evangelion* is more than just negative. *Evangelion* should be understood not only ironically, but literally as "good news," as the word suggests. The animation frequently replicates the tragedy by repeating the main characters' resolution and frustration in one story and then re-repeating the story. At first glance, it seems like it just forces a dismal story on the audience. However, it encourages people not to be discouraged and battle against suffering, be it ever so harsh. The fact that *Evangelion* didn't end with *Neon Genesis Evangelion* and *The End of Evangelion* alone reflects that this work is a story of will. In *Evangelion*, each character's decisions and choices are depicted valuably by being repeated in multiple works. Shinji, in *Neon Genesis Evangelion,* gave up to save Ayanami from Angels, but in *Evangelion: 2.0 You Can (Not) Advance* (2009), he challenges the enemy and gets her back.

While appreciating each work of *Evangelion*, we must simultaneously examine the fact that the story is frequently repeated: specifically, that *Evangelion* should be appreciated as a complete body of work. Only then can we continue to think about the meaning of *Evangelion* in accordance with its creator's intentions. Audiences also continue to replay *Evangelion*. It therefore allows them to reflect on *Evangelion* from different perspectives each time. Audiences know each *Evangelion*, so they can re-evaluate each others' stories.

In the End

By appreciating *Evangelion* from the perspective of repeated tragedies, a deeper message can be found in the work. *Evangelion* isn't just a tragedy or mecha anime. Repetition becomes the core of *Evangelion*, demonstrating the positive and negative aspects of repetition of past regrets and the repetition of characters' new challenges. It's centered on Shinji, Rei,

Asuka, who are repeatedly challenged and repeatedly fail; then three other children are challenged again in another work.

What's unique about the *Evangelion* series, as well as repetition within these works, is that the work itself is repeated, each time with a different ending. These different endings aren't just independent, but encourage audiences to compare the differences. At the same time, this raises aesthetic questions about the ending of the story and what kind of work it is. Repetition within the story and repetition of the story itself are combined to embody the philosophical question of the meaning of life.

Ultimately, what do Shinji, Asuka, Rei, and the people around them find? We must wait for the end to find out.[1]

---

[1] This chapter has benefited greatly from discussions with Jun Kashida, Yu Matsuura, Masahiro Murayama, Daisuke Tanaka; I'm very grateful to them.

9
Shinji's Choice

LUCA CABASSA AND MATTEO CAPARRINI

An eye wrapped up in soft lips and memories come back to haunt, from the tender calm of a dream. An unfamiliar ceiling with no furniture worth driving away the attention of a boy in a hospital room, while he stays focused on something closely similar to himself. Pale blue air and the dull yellow feeling of reality being washed away, almost forgotten.

The most impossible voice echoes in the room, inviting him to do exercise. *He* had no time to practice. One, two, three, four, raise your arms, there you go. From repetition reality emerges, but why should it? Why should anyone follow the crumbs of a dream out into the world?

Reality might be nothing but a routine, a schedule, anyone's timetable for the day. Yet, what if there was an event that is impossible, according to plan? What if that persistent thought the boy is stuck with refers to something left unsaid, not really forgotten, just kept at bay, barely out of sight? What if something happened which the boy had no words for?

He got up and now stays in a corridor, in front of a window. He stares at his arm, trying to find a reason to make a fist of his hand, a motive for action, confusion, intervention. A stretcher is pushed past him. On the stretcher lies a girl, wounded. She's the reason for something that the boy did, but he's not ready to recall just yet. He's brought home by a woman and cheered up, comforted, complimented by her. Lying in his new bed, under another unfamiliar ceiling, the boy hears the distant sound of a rhythmic and obsessive metallic percussion on somebody's skull.

The boy is Shinji Ikari, the girl Rei Ayanami, the woman Misato Katsuragi, three of the many characters of the *Evangelion* series. When Shinji jumps into the Entry Plug of the EVA-01 for the first time, he does it to prevent Rei from having to do so in his stead. Under Misato's command and his father Gendo's supervision, Shinji, with no training whatsoever, is sent into battle against Sachiel, the first Angel we see. It is also the first time we hear the EVA-01 screaming, a sound that shocks and accompanies the viewer episode after episode. The scream of the EVA-01 is the announcement of its going *Berserk*.

The *Berserk* is a state of rage that puts the *mecha* beyond the pilot's control, yet having to show more discernment and resolution in return. When Shinji is incapable of defeating the Angel, it looks like the EVA-01 takes matters into its own hands, for his sake and humanity's, to destroy the enemy. In a fury, its movements are more fluid than before, its combat skills multiplied by a significant factor. Fury is a complexion wherein tasks can be completed without a meaningful explanation of the means involved. Skills are used thereby which one didn't imagine to possess. When we lose control, we accomplish things we deemed unreachable before. Loss of control is sometimes our only response in the face of a dreadful danger.

What Have We Done?

The sensation of being exonerated brings about the shame of having lost control. Soon enough, bitterness sets in and we cannot believe what just happened. Something had unveiled which ought to have stayed concealed. Are we just showing off? Was it really us acting? Was it really us naked in front of a menace with equipment we didn't realize we were wearing? We have the gut feeling that when we're not in control, we stop being ourselves. *I lost it, I wasn't being myself.* Even so, we ask for forgiveness for the things *we* did. We have the eerie feeling that even the most outrageous and furious deeds are somehow ours to take full responsibility for.

In this grey area, it's unclear whether we are fully in control of our own actions or being directed by others. When Shinji refuses to fight Bardiel, the Angel that takes control over the EVA-03 with Toji Suzuhara still onboard, his father gives the order to bypass Shinji and shift pilotage to the Dummy System, an artificial Entry Plug with enough vitality to pilot the EVA. Shinji sits there, watching EVA-01 destroying the enemy and his friend Toji with it. EVA-01 is in a state resembling that of *Berserk*. Shinji has to face the fact that he's piloting something capable of cruel destruction and annihilation beyond imagining. The movements of the *mecha* are beastly and gruesome and Shinji is horrified by the sheer brutality of the situation. Brutality has its origin in someone else's firm grip on you. In this case, it's Gendo, Shinji's own father.

Being able to intervene allows Shinji to break free of his situation. It seems that he desires to intervene when watching his own mecha perform atrocities, but his loss of control prevents him from doing so. If this means someone else has taken over, including a dummy, and makes you do something atrocious and unbearable, it's unclear what choice is available. It's safest to opt out then. You need to avoid being instrumentalized, to be led to act on terms that aren't yours. This is the necessary liberation that this loss of control affords you.

If and when Shinji decides to opt in once again, it's not to act because of his father's orders, but in spite of them. He rewrites the form of intervention required. He realizes that there is so much more to it than what is requested from his father. When Shinji decides to enter the EVA-01 to fight against Zeruel, his hand becomes a fist, he's made his choice. He had sworn not to fight in an Evangelion ever again, but he contravenes his very own resolution. He resolves the impasse that he'd put himself into by accepting that both external conditions and his heart drive him to the field of battle.

The results of Shinji's choice are astounding. We witness an unprecedented state of *Berserk*. The EVA-01 turns into a force that can bring about unimaginable results. When its internal batteries run down, the Evangelion Unit continues to function in spite of not having any power left. Its scream is now an ominous growl, while it literally tears the Angel apart. The EVA's loss of control doesn't mean that Shinji has lost control, but is an expression of Shinji's internal drive.

The Will to Survive

Shinji is driven by the piece of advice Misato gives him throughout the series: *Don't give in, fight on!* Communication between human beings is possible without intending to control each other. We encourage others so that they may survive. Misato encourages Shinji so that he may survive—so that humanity may survive. Humans can't remain in isolation if they want to survive since we are sometimes our own enemies when attempting to overcome obstacles. We can't give in.

We also rely upon others to determine the projects that give our lives meaning. If the first attempt at communicating takes the shape of even a cliché, then the person is primed for action. The simple message begins to grow over time to motivate us to take control of our own lives. When Shinji and Misato find themselves together along Lake Ashi, after Shinji defeated and killed Kaworu Nagisa, who turned out to be an Angel but had first made friends with Shinji, Misato tells Shinji that he survived because he resorted to the will to live. Kaworu chose death. The message is still the same, that you need to fight on, but now Shinji and Misato are able to see something through the mere words that were said. They've grown around that message, around that piece of information that is the symbol of their relationship.

Humans can't avoid being impacted by and impacting others. We leave our marks on each other. They do without the traces others leave in them, but they can't do without leaving their own traces either. It's because of these impressions that our will, desires, and dreams become reality. It's because of these impressions that we can better understand our capacity to make impressions in the world. The cost of doing so may require losing control. Sometimes going *Berserk* is the only way to gain control over our dreams and create a new reality.

Just what kind of reality is there for Shinji?

The City with a Will

Antarctica disappeared fifteen years ago, along with half of the world population. A silent red sea waits for the ones who dare to go to the South Pole, a pole which is not where you'd expect to find it anymore, due to the different tilt Earth's axis displays after Second Impact. It's an unworldly sight, where only Angels can spread their wings. There are no seasons for humans anymore. Earth has become a tropical nightmare.

Do radical changes exist? Can the death of a loved one, a natural cataclysm or a man-made disaster bring about radical destruction and an equally radical (re)birth? Are traumas resolved by tracing back to the equilibrium prior to the fall? How did society react to the Second Impact? How did mourning and reconstruction happen? Where does each person find the motivation to keep on living after experiencing such a trauma?

Answers to these questions are not mere conjectures of a fan scouting an imaginary world for a shelter. Hidden deep in complex occult symbolism, incomplete at best and most often just hinted at, Hideaki Anno does provide us with answers that allow for an understanding of the apocalyptic questions and values that are at stake in *Neon Genesis Evangelion*.

Survival as a guiding principle involves the guarantee and maintenance of the delicate balance resulting from the fragile condition of the world, just as well as the effectiveness of its citizens intervening in response to external and unknown threats. The city of Neo Tokyo-3 is the perfect example of a society guided by the strenuous and sheer will to survive. It's an efficient machine capable of fulfilling all its tasks thanks to automatisms directed by a latest generation supercomputer system: the MAGIs.

The MAGIs are equipped with near-unlimited computation capacity and programmed to make decisions in accordance with the majority rule. With no margin of indecision or arbitrariness, they solve the daily management problems of Neo-Tokyo 3. Everything that is useful and aimed at preserving the basic functions of the city can be calculated and automated. When it's under attack, Neo Tokyo-3 is converted into a giant military machine, shields and weapons altogether, controlled by Japanese armed forces and, if the enemy is something more than just other humans, by a special organization: NERV.

Survival at any cost is the will of the city. Survival not just of its inhabitants but of the entire human species. The city and NERV are able to drain resources from all Japan and the world to meet this goal. Individual drives are unified under the brutal consequentialist principle of survival at all cost and each individual is called upon to do their bit inside the great picture. *Don't think, survive.* This might be Neo Tokyo-3's motto. It's the regression to a single gig that society must perform: keeping humans alive. Questions about how and why to survive and who this survival is going to affect are utterly disabled. The drive is outsourced, it doesn't arise from within. It's become an ancestral legacy surging from and implemented in response to the Second Impact.

In the intentions of the ones who built the city, this doesn't completely rule out the subjective point of view. Only that the true meaning of individuality isn't to be found in the present. It lies at the beginning and at the end. Aspirations, happiness, and pleasure are delusions leading to dissatisfaction and loneliness. Individual drives are better defined by their belonging to the human species. Each individual is a candidate for sacrifice.

Is it possible to accept the radicality of these ideas? No individual person can consistently hold to these principles. But these ideas have an inescapable characteristic of necessity. Accepting them is the only way someone can go about in the world of *Evangelion*. This is where the Human Instrumentality Project takes shape. If no human can accept these ideas but they are nonetheless necessary, then humans must be changed to make them recognize the inescapability of the principle of survival.

The only solution is for each person to accept the loss of control, that is their individuality, in the name of the entire human species. Human Instrumentality is thus the project whose goal is the artificial evolution of humans, it's the plan for the becoming one of mankind. It'd entail the creation of a single sphere of singularity, where all individuals become one. Where all individuals survive as one.

This drive to survive at any cost is what guides the actions of SEELE, the organization behind NERV. Humanity has done nothing but deepen its fall from an original state of indeterminacy, and SEELE aims to fix this error. SEELE recognizes that we're condemned to be separated from one another, to suffer, and to conquer our individuality. The Human Instrumentality Project entails accepting a concrete and radical intervention on this state of affairs that is outside our individual control.

SEELE is a mere tool for the implementation of this project as it's written in the Dead Sea Scrolls, mysterious sacred texts that seem to predict the events leading to the Third Impact, which are needed to set Instrumentality in motion. SEELE knows this mysterious truth and aims at accelerating a change that is considered inevitable. For them, individual drives make questions arise whose answers cannot be individual. Humans are distributed along the sides of a Möbius strip which needs to be created when the project reaches its final stage.

All members of SEELE are elderly, accustomed to power, and wealthy. Their leader appears to be Keel Lorenz, who later turns out to be a cyborg prosthetically prolonging his life with gears and artificial tissues. What does this disclose? Perhaps Instrumentality is an attempt to go beyond not so much of individuality, but of death itself. (Inspiration for the character of Keel is Konrad Lorenz, Nobel Prize for medicine and ethologist known for his studies on imprinting and evolutionary epistemology. But equally well known for his problematic stance on the roles of natural selection and domestication in the improvement of the human species.) Keel is obsessed with the idea of immortality. Individual unhappiness and the perpetual conflicts between individuals are but a façade. Assuming the role of interpreters of an inevitable change allows SEELE members to hide and carry out selfish interests. We could argue that Keel and SEELE's desire is not the state of affairs which Instrumentality would realize, but the rite of passage that leads to it, that libidinous feeling that we obtain by playing with death. This is why the death of single individuals, like Ryoji Kaji, can be accepted and ordered by SEELE. It's the affirmation of their immortality that matters. Individuals can be sacrificed along the way.

The Boy Cannot Know What Awaits Him Down the Road

Instrumentality allows us to imagine a world in which the present is obsolete. Our world, populated by different drives in conflict, must disappear. Individuality is what we must sacrifice to this cause. In return, we'd get a world with no contradictions where we'd be one with the others. Drives like the message Misato conveys to Shinji wouldn't be necessary. *Don't give in, fight on!* Relationships between individuals would happen with no need for intervention. There would be no connection, really, just unity. Individuals along with the present would become obsolete.

One last intervention and then peace. Being afraid of losing control wouldn't be necessary. Nobody would be there to take the risk of opening themselves to others. Resorting to strengths which come from within wouldn't be an option and all the problems that come with it would be suspended. The fear of losing control and being controlled by others is destroyed along with individual autonomy. In instrumentality, loneliness and the fear of hurting others by using them as mere means to our own pleasures would be destroyed. Is this a good thing?

The dynamics of dream and reality would be resolved once and for all. The dream is something that acts without asking permission. It realizes itself where control over ourselves fades. It's not that in the dream we're inactive. It's actually where we're the most, where we push ourselves towards the world and other inhabitants. Control is the barrier that we build around us and limits the form and extent of our interventions. SEELE's project is to fashion reality after the dream, to make reality the ultimate dream. All dreams would be fulfilled and vanish into the thin air outside the sphere of LCL where all souls are united, never to come back again. What would be a reality without dreams? A reality without interventions, where dreams don't come back to haunt us. Messages from others wouldn't require interpretation since there'd be nothing with which to communicate.

The Birth of Meaning

A message does not convey a unique meaning. It's not a command or a phrase whose meaning is straightforward. Messages are neither objects nor tools. They inhabit the border area between self and other. A message doesn't point to a specific goal. It's the medium through which our will to intervene in the world is expressed. A sign is not its meaning. A sign *refers to* a meaning. Similarly, we must think of the message's inception as the establishment of a relationship between self and other. Drives are thus vectors that point from dream to reality. They find themselves in the phase space between others and me. Yet, what good is a message if there is no other?

Mechas are the translators and messengers. Evangelion Units allow for the connection to this phase space. It's not an irrelevant characteristic of theirs that they contain each pilot's mother's soul. The mother is the first mediation with the world that everyone's presented with. The mother is the first bond, the first constraint. It makes you stumble upon a limit to your freedom to move, right at the beginning of your story. Yet this limit enables access, other than to life itself, to a community of relations. Moreover, it enhances the bond it creates. Life is but a repetition of this bond which strengthens and deepens it, while progressively removing its consequences in terms of dependence. Seeing the mother as the source of all pleasure and meaning, as the Mother of Life, is an attitude that stems from the misunderstanding of the focus of the relationship. The mother is just one of the two poles of the system and not the system itself. The search for an access to an indeterminate state, a return to the maternal womb takes the origin of a relationship as the end of all behavior. Being born is an eternally unsolvable trauma that we must get rid of.

Conceiving of birth as a trauma doesn't entail choosing death over life, as Kaworu does. The trauma of birth constitutes but doesn't exhaust the phase space of our lives. In the relationships we have with others, we are not condemned to repeat the same original trauma of detachment from the womb. Life is about coping with the recurrence of traumas that manifest themselves in different forms. Death would be the utter negation of the limits that being born involves, a mere solution or removal of the trauma. Instead, the traumatic nature of birth gives rise to the possibility of thinking of a continual rebirth. What we mean by rebirth is actual change. To change something doesn't entail burning it to the ground and shaping something else from the ashes of what it once was. Change is about intervening in a process and giving it a new direction.

What allows a substantial enough change to occur such that a person does not have to re-experience the original trauma?

Actual change becomes possible when we accept that there's work to be done to build a connection, that relationships aren't granted in virtue of an original bond. There is no (re)turning to the womb. For Shinji, this change has the form of recognizing his disgusting self looking back at himself from the reflection in Asuka's eyes. It took all his energies to get to a beach where affection and care could be denied to him. The acceptance of a traumatic bond, that is, of the impossibility of coping with the same trauma over and over again, establishes the bonds of a future relationship.

The Beast Shouted 'World' at the Heart of the 'I'

What is Shinji doing during the state of *Berserk*? He's faced by an unimaginable reality in front of which his individuality crumbles, as though perpetually returning to the same dream. What's dreaming? It's the regression to a point in which subject and object, the self and the world, stay in a precarious balance which is ultimately untenable. It's to resort to energies beyond one's control that enable the intervention on reality. What's reality? It's the continuous recurrence of a trauma that cannot be simply denied, the unceasing adjustment of a bond that drives our behavior to the refusal of assimilation and disruption.

Others can never be a body of which we dispose. They're always immersed in a fantasy, a dream that constitutes them as real. In the disturbing first scene of *The End of Evangelion*, when Shinji masturbates while looking at Asuka's comatose body, her body is so unreal that it can act as the material of his delusion to claim the whole world for himself. For Shinji, Asuka represents vital and libidinous experiences that he wants to make his own. Yet, without any response from her, her body is just the support for a desire that wants to be satisfied. It's an object whose meaning rests upon the fulfillment of a need. Once orgasm is reached, desire can go back to being inert. Attention then turns to the bestial nature of what has been done. Shinji realizes that he wasn't establishing any relationship whatsoever with Asuka. He was just trying to take control over something. He was running away from the feeling of not having control of himself and his life.

Later on in the movie, when Shinji clings to Asuka's neck and the song *Komm süßer Tod* (*Come, Sweet Death*) starts, he clings to her out of despair. The other must be annihilated, consumed, emptied of the last bit of vitality. The static picture of the world, constructed by the self, exhausts all that is significant. Asuka must be able to help him. If she doesn't, if she doesn't help him achieve pleasure, then she's useless. So, she must, or rather *it* must, die. Why should others exist if not to be with us? Why, if not to make us complete? *Help me!* I need to be in control. I need to foresee what's going to happen when I open myself to you. I must know that my intervention into the world won't face resistance.

But Asuka is more than that. The world is more than that. Shinji knows, and we do too. This is the reason why he refuses to let Instrumentality be completed. His choice is to allow the ones who choose so to emerge from the sphere of LCL where they've been united. Asuka is with him, on the beach along the red sea that washes the shores of the world after Third Impact and Instrumentality. Asuka is there because, of all voices Shinji heard during the catastrophe, she was the one who opposed the sharpest refusal to the invitation to join him in the world created by Instrumentality.

Change begins with conflict. Shinji has the blurry premonition that being one with others would mean prolonging his traumas in the endless loop of eternity. It'd be like hanging on to the very traumas from which he strives to find a way out. What we are looking for is a better world. We don't want and cannot run away into our dreams. Dreams don't allow us to. They keep placing us back into reality. A relationship with Asuka cannot be obtained in Shinji's dream. It needs to happen for real. It needs the radical awareness of not being alone. And that entails the possibility of being refused, pushed to the side, hated or despised even, and hurt.

Others can hold us in check because of the mistakes we make. Our beastly behaviors are put up against the wall. The final words Asuka addresses Shinji with are of the same stuff any change is made of: *How disgusting*.

III

How to Think When You Are (Not) Alone

10

When You Have Two Right Hands and They're Both in Flames

DAVID FAJARDO-CHICA

NERV headquarters have a strict protocol for when an Angel arrives in Tokyo-3. The alarms start buzzing, red lights go on, and their frenetic pulse reflects everybody's anxiety.

Look out for the pilots. There they are, rushing to put on their Plug Suits and getting to the EVA's Entry Plug on time. Asuka sits down in the capsule, puts on her A10 Nerve Clips, and then the LCL fluid starts to fill the entire place. These are the preliminaries for the synchronization process.

Thanks to synchronization, the pilot's mind and the EVA's body interconnect. They do it in two directions. First, the pilot moves, controls, and fights with the EVA's body as her own body. Second, the pilot experiences the EVA's bodily damage as her own. What is it for the pilot to be in the EVA's body?

The Inner Workings of the Synchronization Link

Synchronization is a process which merges the pilot to the EVA Unit. The Pilot and the EVA are two different individuals, two different bodies. However, when the pilot is controlling the EVA Unit, she is not different from it. That is possible thanks to the embodied character of the mind. This phenomenon may have a deep significance for the pilot. After all, it means a disruptive and total body change. It is a mentally transformative experience. Whether the pilot was affected holistically is open for the viewer's interpretation. What's the physical nature of this process? Even if the word "soul" appears many times mentioned on these matters, in this context it is only another way of talking about the pilot's "mind" (as in the French *esprit* for "mind").

Synchronization requires the careful implementation of a protocol mediated by a series of devices: the Plug Suit (elastic and colorful), the Entry Plug (the capsule where the pilot lies inside the EVA), the LCL (the orange liquid which fills the capsule and the pilot's lungs), and the A10 Nerve Clips (an interface headset). Synchronization is a neurophysical process in the sense that it involves the pilot's brain and pieces of technology. More importantly, it is also a cognitive process.

Cognitive scientists see bodies and their brains as organic machines whose function is to enable adaptive behavior in hostile circumstances. Researchers differ in their focus. The more brain-centered ones claim that the mind's activities are identical to some informational operations made and integrated by the brain. The more bodily-centered ones claim that the body's role is not peripheral, that the mind is embodied. What is important here is that NERV's gigantic bio machines may also realize all the operations implemented by animal brains and bodies. As far as significative connection is concerned, the EVA Unit's hands seem closer to the pilot than her own hands. Synchronization allows the pilot's mental cognitive appropriation of the EVA Unit.

Think of the everyday use of language as one of many mental cognitive operations. When someone asks you what time it is, your brain performs a complex cognitive task. The auditive message in the form of an electric signal is rapidly transformed in an appropriate outcome: the precise movements required for looking at your watch, a detailed visual perception processing and a verbal report. That's just some of the brain's cognitive power. The crucial role of language in thought underlies the use of language made by the pilots when controlling an EVA. Remember that the Unit 02 was specially designed to be controlled by a pilot whose language was not Japanese. The pilot and the EVA maintain a connection which is cognitive in nature. The synchronization process integrates information coming from the pilot's mind and from both the EVA's and the pilot's bodies in a particular way that result in the pilot owning the EVA's body.

Bioengineers at NERV behind the EVA's biotech developments faced challenges that Nature has already faced in the evolutionary history of animals. Biological adaptations in creatures; anatomies and their behaviors are specific natural designs of biological machines that can be understood as solutions from Nature to specific environmental challenges. This is why the word "selection" features in "natural selection." Charles Darwin, evolution's great proponent, famously argued that Nature "selects" the best answer to solve a certain problem. When NERV bioengineers wanted to equip pilots with

EVA's super-capable bodies, they probably first looked at what they knew about how human and animal brains relate to their bodies. Better understanding of how the human mind controls the the human body may have been a guide for designing a biotechnological interface which allowed minds to control another body, for instance, the EVA's body.

Owning and Controlling a Body

An EVA's pilot is not a pilot in the same sense that a driver is a car's pilot. There is a difference between the usual causal relationship between a common driver and her vehicle and the relationship between an EVA's pilot and her EVA. In the former, the pilot mind causes physical changes in the machine through some intermediaries: the pilot's body (her hands) and the vehicle input devices (the handles). In the latter, the pilot acts on the biomachine without intermediaries. The pilot need only think for the EVA to execute the movements he desires, similarly to how we move our bodies according to our desires just by thinking it. The relation between body and mind is so tight that it's not precisely a desire that's involved. Perhaps it's better described simply as the operation of our agency over our own body. This is one of the motivations behind what is now called 'the embodied perspective' of the mind. It doesn't seem that the mind is different from the body. The mind is extended beyond the limits of the brain to the complete body.

We are the owners of our bodies. That's why we have this privileged ability to control them. When Rei Ayanami is inside the entry plug, she moves the EVA's body in the same way that she moves her own body. At the same time, she experiences the EVA's body as her own body. The relationship between the pilot's mind and the EVA's body is known as bodily ownership, which is the relationship each person has with her own body.

The Pilot's Mind Needs to Know Things about the Body

Animal senses are information channels from the exterior world to the mind. Perception takes place thanks to specialized devices in bodies: eyes, noses, hands, skins, tongues, mouths, and ears. The information from the exterior world is transformed by them into electric impulses that are computed by the brain, another specialized device which integrates the information for the production of appropriate behavior. The purpose of a mind is to integrate data from the outside to produce an appropriate behavior that guarantees the organism's survival. That's the key of every EVA's design purpose: survival. Every organism must know things about the environment they live in. It is very valuable to adequately distinguish the food from the danger, the prey from the hunter, the enemy's weakness from the right time to run away. The EVAs also have these perceptive abilities. The pilot's mind gets perceptual information from the EVA's sensory channels.

Bodies (human or EVA) and minds work together in such a way thanks either to the adequate production of bodily representations or to minds having the right degree of embodiment. These are the mental items which are being manipulated in brains to properly deal with many different bodily issues. Feeling an itch, following choreography, experiencing a leg as yours, being able to answer where is your biggest mole, all of them are things that we experience thanks to our cognition of bodily representations. There are at least two different kinds of bodily representations, each of them having a different purpose. That is because each one solves a different need. The interface between the pilot's mind and the EVA's body should support both ways of bodily cognition for synchronization to occur.

Survival requires organisms' knowledge of their own body. The animal mind has many challengers that are met with particular kinds of bodily perceptions. Tactile information provided by specialized sensors all over the skin is a primary source for data on what is happening on the body's surface. If someone touches your left arm, the mind needs to know many things. In the same way, if an Angel catches the left arm of an EVA, the pilot needs to know many things about the EVA's body to offer an adequate response. For example, the identification of the bodily part (what has been caught?), the bodily posture (where is the left arm?), the specific spot that got caught (where in my arm have I been caught?), or the position of the arm in relation to the other arm.

These questions need a solution if we want an EVA to have a chance to survive in a fight. The answers are solved by the mind in the way of a *body map*. The brain creates the map to integrate and trace the stimuli location and the body parts. The pilot should have access to the information required to build up the map of the EVA's body within the pilot's mind.

The Mind Needs to Control the Body

Bodily cognition is not only a matter of passive searching in a map. The mind also exercises its agency by controlling the body. You need a certain kind of knowledge about how a machine functions to be able to put it to work. It's a similar situation in the case of the mind and the body. The mind needs a practical guide to know how to move in the best possible way. The pilot should act upon the EVA's body similarly by using patterns of action that require different bodily mental items. These mental items about the EVA's body are created from the information provided by the bodily perceptual capacities. This information is obtained from different channels and it's diverse in nature. That is why synchronization is not a matter of black and white. It's a graded process, as reflected by the luminous progress bar each time a pilot enters to the EVA Unit.

Studies of humans show that some people may have lost their ability to control their bodies without losing any ability to know things about their bodies. These abilities look at different capacities with dissociable functions. NERV bioengineers should have noted that some patients are able to recognize their body parts, even to feel pain, but yet be blind to their limb positions. This is a syndrome called *peripheral deafferentation*.

Other patients have a bodily control problem called *apraxia,* it consists of forgetting how to do particular actions: how to tie your shoes or to use a screwdriver. The development of the sychronization process must have considered the many different ways in which body and mind are connected, from different forms of *cartographical* knowledge (where is my leg right now?) to the diverse range of *practical* knowledge (how to fight with a Progressive Knife?).

From 10% to 100% and from 101% to 400%

We can now see why the synchronization "levels" are frequently expressed in percentages. Different scales could be offered as an estimation of how well integrated the pilot's mind and the EVA's body are, as synchronization levels reflect. First, there is the *input* connection. Bioengineers incorporate all perceptive channels from the EVA's body to the pilot's mind. Secondly, there is the output connection which determines the production of successful behavior according to the situation. And thirdly, there's the creation of internal bodily representations from the feedback loops of sensory input and behavioral output. The internal body representation is strengthened with the existence of this *sensorimotor loop*. Any new data about the body adds detail to the image, and every effective movement helps to solidify the learning of that particular way in which the body could be moved.

What would it mean that the pilot's mind and the EVA's body are well-connected enough to have a reading beyond one hundred percent? My bet is that even if 100 percent is the estimated maximum of synchronization on the sensorimotor loop, there are other possible connections between a mind and a body that could explain why on some occasions the synchronization levels are over 100 percent. Even if the brain were an organ primarily related to motor control, there are higher brain capacities than motor capacities. A pilot's mind could be in touch with different aspects of the EVA. For example, we are not aware of the pilot's own subjective experience that is produced by the EVA's senses. Emotion, memory, motivation, all of them are different aspects of the relationship between the pilot's mind and the EVA's body that are beyond the sensorimotor loops.

Many Bodies for One Piloting Mind

The pilot's movements are not only reflected in the EVA's body. The pilot's body itself moves too at the same time. Remember Shinji firing the EVA's weapon against the fourth Angel, "Eye in the target, pull the trigger; eye in the target, pull the trigger." While Shinji's mind is focused in targeting and shooting Shamsel, Shinji's body and the EVA's body are doing the same action: moving their right index fingers.

Does Shinji own two bodies? I don't see any reason for rejecting the claim that he does. The synchronization between Shinji and the EVA allows that. The bodily representations used in Shinji's mind to move the EVA are now integrated into the bodily representations used to move Shinij's body. We see repeatedly how the pilot's body moves synchronously to EVA's. At the same time that EVA's arm moves the progressive knife against the Angel, Asuka's body is doing the same movement. In other words, the pilot's mind moves both bodies in perfect temporal correspondence. This is why it makes sense to think of this event in terms of merged bodily representations.

It's more efficient for Shinji's brain to work over only one kind of bodily representation at a time, even if they are merged. Every other option would cost more cognitive resources. The pilot's mind already owns a body. In cognitive terms, the pilot's mind already knows how to control one body. The EVA Unit is a new body to control. It is better if the bodily representations are merged. That way, there are fewer opportunities for making mistakes in the production of rapid responses. It would be more effective exploiting the already well-suited connection between the pilot's mind and her own body than starting the process from scratch. From Shinji's subjective perspective, the body is also experienced as merged. In his fight against Shamshel, Unit 01 suffers an injury on its hands, and a mixing hand (half-EVA Unit, half-human) represents Shinji's suffering (Episode 3, "The Silent Phone").

Managing two bodies could be a stressful task. You think as if you need to move only one body since the bodily representations are synchronized, but at the same time, you receive the sensory input from two distinct bodies. A pilot's mind received input of the pilot's body and the EVA's body. Even if the pilot's brain only needs to produce one response, managing the multiple sources of information could be stressful and confusing. There could be a related function for the LCL liquid, though. The LCL liquid fills every sensory receptor in the pilot's body: the skin, the eyes, the ears, the nose, and the mouth. In that situation the sensory input from the pilot's body is quite nonexistent. The information coming from the immediate outer world of the pilot's mind is neutralized by floating in this substance.

That's a very similar strategy to the one used by psychologists in the 1960s experimenting with psychedelics. They put their experimental participants in tanks for *sensory deprivation*. These tanks were filled with salted water in such a way that the person would effortlessly float while being relaxed and isolated from normal sensory stimuli. The idea was to find the effects of psychedelics on the mind without any interference from the senses, including noises coming from the outer world. The LCL may serve similar purposes by isolating the pilot's mind from the pilot's body sensory information. Being submerged in LCL may alleviate the sensory charge in the pilot's mind, helping it to address the huge load of new sensory information from the EVA Unit's body.

Feeling the EVA's Pain

Having a body is often a painful experience. Think about Shinji's fight against Shamsel. Shinji experiences a lot of pain when the Fourth Angel grabs the EVA's left arm (Episode 3, "The Silent Phone"). One of the most salient features of Shinji's bodily suffering in this scene is his facial expression. It indicated something important about synchronization and the sensorimotor loop. Bodily gestures, facial expressions, motor reflexes, and some groaning may not be due to the presence of the complex mental state that we know as pain. They may be the result of a previous stage of signal processing called *nociception*, a primitive response that occurs in the spinal cord. Evolutionarily speaking nociception is older than the brain itself. For synchronicity to run deeply, the pilot's spinal cord computes the responses produced by the receptors in EVA's body.

Once the damage is inflicted upon the body, a signal goes to the spinal cord, and then to the brain, where the pain is produced as a subjective experience. Shinji clearly suffers from the EVA's injuries. Is that a good design idea? Wouldn't it be better if the pilot were insensitive to the EVA's bodily damage? We may think he would be better suited to fight against his enemy without the heavy burden of the distress of that pain. However, this line of thought has proven to be false. Painless life isn't a superhero's dream life. If you don't feel your pain, your body is less relevant to you. Having a body implies the requirement of taking care of it. The biological strategy for this complicated task is the development of pain production systems. People born without the right functioning of these systems have many problems living a healthy life. Most of them die young. Pain motivates us to do certain things that are crucial for preserving the integrity of bodily tissues: avoiding the potential sources of damage, preventing a pernicious movement, and restricting limb use for recovery.

Pain can indeed be incapacitating. When the Fourth Angel took and twisted Unit 01's arms in a way that they appear broken, Shinji's suffering was overwhelming. Misato had to yell at him, making him remember that it wasn't his own body that was being harmed. "Shinji-kun, calm down! That's not your arm! It is just a sensation!" (Episode 2, "Unfamiliar Ceilings"). Shinji's experience must be very similar to having pain in his own arm. But Shinji is not confused, the synchronization process makes his brain treat the EVA's body as his own body.

That tremendous pain prevents Shinji from taking a course of action against his enemy. It looks like an obstacle more than a design advantage. However, there is a fair trade-off between the disturbing nature of pain and its value for rapid responses to the Angels' attacks. Without the capability for experiencing the EVA's pain, the pilot wouldn't have such a marvelous tool for his fight. It consists of a biotechnological strategy that copied the best solution of Nature to an analogous challenge: a strong internal motivation to avoid damage.

Pain Modulation to Fight Back

Sometimes painful experiences don't help. An animal facing its predator doesn't need internal motivation for protecting its limbs. What the animal needs is to be in full capacity to run away to survive. The pain system should integrate a way to turn off the pain production. People's bodies used to find ways to disconnect pain in dangerous situations. In his fight against Ramiel, Shinji is capable of surpassing a terrible physical pain: two tentacles are passing through EVA's viscera (his own viscera in his mind). After a furious scream, Shinji is able to move and counterattack the fifth Angel. If the debilitating pain were not experienced for a brief moment, Shinji wouldn't have been able to kill the Angel and survive.

The very presence of pain modulation in the pilot's mind related to damage in the EVA's body suggests deep levels of synchronization. Some operations of the mind, including meditation, can produce pain alleviation. When some belief, desire, or expectation turns off the pain, it shows that the pilot's mind is acting on the pain. Actually, it is acting also over both the pilot's and EVA's body.

The automatic responses caused by nociception are inhibited in both cases. The behavioral part of the regular sensorimotor loop produced by pain is not activated. There is not automatic avoidance of the damaging situation. Pain modulation is also deeply related to emotions. Anger, rage, and fear all have an analgesic effect. The possibility of having an emotion through the EVA's body shows how deep the synchronization between pilot and EVA can run. If Shinji can experience emotions by triggering events happening to the EVA's body, then many paths of pain modulation and analgesia for combat are available.

Are the EVA and the pilot sharing the same pain or are they experiencing two independent pains? That is a tricky question. Imagine that the EVA receives a hit in the leg. Shinji's face expresses suffering and his motor reflex also shows that the injury affects both: EVA's body and Shinji's body. But it doesn't mean that there are two pains in that situation. There is only one body mental map. Pain happens in that cognitive construction that is supported by the pilot's brain.

As far as there is only one pilot's mind, there is only one pain. Bodily responses in the pilot's and the EVA's body are not the result of any mental process. That is why their presence is not a guide to the existence of pain. Reflexes and motor action are more of a corporal matter, and pain is a mental one. That is why when Rei, Asuka, and Shinji abandon their EVA units after a battle, they carry scars with them.

11
The Mysterious AT Field

Luka Perušić

At the end of his journey, Shinji experienced the fulfilment of a grand, old idea, an idea of eternal humanity, peaceful and happy.

The leaders of SEELE and NERV made morally questionable choices in the execution of their plans, but ultimately they advanced humanity towards attaining the state of perfect, painless existence. In Shinji's last conversation with Rei in *End of Evangelion*, she told him that it is "a world in which we are all one," that "it is the world you wished for." Similarly, before dying, Asuka realized that her mother never left her side, and although she was fueled with hatred to the last second in the fight against mass production EVAs, she appeared to have made peace with herself. So why did Shinji and Asuka—an anguished boy and girl seeking acceptance, comfort, love and approval in their struggle to find purpose in the world—reject the Human Instrumentality Project, only to continue to dwell in their woes?

Regardless of his wish being fulfilled, Shinji told Rei that Human Instrumentality "isn't right," that "it feels wrong." Rei warned Shinji that fear would return to the hearts of human beings if Human Instrumentality got destroyed, yet Shinji did precisely that. He was also the first to experience the consequences. In the last frames of their story, Shinji was miserable and violent towards Asuka, and she was frustratingly ambiguous towards him, caring and hostile at the same time, precisely the way they always were. This may mean that, for Shinji and Asuka, living in fear, misery and enmity feels *less wrong* and *more to be desired* than the peace and happiness experienced in the Human Instrumentality.

But how could that be their final decision, something so opposite of what they yearned for, so unfulfilling?

There's no direct explanation for their choices, which means that we can't honestly say what kind of understanding of the world they attained. But some other aspects of the story may help us. Even though an AT field often appeared as being merely cool battle mechanics, it continuosly played a role in important scenes and dialogues between characters. So maybe a part of the answer we're looking for lies in understanding the nature of the AT Field.

The Ego Driver

In their last dialogue, Rei told Shinji that the place where they find themselves bounded is "a sea of LCL," a "primordial soup of life," a "place with no AT Fields, where individual forms do not exist." In a single frame in the show's intro, we learn about the possibility that "AT" stands for "Absolute Terror," while supplements in some editions of manga briefly inform us that the AT field *creates* unimaginable, limitless terror.

In the late episodes of the show, we also learn that it is a protective field of energy, projected by the self of each conscious individual. In the scene with Asuka and Arael in Episode 22 ("Staying Human"), in which Asuka experienced a breakdown, we witness what happens when the AT Field gets overtaken.

But isn't it strange to call something that protects you by naming the *adverse effects* it causes? By this logic, something *bulletproof* we'd call a *bulletexciter*. Quite odd. We should take a look at this by examining the manifestation of terror.

Terror is a form of *fear* which begins as a feeling of dread but can reach an extreme state; it is a heightened defense mechanism created by an organism. Another such mechanism is *pain*, which in its extreme form, we often call *agony*. If we apply the idea of an AT Field to our physical protection— bones, nerves, skin—we'd be talking about *absolute agony*, and the scope of its protection we'd call *A. A. Field*. An encounter between two A. A. Fields, for example, a fist-fight between Shinji and Toji, would mean that Toji's body is producing pain to Toji and that it is also the source of pain for Shinji.

So there seems to be a "trade-off" in the way in which our organism functions: to be safe, we have to feel pain and fear. However, it means that our organism "opens up" or even produces weaknesses that define us. It also means that anything overtaking the defensive system can turn it against us; makes us so terrorized and agonized that we can't appropriately respond. Arael's attack on Asaka was such an event. The content of about 270 frames of Asuka's breakdown caused by Arael's attack is, in fact, made of her life—her organism, memories, thoughts, desires, and fears. They are full of anguish, insecurity, and suffering, caused by some terrible experiences, all of them her own.

Since it's the self that projects the AT Field, it means that "AT" is a central point directly present in the self. *Self* is the essence of who we are, comprised of conscious and unconscious content accessible by introspection. If Arael penetrated Asuka's "AT" then it overtook the core of selfhood that up to that point belonged and was available to her *only*. We can think of this "central point," this core," as the *ego*, a domain of our psyche that provides continuity to our conscious existence. Ego nurtures our identity, protects our selfhood, and maintains our ability to communicate with others. In Episode 20 ("Of the Shape and Hearts of Humans"), characters refer to the limit of the AT Field as the *ego-border*.

How is it, then, that the core of who I am, who all of us are, the ego and the soul, could be something so horrible that it produces *absolute terror*?

There, in the Depths of Human Souls

By overtaking Asuka's ego, we can say that Arael "cast" a "light" on Asuka's "darkness." Arael's name may be signifiant since it is derived from Hebrew אראל, which can be translated as "light of God." Arael brought her most profound weaknesses into the unwanted spotlight. More importantly, Arael illuminated the borders of Asuka's selfhood, the "place" where "I" ends.

Revealing such borders would mean either that we can see beyond them too, or that we are but a whiff from the whole of the unknown. In the deepest layer of our soul, it's not that we find something utterly mysterious that defines us, it's the border we encounter, we face the *end* of our being. It seems, then, that the ego, the AT Field, protects not against others but against *what crawls into us* when the ego is negated, brought to its end. It would also mean that it is a protection against *what crawls through us* when we invade another AT Field.

In real life, every encounter with a stranger, or with something alien or unknown, creates physical and mental terror, subtle or great, until identities are communicated, and security reaffirmed. It's "absolute terror" because an encounter of two selfhoods is an exchange in which one identity can negate the other, take it over, or subdue it under its dominance, and reveal its limits. The deeper the dependence or intrusion, the higher the terror of the other I—because being replaced in identity— losing your memories, thoughts, feelings, desires, fears, and consciousness—may be just the same as dying or not existing at all. This is why Kaworu said that "death of the Self, removal of the AT Field, that is the only absolute freedom." As long as we struggle with ourselves or others, we can't act freely, we are always conditioned.

However, the price paid for the removal of the AT Field is the loss of autonomous identity. This is a direct consequence of the "Anti-AT Field" projected by the merging of Rei, Adam, and Lilith that allowed for the creation of unity. The AT Field was also the ultimate obstacle that SEELE and NERV tried to overcome: to achieve absolute freedom without losing the identity and meaning of human existence, to remove defensive systems without destroying the rest the essence of humanity.

What would be this *thing* that "crawls" from beyond our self, that creates the terror and makes us terrified; against which we struggle, but which establishes our identity? To look for the answers, we need to take a few steps outside our AT Field.

A Step Backward, into Terror

In the universe, *life* is unique because it has a self-emergent power to govern and maintain itself purposely. The realization of the difference between life and other forms of matter motivated Humberto Maturana, a Chilean biologist and philosopher, to understand life as a distinct material system depending on three features: it gathers energy to spend on its abilities, transforms its environment to suit its needs, and reproduces itself to overcome decay. This complex behavior Maturana called *autopoiesis* (*self-creation*). For our problem, what is important is the emergence of *animus*, or "motivated spirit." When we act with animus, we act with motive and form *intentions*. Descendants of both Lilith and Adam are autopoietic systems, and both Angels and humans have animus.

Intention is a very interesting word. It comes from the Latin word *intendere*, meaning *to stretch out*. The underlying sense tells us that intentional actions, having a reason and purpose, are the mental extension of our physical stretching, like when we stretch our hand across the table to give our friend a book. Since animus represents the sphere of our meaningful action, for example, giving the book because the person is liked, it is directly infused with our ego. This may be why AT Field battles in *Neon Genesis Evangelion* are represented as various forms of stretching and withdrawing, expanding and contracting.

Human beings, however, would be different in their animus from Angels because we do not have an infinite source of power, We need to *feed* upon other life-forms. In contrast, Angels/Apostles possess the *Fruit of Life*. According to Episode 19 ("A Man's Battle"), Fruit of Life—or S^2 *Engine*—is an organic component of Angel's core that provides infinite power. "Infinite power" might mean an infinite source of energy to exist and sustain itself. This makes Angels a completely unreachable lifeform that may have tried to destroy life on Earth only because of the directive given by the First Ancestral Race. The transformation of EVA-01 into a god-like being happened when, within one entity, the two "Fruits" from the Seed of Life—S^2 engine and the *Fruit of Knowledge* (an unidentified component, probably human soul or brain)—merged through feeding.

Humans are different from other Lilithians too because we have a deeply developed self-awareness, we can understand our "stretching out." This awareness creates a sense of *existence*, a sense of "coming forth" and "standing out" from otherwise inanimate matter. It further creates a sense of "being here," which awakens the sense of time.

French-Romanian philosopher Émil Cioran once described the becoming of human beings as the spiritual suffering of denying the animal within. Whatever is or might be happening within the almost terrifying blend of soul, organs and machinery in EVAs might be the effects of balancing on the thin lines among various forms of existence. It would explain the beastly twitching behaviour of EVAs who most of the time seem to be frustrated and in pain.

German philosopher Martin Heidegger argued that human beings create the dimension of time by utilizing self-consciousness. It would mean that we are not "in time," rather we *are* time itself. Time is not to be understood as a material container in which we find ourselves to be moving through an irreversible succession of events. It is also not an invention for establishing the position between two events and tracking their course and length. Instead, we as time "stretch out" through the universe, through the entire "Being," as its self-awareness. We are the "here" and "now" of Being and the "then" and "there" of Being that *records* its stretching out. But there is a difference between "mere" human beings and human beings who are what Heidegger called *Dasein* (*Here-Being*), the "clearings in the forest of Being," the passages in the universe, in that mere human beings aren't unified with the cosmos.

A Step Backward, into Absolute Terror

Our burden of existence comes from realizing that our stretching out—our standing out—has limits: if we do not perpetuate the three mechanisms of autopoiesis, we die. Time is what makes us human beings, but having time means being aware of the passing of life, of ceasing to be a living being. It means the failure of autopoiesis whose *only* drive is to sustain and create continuously. This could be the cause of ego responding viciously in being pushed to its borders, where it meets with its non-existence, with its end. Ego protecting itself, the AT Field, can then be understood as an extension of the much deeper drive to remain existent, to remain "standing out," invented by life from life itself, in a transformation of a much deeper principle in nature.

Arthur Schopenhauer argued that there's an inherent force in living nature that drives life to persist, which in turn tricks individual beings into continuing to exist. Misato's motivation to work in NERV is the perfect example: she explained in Episode 12 ("A Miracle's Worth") that she is tied to the Human Instrumentality because her father neglected her, yet saved her from death during the Second Impact, at the very last moment. She speculated that "it might be that I still hate him, and just want to avenge my father so that I can free myself of him."

Schopenhauer's force is a refined version of the universal Will that we can understand as an absolute mindless drive lacking all motive but setting everything into effect. Autopoietic beings transform this drive into the positive impulse of sustaining themselves. However, it is also the pathway to what is the cause of absolute terror because the ego *emerges* from the drive but posits itself *against* it.

On the one hand, absolute terror is the fatal, limitless *void* beyond the barricaded ego, the immensely destructive universe, driven by an unstoppable force and shrouded in the darkness of its unconsciousness, leaned on us without ever receding. On the other hand, the only other thing we encounter is the world of the living—and it is the world where we need to feed upon another to sustain ourselves. So, we *too* are the terror, *ourselves*, and our ego, our AT, the border of that terror.

In Episode 25 ("The Ending World"), Ritsuko said that there is "an emptiness in our souls, a fundamental incompleteness that has haunted all beings since the very first thought. On a primal level, humans know of the darkness at the core of their mind. We have sought to escape this void and the fear it causes. All of humankind's accomplishment stems from the hope of filling it. The darkness will never vanish as long as humankind is merely human." So the victorious alternative to our existence is as old as the idea of an afterlife: living, eternally.

Today, ideas such as human enhancement, morphological freedom, mind uploading and singularity are resting upon the same desire to ascend into a higher plane of existence, overcoming human limits with human potential. From the perspective of *Neon Genesis* it is a natural utilization of the Fruit of Knowledge. Ancient Greek philosopher Plato tried to explain this relationship between technology and humanity in his dialogue *Gorgias*, through the myth of Epimetheus who forgot to give humanity purpose when the time was ripe to provide each living being with their reason and cause, so his brother Prometheus stole the arts (*technai*) from Hephaestus and Athena to help them develop their purpose. It's why Misato said that we are those beings that "utilize even the things that try to destroy them." We learn the technics of the universe and turn this knowledge into instruments against it.

Ultimately, this struggle is what makes our identity. From the perspective of the universe, it's normal not to persist, it's normal to change, decay, and dissipate; to persist and create— *that* is abnormal, *that* takes guts and energy. In return, it is the future we make, in which we stretch out and stand out, to confirm the value of our existence. Here lies the possible answer to why Shinji and Asuka returned to the world.

The Gentle Angel

Søren Kierkegaard said that human beings are crucified between the finite and the infinite, that our struggle revolves around what's necessary and what's possible. In the uncertain possibility lies the potency for freedom. As Misato and Yui said to Shinji and Gendo in Episode 20, the decisions made don't change the fact that we can decide again—as long as we live, we have a chance of being happy. But SEELE's final goal was to be as eternal as the universe, to be in its image, without disappearing. That is, to be god-like: to secure the permanent awareness of our species' identity by freeing us from death, terror, and pain. In such a state, however, time ceased to be. There is no future in eternity; in eternity, you simply are.

Surprisingly, Kaworu concluded that we "are not the existence that should die," that all of us "need the future." He realized that what is of no value to the Angels precisely makes human beings worthy of existence—the time we create. But Kaworu as an Angel actually sided with NERV and SEELE. In *The End of Evangelion*, it is humankind that initiated a conflict against itself, for its future, finally transforming itself into a self-made Angel—Lilin. This means that Asuka and Shinji, in fact, completed their duty. By reversing Human Instrumentality, they destroyed the final Angel—humankind eternal—and protected the existence of "mere humanity."

Human Instrumentality missed a crucial point; Kaworu did too. In Shinji, who became the symbol for a real human being, in all its strengths and weaknesses, the sense of wrongness in being eternally at peace comes from his unhealed ego. Humanity defeated the absolute terror, yet that process didn't solve Shinji's or Asuka's issues: Shinji wanted to *earn* his worth and wanted to show his worth *through* his endeavors, and Asuka pledged to herself to succeed *on her own*. In the end, Human Instrumentality denied them that.

MAGI Consensus

The problem may become clearer if we compare *The End of Evangelion* with the original Episode 26 ("The Beast that Shouted 'I' at the Heart of the World"). In the original, we witnessed Shinji's internal reasoning by which he concluded that he *does* hate himself, but that he *could* love himself. If the two versions aren't completely disparate, then the aftermath of Shinji's positive attitude in Episode 26 has to be the anguish seen in the last scene of *The End of Evangelion* for him to be able to *try* to love himself. The point wasn't to be loved or worthy of someone's love; it was to be *worthy* of your *own* love.

For that to make sense, Shinji had to revolt against Human Instrumentality, and he did so precisely because of his ego. In Episode 20, Yui said that only those who live could achieve happiness. But eternal life is not life at all, because life as we human beings constitute it has to cease to exist to be considered a life. In Christianity, to give an example, God became "a living god" only by His materialization as a being who can die. So Shinji and Asuka rejected the eternity of peace because only through the hardship of struggle, against all the odds and all the evils, can they attain the life worth having for themselves, as a possibility in the future. For the possibility to achieve happiness, the AT Field needs to stand on its own.

If I can understand at least a part of *Evangelion*'s story of revolt, in refusing the harmonized unity before coming to terms with yourself, it would be that we, as individuals, owe nothing to the world and that the world has no right to ask anything from us. There's no higher purpose but the one we create from within ourselves.

We were pushed into this existence by choices made by others, and in this existence, things that don't originate from our choices, including our own constitution, are sources of terror we have to overcome. To do that, we have to contemplate the deepest recesses of our ego, which can be our foe and our friend, and consider the causes and reasons for who we might be, to attain peace within, for ourselves, until the end. Then, the end disappears in the eternity we created.

12
Coping with Loneliness, or How to Grow Watermelons

YOSHIHIRO TANIGAWA

In Episode 17 ("Fourth Child"), Gendo Ikari and Dr. Kozo Fuyutsuki wax philosophical as their train rushes through Tokyo-3.

FUYUTSUKI: The city. A paradise built by the hands of man.

GENDO: Man was cast out of the Garden of Eden and forced to flee into a world where death could come at any moment. He created his own Garden of Eden using the knowledge he was forced to gain as the weakest of all lifeforms.

FUYUTSUKI: A Paradise we built for ourselves to insulate our kind from the terror of death and satisfy our carnal desires? This city is a stellar example of that. An armed city, built for our protection.

GENDO: It's a city of cowards. Shelter for those fleeing an outside world full of enemies.

The pair are talking about the city drifting past them. But hidden in their words is an important point about the self. In *Neon Genesis Evangelion*, we find a complex (and notoriously confounding) treatment of how we as individuals maintain and change our egos, and how we, *as* individuals, learn to deal with other people.

Some of us, like Asuka Langley Sohryu, disguise our weaknesses and loneliness, arming ourselves with combative words and actions. To protect ourselves, we sometimes become authoritative and overbearing. And yet at other times, we see no other option but to run away, deserting our jobs and obligations. Not to single out Asuka, *every* EVA pilot loses a grip on their egos, succumbing to their social anxieties, irritations, feelings of isolation, senses of loss, desires for recognition, fears of death, stress, and the incredible gap between what they are and what they want to be. And they frequently respond by putting up an inner barrier, their own personal AT Field, as it were.

Hannah Arendt, author of *The Origins of Totalitarianism*, insists that loneliness and solitude are quite different, praising Epictetus, the emancipated slave-philosopher of Greece for his discovery of the difference:

> As Epictetus sees it (*Dissertationes*, Book 3, chapter 13) the lonely man (*eremos*) finds himself surrounded by others with whom he cannot establish contact or to whose hostility he is exposed. The solitary man, on the contrary, is alone and therefore "can be together with himself" since men have the capacity of "talking with themselves." In solitude, in other words, I am "by myself" together with my self, and therefore two-in-one, whereas in loneliness I am actually one, deserted by all others. (*Origins of Totalitarianism*, p. 476)

Lonely people are those who can't bear being together with their selves, who can't face and endure conversation with their own egos. Instead, ironically, the lonely depend completely on others. But this doesn't mean we all show this dependency in the same way. While some of us are clearly craving for some form of basic human kindness, others show only hostility.

The characters of *Neon Genesis Evangelion* are lonely people. They live in Tokyo-3, a crowded and bustling hyper-modern city. And while surrounded by others, working in close proximity and sharing plenty of conversation, they don't live with their *selves*. They dread the thought of being alone. In Episode 23 ("Rei III") there's a revealing interaction between the thirteenth Angel (Almisael) and Rei Ayanami. The Angel invades her psyche and tries to understand her soul by generating another Ayanami as an interface for communication.

AYANAMI: Aching? No, that's not it. It's lonely.

ANOTHER AYANAMI: Yes, that's it. It's lonely. Lonely? I don't understand. You don't want to be alone. There are many of us. But you're alone and you hate it.

AYANAMI: That is what we call "loneliness."

ANOTHER AYANAMI: That's your heart you're feeling. It's yours that is full of sadness. Your own heart.

AYANAMI: These are tears! The one that's crying . . . is me?

Ayanami hadn't realized her feelings of loneliness until this dialogue with her alter ego. That is, until the Angel forced her to 'talk with herself.'

In another example from Episode 23, Misato Katsuragi and Shinji Ikari learn the shocking details about Ayanami and SEELE. Returning home, Misato notices that Shinji is looking pretty down. Herself still reeling from losing her partner, she tries to reach out to him with comfort only to be rejected. In Misato's monologue, we again find the topic of 'loneliness':

> MISATO: He has to be feeling lonely . . . Maybe he's scared of women. No, what he's scared of is intimacy with others. . . . Pen Pen, come here. [Pen Pen rejects her.] Oh, now I get it. Anybody will do. The one that was feeling lonely is me.

The characters act and react toward others by setting up an inner barrier. They retreat within their own private fortress cities, much like how they've barricaded themselves as a community in the strategic base of Tokyo-3. According to Arendt, this is precisely why they cannot come to terms with their loneliness. Loneliness is a phenomenon that appears when people are *together*. In other words, they can't bear true solitude. And without solitude, they have no chance to enter into dialogue with their *selves*. So, if loneliness is a symptom, the story of *Neon Genesis Evangelion* presents us with two strategies for treating the underlying disease. We need to get back to the question raised by Gendo and Fuyutsuki above. What kind of 'city' do these lonely people inhabit?

Tokyo-centrism and the Image of a City

Japanese society has a bad habit. Anthropologist Yoshiyuki Tsurumi calls it "Tokyo-centrism." For example, every year somewhere between July and October, typhoons besiege Japan. Millions of people, then, tune into the weather forecasts to stay up to date with the latest conditions. Tsurumi noticed that weather forecasters regularly said that a typhoon "has passed" after it passed Tokyo. And that's even if the typhoon was currently pounding the northern island of Hokkaido, which, by the way, is still very much a part of Japan!

Such examples are ubiquitous, and contemporary Japanese culture all too often organizes itself around the local circumstances of Tokyo. Japanese pop culture is no exception. Sui Ishida's *Tokyo Ghoul* (2011–2018), Atsushi Okubo's *Fire Force* (2015), and the Makoto Shinkai-directed hit, *Weathering with You* (2019), are some noteworthy examples of works set (at least primarily) in Tokyo. In *Fire Force*, Tokyo-centrism is particularly profound. There, survivors of the apocalyptic 'Great

Disaster' take refuge in the 'Tokyo Empire.' In some Japanese popular works, Tokyo is literally all there is!

But what is it about Tokyo that has captured the imaginations of an entire nation of Japanese? What is it that makes Tokyo *Tokyo*? Does it even make sense to ask this question? According to philosopher Hiroki Azuma: no. At least not anymore. Surveying issues of the architectural magazine *10+1* that featured Tokyo, Azuma noticed an interesting trend. In the issues dating from the end of the twentieth century, intellectuals and architects discussed Tokyo as a whole. They tried to define its essence and construct a theory of the city. But attitudes began to change in the dawn of the new century. Now, people seem more likely to center their *lifestyles* in Tokyo or the images of *particular places* in Tokyo, like Shibuya or Shinjuku. Gone is the image of Tokyo as a unified whole. Azuma diagnosed this as a kind of "aphasia," a lack of coherent image. He interpreted this to be part of the collapse of 'grand narratives,' or large-scale ideas about the world. Grand narratives about, say, the progress of history or the omnipotence of science have little currency these days. Likewise, comprehensive images of Tokyo too seem to be losing their grip. Even so, the cultural trend noted above seems to contradict this theory. *Fire Force* and *Tokyo Ghoul* still seem comfortable centering 'Tokyo' in their narratives.

To figure out why, we should take into account the socio-economic effects globalization has on major cities. Globalization causes a strong tendency toward urban concentration. As social and economic functions gather in a city, the felt cultural presence of major cities snowballs. A city like Tokyo comes to represent its country, not only to itself, but to the world. Pop culture responds to these dynamics and so in many works, Tokyo becomes almost synonymous for Japan.

But if defining or not defining, centering or not centering Tokyo is so problematic, why worry about the place at all? In Western philosophy we can find a long tradition concerned with history. In the early twentieth century, Martin Heidegger took up the mantle by arguing that we must understand human existence in terms of time or "temporality." How does *when* we exist impact our existence? Tetsuro Watsuji, a philosopher of the Kyoto School, challenged this idea and stressed that we must also look to our "spatiality." How does *where* we exist impact our existence? Watsuji has since come under harsh criticism for falling into cultural stereotypes and a problematic kind of determinism. But his point is still worth taking note of. For example, French geographer Augustin Berque inherits Watsuji's project and tries to work out the "senses of a city." According to Berque, these "senses" consist of both existences and images. What a city *means* is constituted by its natural and cultural space. For us, then, it's worth asking, what 'senses of the city' are there in the Tokyo(s) of *Neon Genesis Evangelion*?

Scheming, Global Tokyo

We begin in 2000. SEELE and Gendo Ikari conduct an experiment that triggers the awakening of Adam (the first Angel). A resulting explosion melts the Antarctic ice caps and shifts the Earth's axis. Sea-level rise and tsunamis submerge many coastal cities, including parts of Tokyo. Armed conflicts break out as some nations try to take advantage of the disorder. Finally, Tokyo is violently destroyed by a nuclear bomb. Five hundred thousand people are killed. Tokyo, or Tokyo-1 as it was to be called, is gone and so in a quite literal fashion, the twenty-first century marks the end of talking about Tokyo as a whole.

Following the destruction of the Second Impact, the Japanese government abandons Tokyo-1, re-establishing the capital in Matsumoto City, Nagano Prefecture in 2001. The city is renamed "Tokyo-2." With New York City submerged, the new headquarters of the United Nations are provisionally relocated here.

2006, Hakone City, Kanagawa Prefecture: the government starts to build the massive subterranean cavity known as the "GeoFront." Surrounded by sensor posts and missile stations, the GeoFront is a fortress designed to intercept all incoming Angels and thereby protect humanity from certain doom. Attracting global attention and investment, this last bastion of hope for humanity is called "Tokyo-3."

Tokyo-3 is home to our heroes and station to the NERV organization and Evangelion Units. By governmental decree, the city is assigned to be the next capital upon its projected completion in 2015.

Shrouded by a thick cloud of conspiracy, however, the true agent behind this latest relocation project is SEELE. This globally-organized, secret society intends to secure a budget for their hidden plot: the Human Instrumentality Project. Tokyo-3 is, as Fuyutsuki says, "NERV's camouflaged Angel interception fortress city. The endlessly-delayed seventh construction phase is finally ending. The city is finally complete" (Episode 17). The story of *Evangelion* begins in 2015. Thus, in this world, Tokyo is the center of rationality. It is here that advanced technology and econo-political powers gather and global actors attempt to realize their schemes.

Kyoto in Disguise

So does *Evangelion* too suffer from Tokyo-centrism? Let's not be hasty. What's obscured behind these images of a conniving, power-drunk Tokyo? *Kyoto.* Covert agent Ryoji Kaji is the one to expose this secret. In Episode 15 ("Those Women Longed for the Touch of Others' Lips, and Thus Invited Their Kisses"), he visits Kyoto City to search for evidence of a conspiracy related to the Marduk Institute. Although he officially belongs to the Department of Special Inspections, Special Agency NERV, he is really a spy for the Japanese Home Ministry's Department of Investigations. His mission is to investigate the ruse hatched by commander Gendo Ikari and Fuyutsuki. Kaji explains: "The Marduk Institute: an advisory body directly under the Human Instrumentality Council that was established to find potential Evangelion pilots. Its true nature is still shrouded in mystery." His investigations reveal that the Marduk is a dummy committee composed of one hundred and eight front companies. They are attempting to conceal the true operations of the Human Instrumentality Project.

In Episode 21 ("He Was Aware that He Was Still a Child"), more is revealed through Dr. Fuyutsuki's flashbacks. We return to Kyoto, 1999. Before the Second Impact, the doctor was a professor at Kyoto University near Kamogawa River. There, Fuyutsuki met the young and brilliant bioengineer, Yui Ikari and became her sensei in "metaphysical biology." Yui, we discover, is the daughter of a prominent member of SEELE. Approached by Gendo Rokubungi for her talent and SEELE connections, the two are eventually married.

Thus, Kyoto sets the backdrop for the meeting of these characters who are to be key for Project-E, the scheme to create the Evangelion Units from Adam. In Episode 23, Ritsuko Akagi explains the project as follows:

> Mankind stumbled across God. Overjoyed, we tried to possess it. And so, we were punished. That happened fifteen years ago. The God we were so excited about vanished. Undeterred, we then tried to resurrect God. That was Adam. We made humans from Adam in God's image. Those are the EVAs.

Project-E sets the stage for the next strategic move: the Human Instrumentality Project. Now, the exact nature of this project is murky, due to the differing aims of Gendo and Fuyutsuki and of the SEELE mainstream. Nevertheless, Episode 20 ("Weaving a Story 2: Oral Stage") hints at what these men are after: the dissolution of the ego's boundaries.

The fictional Tokyos of *Tokyo Ghoul*, *Fire Force*, and *Weather with You* are located in our Tokyo. They are the Tokyos of *modernity*, which far from aspiring to the melting of the ego's boundaries, demand that we form clearly delineated self-identities. In contrast, *Neon Genesis Evangelion*'s Tokyo is not Tokyo, but a series of quasi-Tokyos that follow the annihilation of the original in the Second Impact. And rather than drawing on the city of modernity, this story constructs its global center, Tokyo-3, through images of *ecstasy* peculiar to *Kyoto*. In short, we can see this as an attempt to *overcome* Tokyo-centrism precisely by *reconfiguring* Tokyo's imagery.

Ecstasy and the Fleshpot

The Human Instrumentality Project deals with the dissolution of the ego's boundary or melting of an AT Field. From the standpoint of Japanese philosophy, the idea of the dissolution of self has its origins in Kyoto, not Tokyo. Tokyo and Kyoto are two major cities in Japan. The former is regarded as advanced and modern; the latter as traditional and historic. Movie critic Mikiro Kato follows this contrast in his study of Japanese films:

> *Clothes of Deception* [(1951) directed by Kozaburo Yoshimura] is a fleshpot film starring Machiko Kyo . . . Though this movie was created more than fifty years ago, the scenes of Kyoto today are almost unchanged from those of Kyoto in the film. And this is the big difference between Tokyo and Kyoto. Kyoto is the [historic] city of the ancient capital, while Tokyo is the [advanced] city of 'scrap and build'.
> (Mikiro Kato, Eiga no Ryobun [*The Territory of Films*], p. 103)

Tokyo is a changing city that follows the cutting edge of modernity; Kyoto is not. This contrasting image seems to hold for *Neon Genesis Evangelion*. Importantly for our purposes, Kato mentions a "fleshpot" (*kagai, hanamachi*), or geisha quarter in Kyoto. Many "Kyoto" philosophers drew inspiration from this aspect of the city.

Shuzo Kuki, a well-known philosopher of the Kyoto School, wrote an essay on cherry blossom viewing (*hanami*) in Gion, an iconic fleshpot of Kyoto. In "The Weeping Cherry in Gion," he writes of the dissolution of the boundaries between people. He reports that people of all classes, sexualities, and philosophies could have an ecstatic moment through the drink and dance that surround *hanami* (*Kuki Shuzo Zuihitsushu* [*Selected Essays of Shuzo Kiki*], pp. 39–42). Another philosopher, Kiyokazu Washida, characterizes Kyoto as a city familiar with ecstasy. He takes up many examples of the "other-worldly" moments in Kyoto with reference to Kuki and Gion:

At one time, a certain professor of philosophy went by taxi to Kyoto University from Gion; a certain student, having drank too much, climbed over the wall of Ginkaku Temple and into the garden on the snowy new year eve, resulting in death by hypothermia; a certain group of students furtively waited for the ceremonial bonfire on the mountain called Okuribi and tried to hack the meaning of the bonfire by changing its shape. I bet some students lost their virginity in Kyoto. There were few theaters for popular movies, but plenty of theaters cozy and old . . . holiness, lovemaking, and playfulness were and are intertwined into the unique senses of this city. (Kyoto no Heinetsu [*The Normal Temperature of Kyoto*], pp. 4–5)

Washida describes three major ecstatic moments of Kyoto: "These senses of the city suggest that Kyoto is open to the worlds of the 'other side'. The world of religious ecstasy (shrines and temples). The world of inferential ecstasy (universities and colleges). The world of euphoric ecstasy (fleshpots and recreation)" (p. 5). Each of these contributes to dissolving the established boundary of the modern ego.

Kyoto City is so small that one can go by bicycle from one end to the other. And yet this compact space contains a variety of historic spots, religious architectures, universities, amusement facilities, and, of course, fleshpots. Washida gestures to this variety in characterizing Kyoto as a place full of opportunity for ecstatic experiences, the dissolution of ego boundaries. And of course the theories of the legendary Kitaro Nishida lie in the same intellectual genealogy. The religious ecstatic experiences he achieved through Zen served as one of the triggers for his unique notion of "pure experience" (*An Inquiry into the Good*).

Kei'ichi Sakuta, a sociologist at Kyoto University, takes up Sigmund Freud and draws on the arguments of Henri-Louis Bergson to develop a theory of the "dissolving experience" (*Seisei no Shakaugaku wo Mezashite [Toward the Generative Sociology]*). Sakuta mentions the famed "oceanic feeling" as a typical example of the "dissolving experience" that melts the boundary of the self.

In Episode 20, we find an incredibly similar description as one of NERV's main computer technicians, Maya Ibuki, and Ritsuko Akagi discuss Shinji's dissolution of self:

MAYA: We hypothesize that Shinji's body has lost its ego boundary delineation and he's drifting in the Entry Plug [*a capsule-like cockpit that houses the EVA pilot*] in a quantum state.

MISATO: You're saying that Shinji's been transformed into a state that we can't detect visually?

MAYA: Yes, ma'am. The makeup of the LCL [*something akin to amniotic fluid in which the pilot is suspended*] in the Entry Plug has undergone a chemical change. It's now very similar to seawater on primitive Earth.

MISATO: The primordial soup, huh?

RITSUKO: All the matter that comprises Shinji is still preserved within the plug, what can be called his soul is also still there. The proof is that his mental self-image is manifesting a facsimile of his suit. So by "salvage operation," we mean reconstituting his body and affixing his psyche inside it.

In the battle with the fourteenth Angel, Zeruel, Shinji's EVA-01 goes "Beserk," causing his body and mind to dissolve into the primordial ocean of LCL. As it turns out, his mother's soul somehow inhabits EVA-01. As his ego dissolves, Shinji sees an image of the "soup" of primordial Earth and catches the scent of his mother. Assimilated into EVA-01 (that is, *his mother*) and blended into the sea of LCL, he has all the symptoms of an 'oceanic feeling'!

Neon Genesis Evangelion weaves (dare I say, *unconsciously*) the philosophical tradition of ecstasy characteristic of Kyoto into the core story theme of ego-dissolution. In other words, Kyoto's connection to the Human Instrumentality Project penetrates all the way to the issue of complete ecstasy. And it's here that we find it as a strategy to combat modern loneliness. When the self is dissolved and melted into the feeling of fullness, loneliness itself dissolves, as it were. Lacking the consciousness-melting technology of the Human Instrumentality Project and armed with (arguably) better moral compasses, we find little resolved in this 'solution.' Yet, if we take the aim of the Project to be losing our "selves" in a "feeling as something limitless, unbounded," we come close to what the ancients called 'ataraxia,' or complete peace. Practically speaking however, are we any better off? How many of us could manage the life of a sage? What remains is the problem of how to manage our "this-worldly" desires, our carnal appetites.

Growing Watermelons at the End of the World

If we may assume that this primary ego-feeling has, to a greater or lesser degree, been preserved in the more mental life of many people, it would stand beside the more narrowly and sharply demarcated ego-feeling of maturity as a sort of counterpart, and the ideational contents appropriate to it would be precisely those of unboundedness and connection with the universe—the same ones with which my friend explains the "oceanic" feeling. (*Civilization and Its Discontents*, p, 48)

According to Freud, ego boundary goes hand in hand with "maturity." Yet, while maturity and boundary go together, he also suggests that the oceanic, ecstatic feeling is fundamental to the construction of the ego. Our desire for ecstatic moments might turn out to be basic, since our fundamental weaknesses force us to seek some haven from anxieties. This idea gets picked up in the story. Let's return to a conversation from earlier (Episode 17).

> **GENDO:** Man was cast out of the Garden of Eden and forced to flee into a world where death could come at any moment. He created his own Garden of Eden using the knowledge he was forced to gain as the weakest of all lifeforms.
>
> **FUYUTSUKI:** A Paradise we built for ourselves to insulate our kind from the terror of death and satisfy our carnal desires? This city is a stellar example of that. An armed city, built for our protection.
>
> **GENDO:** It's a city of cowards. Shelter for those fleeing an outside world full of enemies.

The protective and satisfying aspects of the city demarcate an outline of its "ego." With such a defined line or shape, it can offer us a haven by keeping anxieties at a distance. The city lulls people into the belief that fear is shut out behind closed doors. And yet, these boundaries—which gather people together—can't eliminate, and may indeed cause, a different anxiety: loneliness. Loneliness stems from being together with others. Humans gather together because they're weak, and humans feel lonely because they live together. One weakness causes another. Gendo, and perhaps also Fuyutsuki, believes this basic human condition must be eliminated, and they commit themselves to their ego-dissolving project in order to overcome our fundamental cowardice.

But isn't there any other way? In Episode 20, Ryoji Kaji mentions indulging in "carnal desires" to manage the difficult conditions that come with his spycraft. Kaji's attitude toward "desires" is markedly different from Fuyutsuki's. In Episode 21, Gendo describes Fuyutsuki with scrupulous honesty. Fuyutsuki has a strong inclination toward puritanism, and this motivation may be the driving force behind the Project. If the goal is to bring humanity into a whole, complete, pure entity, then Fuyutsuki and Gendo appear to be after some nirvana, the "oceanic" bliss of eternal peace. We could say that this puritan hostility toward carnal desires leads straightaway to the dissolution of the modern self.

But what of Kaji? Well, his position is a bit more nuanced. In Episode 20, Kaji says to Misato, "You're truer to the human condition when you indulge in carnal desires. The deception should hold for a while. The deception against yourself." Yet, literal indulgence in carnality is not the path Kaji ends up supporting, but rather the *cultivation* of his own desires in this world. What does this attitude take him to? In Episode 17, Kaji invites Shinji for a walk and notices his depressed state. In conversation, he comes up with the idea of showing him "something special": his personal hobby.

> **SHINJI:** Are these . . . watermelons?
>
> **KAJI:** Yeah. Cute, huh? They're my hobby. Don't tell anybody, okay? It's great to make something, to grow something. You will notice things and figure stuff out. Things you enjoy, for example.

Kaji recommends creating something, and not just anything, but something free from all the *things you have to do*. In other words, we need to do something that's not bound up with the logic of utility. Buying a watermelon in summer is a modest luxury for Japanese people. Japan is small; watermelons are big. Worse yet, they're filled with water and supply almost no nutritional benefit. Growing them seems pretty useless from the perspective of economic utility that dominates today's society. But for Kaji, it's a private desire. It's connected neither to the logic of utility nor to the things he has to do. It's that peculiar form of human action he calls a "hobby." He believes that having a hobby will open up possibilities for "noticing" and "figuring out" stuff about *his own self*. A hobby gives us a chance to make use of our "capacity to talk with ourselves," as Arendt says. Kaji seems to suggest that a hobby lets us be with ourselves, to have a dialogue between myself and me (two-in-one), no matter how lonely we feel (*Origins of Totalitarianism*, p. 476).

The issue of "hobby" clarifies why Kaji lectures Shinji in Episode 18 ("Ambivalence"):

> **SHINJI:** I've learned a fair amount lately. About my father. About his job. About my mother. So I thought—
>
> **KAJI:** No, that's where you're wrong. You only think you learned something. Nobody can ever completely understand another person. Good luck even understanding yourself. Complete understanding

between two people is impossible. That's why people try so hard to understand themselves and others. It's one of the things that makes life interesting.

Kaji is trying to show Shinji, and us, our "unhandsome" condition. "Unhandsome" is a term favored by American philosopher Stanley Cavell, who uses it to remind us of our finitude. In praise of Ralph Waldo Emerson, Cavell says, "Emerson's 'partiality' of thinking is, or accounts for, the inflections of partial as 'not whole,' together with partial as 'favoring or biased toward' something or someone" (*Conditions Handsome and Unhandsome*, p. 41). We're constantly reminded that this partiality of our understanding is inevitable. In fact, during the above discussion, Shinji was clueless as to the identity of the fourth pilot, who, as it turns out, was his friend. Of the main characters, Shinji is the only person who does not know this fact during the combat. Marked by his own "partiality," Shinji nearly killed his friend in combat.

Having a personal "hobby," then, precludes the kind of passive cynicism we incline to when faced with the impossibility of complete knowledge. Indeed, we never see Kaji as spiritless or apathetic. In Episode 19, Kaji adds another layer to this story when he meets Shinji during the battle against the fourteenth Angel, Zeruel.

> KAJI: They [SEELE] found out about my side job. Now I don't have a station to man during combat. I've been stuck watering my plants ever since.
>
> SHINJI: At a time like this?
>
> KAJI: Because it's a time like this. Between Katsuragi's breasts would be nice, but when I die, this is where I really want to be.
>
> SHINJI: Die?

Even as the world is coming to an end, Kaji insists that people should commit themselves to their personal hobbies. Quixotic indeed. But what he's getting at, as is Hannah Arendt, is the importance of time in solitude for gaining knowledge of one's self. A hobby, like growing watermelons, isn't something through which we connect with others. Neither is it something we do *for others*. Instead, it's the solitary place of dialogue between myself and me. Kaji grows watermelons, and he does it *for himself*. Hobbies stem from the desires deeply rooted in our minds and this is suggested when Kaji asks Shinji to keep his hobby a secret ("Don't tell anybody, okay?"). To have a hobby, one has to "cultivate" one's fundamental desires *in this world*. For Kaji, growing watermelons is an action sprouting from his "this-worldly," carnal desires. So then, having a hobby could be another strategy against modern loneliness. But how is that so?

Ooh, That's a Philosophy!

As we've seen, Kaji was more comfortable with human desires, Fuyutsuki more hostile. And while the latter tries to annihilate desires in some kind of nirvana, the former encourages us to cultivate our carnal desires through a personal hobby. The key is solitude. We need time to come to know our "selves" through dialogue. With our hobbies, we might just be able to bear the loneliness that we often feel when we are with others. And while we may never know all the dark corners of the ego, it's always worth trying to know more:

> KAJI: Complete understanding between two people is impossible. That's why people try so hard to understand themselves and others. It's one of the things that makes life interesting. (Episode 18)

Kaji even invites us to embrace the negative aspects residing in us, since this too may prove fruitful for life:

> KAJI: If you have your hobby, you notice things and figure stuff out. Things you enjoy, for example.
>
> SHINJI: And things that hurt.
>
> KAJI: You don't like being hurt?
>
> SHINJI: I don't care for it.
>
> KAJI: Did you find something you enjoy?
>
> SHINJI: [Silence]
>
> KAJI: That's all well and good. But listen, people who know what pain is are kinder to others because of it. That's not the same thing as being weak.

Kaji never gives us any rock-solid argument for his case. He merely suggests that to be kinder, *to live better*, is good for its own sake. Kaji's own life demonstrates to us what it's like to live with one's personal hobby and the consequences this has for a better life. We could even call this a kind of "perfection-ism" like that espoused by Stanley Cavell.

The motif of the "ego" runs parallel with the "city." And so what Kaji says about the self should well be applied to the city. Humans are forced to gather because of their weakness, but loneliness in the city brings hostility to one another. When filled with fear, they rush into little fortresses built against supposed enemies. When filled with loneliness, they rush toward visions of melting boundaries. In contrast, Kaji's suggestion doesn't include any total elimination of negativity, or the "things that hurt." He demands we live with fear, with sadness, loneliness, and pain, and with all the other shades of human negativity. The city is no sanctuary from these negative emotions, since their causes are linked to "others." Thus, we must learn to manage them, live with them, that is, *cope with them*.

This message is echoed in Episode 11 ("In the Still Darkness"). Asuka and Ayanami talk during a power outage brought by the destruction of battle:

ASUKA: Yeah, well, without those lights the place looks deserted. [System restored] See? You feel safer this way.

AYANAMI: Man fears the darkness, and so man scrapes away at the edges of it with fire.

ASUKA: Ooh, how profound!

Plunged in darkness, we feel unsafe and crave light. Yet even if we harness the power of fire or electricity, darkness remains. Where light falls, shadows prevail. The city in particular can't cast off darkness completely. Technology fails. And even when it's working, there's always the threat suggested by the off switch. Nevertheless, it's true that we "scrape away at the edges" of darkness. Darkness will never fully recede, but we can learn to *cope with it*. We can, *and do*, survive with it. And since the ever-remaining darkness encourages us to scrape away at yet another part, the result may not be so bad. After all, that's one of the things that makes the city interesting.

Growing watermelons means learning to manage negative feelings. Coping with the darkness, then, means having a personal "hobby." With a hobby, we escape the economy of utility and create the opportunity to talk with our selves. And so, if we are to advance as a city, or a collective society, we would do well not to rush to the logic of utility. To survive in the city, we need solitude, the private place where we can manage our loneliness. And if we were to translate what

Asuka says in the last line above literally, it would be "Ooh, that's a philosophy!"

While she may not have intended to say something so truly profound, she in fact points us straight to Kaji's message, and in their conversation we find echoes of the call to manage the darkness and cope with the tragic "things that hurt" in our lives. Now *that's* an Evangelion's philosophy.[1]

---

[1] I would like to thank Sova P.K. Cerda, Kyoto University, for English proofreading and advice. With his assistance, I was able to make my argument much clearer.

13
Evangelion's Terminal Dogma

KHEGAN M. DELPORT

Somewhere on the Moon, there's a god being born. It's just another day in another weird universe. Behind closed doors a transnational cabal is plotting the rebirth of an ancient goddess (as one does). They desire cosmic harmony, at the price of humanity. An absurd enterprise, though not without a certain logic. So, what could go wrong? "God's in his heaven—All's right with the world!" But then again, even NERV isn't drinking the Kool Aid. Angels are attacking. Things are falling apart; the center isn't holding (Yeats). But the "blessed rage for order" (Wallace Stevens) goes on . . .

Black Moon Rising

Early in "You Can (Not) Advance," the second installment of the Rebuild series, Gendo Ikari and Dr. Kōzō Fuyutsuki spot something while they're checking out Tabgha Base. Gendo recognizes a creature known as Evangelion Mark 06; it's a new prototype being developed by SEELE and their somewhat creepy enclave. They are now secretly building advanced EVAs after the unexpected destruction of EVA Units 04 and 05—hence the lunar hangout.

SEELE's plan is moving quickly, and is reaching its final stage: the Human Instrumentality Project. Although stories differ (between say *The End of Evangelion* and the –2 version—as any self-respecting otaku should know), the general picture given is that SEELE wants to bring an end to history by uniting everyone through a destruction of their AT Fields, reducing all beings to a conscious ocean of LCL. This is initiated through a ritual joining of the crucified Lilith and EVA-01, which one of the council members (in *The End of Evangelion*) calls a "sacrament to unite God, humans, and all other life forms in death." All sounds rather esoteric. I did mention this was a weird universe.

Gendo has his own version of Instrumentality. To him, Keel Lorenz and the council are just useful idiots in his own similarly psychotic attempt to reconcile Lilith with Adam. This is all done so that he may be finally reunited with Yui Ikari, his long-suffering, cheated-on wife, who died in an accident at NERV headquarters. Spoiler alert: Gendo gets what he wants, kind of, only to be unceremoniously bisected by a replica of EVA-01.

Anyway, while he and Kōzō are flitting over the lunar surface, they start pontificating on the respective goods of harmony and chaos. On the one side, Kōzō thinks that chaos is a creative energy that always exists in the human heart. On the other, Gendo thinks harmony and order are the deeper phenomena, and that these should be pursued above all else. Now while Kōzō is certainly an enabler of Gendo's egomania most of the time, he doesn't always agree with Gendo. Here and there, Kōzō shows himself as a tempering figure, a yin to Gendo's yang so to speak. This is explained somewhat in Episode 21 ("The Birth of NERV"/"He Was Aware that He Was Still a Child") where we see Kōzō's affection for Yui—one of his most promising students—and his suspicion of the young Gendo (who changes his name from Rokubungi to Gendo, presumably because of his dodgy background).

For instance, in Episode 12 ("A Miracle's Worth"/"She said, 'Don't make others suffer for your personal hatred'."), while surveying the hellish landscape of Antarctica (Ground Zero of the Second Impact), we can see more clearly this philosophical disagreement about whether the fact of plurality itself should be praised or lamented. Gendo longs for a world purged of multiplicity, believing this to be the root of the world's problems. Kōzō is more pragmatic, one who believes the Second Impact was grounded in human arrogance, and that these urges can be managed without the apocalyptic remedy Gendo is suggesting. Gendo looks at the unforgiving scenery of Antarctica and finds "a pristine world untainted by original sin," while Kōzō quips that he would "prefer a world filled with humans, sinful though it may be."

Postmodern Metaphysics—Say What?

What this conversation shows us is that the *Evangelion* saga has a *metaphysical* vision. More specifically, it's what we could call a "postmodern" metaphysics of the unity and plurality of Being. You might think this is some highfalutin, Angelic nonsense, but hang in there.

I'll admit "postmodern" is a bit tricky to define, but in philosophy at least the word usually indicates a feeling that there's something wonky with modernity—and especially its desire for certainty and universal truths. Of course "modern" can also be used in a less judgy way to mean 'contemporary' or 'current,' but the target here is something rather more specific. For many, it's the French philosopher and mathematician René Descartes (1596–1650) who started this mess, most famously with his method of basing certainty on the *cogito*, the thinking thing ("I think, therefore I am"). For postmodern philosophers, like Jacques Derrida (1930–2004) and Jean-François Lyotard (1924–1998), certainty is a pipe-dream. Any attempt at certainty always leaves something left over which isn't accounted for by the given explanation or structure, and this "remainder" will always be there, try as we might to get rid of it.

Think of the meaning of a word or phrase at such-and-such a time or place. It might mean one thing, but as history moves on, it can develop different meanings and associations. (What Gainax does with the word "Evangelion"—Greek for "good news" or "gospel"—isn't the same as the New Testament, for instance). In this setting, the "modern" person would want to emphasize clear and consistent definitions (for science depends on it), while the "postmodern" would want to emphasize the reality of random, unpredictable changes, and therefore that meaning can never be closed or finished.

Neon Genesis Evangelion as a whole does something similar to this, particularly in the way that it ultimately leaves unresolved the relationship between a unity of initiating principles (The First and Third Impacts, for example) and the diversity that comes about because of them (possible worlds in the Evangelion universe which may or may not exist, for example). Gendo and NERV's desire for Instrumentality trades on this since it implies an attempt to reverse the movement of the One toward the Many *back* toward oneness. But anyone who has seen *The End of Evangelion* knows that this is an exercise in futility.

Another way *Evangelion* could be called "postmodern" is that it pastiches, or mixes-up, a variety of styles, methods, and mythologies together. See how the series remixes old religious themes, taken from sources like Christianity and Kabbalah, and jazzes them with the mecha and science-fiction elements of giant robots and MAGI supercomputers. Case in point: the ritual that resurrects Lilith in *The End of Evangelion* combines religious archetypes (the Tree of Life, crucifixion, the "Dead Sea Scrolls") with EVA-01 and Mass Production EVAs that all work together to begin the Third Impact. This mixture of ancient and sci-fi technology is something that continues throughout the TV series and movies.

There's also this term "metaphysics," a word that gets bandied about by a whole range of people from logical positivists to chakra healers. Again, what people mean by this term can be many different things; even in the history of philosophy, this word can be used in all sorts of ways. Aristotle (384–322 B.C.E.) wrote a book that came to be called *Metaphysics*, a name given to it by some of his students. Exactly what this implies isn't entirely clear, and there's some debate about what this title means. But what it seems to suggest is that we know the physical world first, which then leads us to those realities that help explain why there is a world of things in the first place; in other words, we ask questions of meaning and ultimate causes. One moves from the world of everyday interactions to those of a higher, simpler order, which aren't as easy to know as the more immediate, mixed-up stuff we get through our senses. Simply put, metaphysics arises when we think about what makes things be the way they are.

When we're surprised by the behavior of an EVA, like when it goes suddenly into Berserker Mode, we're forced to think about what an EVA really is. We're no longer certain. This provokes us to think about its being, what it is, and why it acts like this. What is an EVA? For Martin Heidegger (1889–1976), it's when things start to break-down and misbehave that we're forced to think about how the stuff around us isn't just useful for this or that, but what things actually are (*Being and Time*, pp. 63–110). This is the beginning of metaphysics.

The One and the Many

To think how this applies to the everyday, here's something Plato said again and again: we experience things most immediately through our senses. Taken alone, this would suggest the world is changing all the time. Things come into being, and they disappear. They evolve and mutate, like a raging bio-mechanoid. To quote Heraclitus (c. 535–c. 475 B.C.E.), one of the Pre-Socratics, you can't step into the same river twice (*Early Greek Philosophy*, p. 70). But Plato argues that if this were all there was, we wouldn't be able to think or understand anything, because just as we tried to grasp something, it would change into something else. There wouldn't be continuity between one state and another. You wouldn't be able to say what something *is*.

So, in order for us to grasp anything, the world must present to us certain forms or ideas that are consistent enough for us to understand. In the *Evangelion* universe there are Angelic beings, all of which are individual and unique. But we have learned to recognize the form of "Angelic beings" in all their terrifying glory, so that we are able to call them "Angels" irrespective of variations in size, appearance, what have you.

But as Aristotle once said, what it means to be something can change, depending on what you're talking about. This creates some paradoxes, which are riffed on in one of Plato's dialogues called the *Parmenides*. This text is a bit of a mind-bender—more devilish than any Cruel Angel's Thesis. What the dialogue argues is that, on the one hand, we encounter many different beings in the world. But, on the other hand, if this is true then in what sense can all these different things be in a singular sense? If "being" is one, then how can we speak of multiple "beings"? But if "being" is many, how can we speak about any individual thing (which counts as "one"), or even about the word "being" itself, which is a singular noun describing different things?

How can we speak about many "Angels" and "EVAs" if we can't speak about what it means to be one "Angel" or one "EVA"? This is perplexing, and isn't really solved at the end of the *Parmenides*: for as the Stranger says "if one is not, nothing is" (*Parmenides* 166c). Plotinus, a Neoplatonic philosopher, once said that "All are beings due to unity" because "if you take away the unity which they are said to be, then they are not those things" (*Enneads* 6.9.1.1–4). Shinji may "contain multitudes" (see Episode 16, "The Sickness Unto Death, and then . . ."/"Splitting of the Breast"), but despite everything we can still recognize him, somehow, as Shinji. This is a bit of a mystery.

Deviant Divine Philosophy

Connected to talk about the one and the many is the age-old idea of the emergence of the universe out of a single principle or substance. We see this all over the place, from the ancient Presocratics, to Christian ideas of creation out of nothing, to modern cosmologies like the Big Bang. This original principle is understood in different ways—as Nature, the Infinite, the One, or God—but throughout there's a single principle that gets everything rolling. This process might not have a beginning, and can take the form of a cyclical and eternal universe, as in Greek cosmology, Buddhism, and Hinduism. The *Evangelion* cosmos itself is created out of cycles of destruction and rebirth, as revealed in "You Can (Not) Redo" (but suggested throughout the franchise). In all these traditions, however, there's some unified thing, idea, or being that helps explain why there's all this other stuff in the universe. *Evangelion* mythology trades on this, with all its talk about the First Impact, the Black Moon of Lilith, the Original Adam, and so on.

It's also present in the imagery of the Tree of Life (the *Sephiroth*), seen in the opening sequence of the TV series and in *The End of Evangelion*. In the Jewish mystical philosophy of Kabbalah, it serves as an image for the creation of the world by God. It symbolizes the emanation, or "flowing-out," from the Absolute (the *"Ein Sof"* or "Limitless") of all the ideas and forces that govern and populate the universe. Tied up with this is the belief that each branch of the tree takes us away from simplicity, and unfolds into a world of diverse beings and principles, like the refraction of light through a prism. This includes the male principle of *Chokhma* ("Wisdom") and the feminine principle of *Binah* ("Understanding"). However, all things eventually return to their source, to a moment when heaven touches earth, and *Kether* ("Crown"), the highest created principle, touches *Malkut* ("Kingdom"), the lowest principle, thereby completing the cycle.

But exactly because each level moves us further from the source, which is both infinite and simple, the possibility of risk and error is opened up. Things become more limited, objects vie for space. Someone's going to get hurt eventually. Origen, an early Christian theologian (and classmate of Plotinus), thought that an exit from the original harmony with God opened the way to evil and sin, and the only way this would be overcome is through a millennia-long process of divine teaching and learning that returns us to God (*On First Principles*, 2.1.1-3, 2.3.1, 3.5.4, 3.6.4). Somewhat differently, SEELE and Gendo Ikari hold to the rather pessimistic view that humanity needs to be overcome so that peace may return to the universe. For them, to quote Jean-Paul Sartre (1905–1980), "Hell is—other people!"

The *Evangelion* myth proposes a cosmology of birth, death and rebirth, order and disorder, as well as many possible worlds and stories. This happens at the higher level of mythology, but it also appears in the way Hideaki Anno (and the Gainax team) put the franchise together, and shows us something of how form and content work in synergy.

You Can (Not) Repeat

The *Evangelion* saga is still continuing and developing. Even though the original TV show is more or less a self-contained entity, and doesn't require the later installments to understand it, Anno has continually revised the saga, holding to a recognizable narrative arc, while changing substantially how that story unfolds. It's somewhat like Akira Kurosawa's movie *Rashomon*: we know something happened, but the stories don't fit. I mean, even *Neon Genesis* leaves things hanging when it suggests in Episode 26 ("The Beast that Shouted 'I' at the Heart of the World"/"Take Care of Yourself") that there's another world available within it. Just after we catch a glimpse of this other reality, we cut to Shinji saying "I get it. This is another possible world. A possibility that's inside me . . . Different versions of me might exist." So what happened? Is Misato really a NERV Commander or a school teacher? Is Shinji an EVA pilot or just another student? I'm not sure. And on top of this, *The End of Evangelion* completely re-imagines Episodes 25 ("The Ending World"/"Do You Love Me?") and 26, while *Evangelion: Death (True)* and *The Rebuild of Evangelion* remixes *Neon Genesis* as a whole. If we were unsure before, everything's now up in the air.

So even at the beginning we have difference, to allude to Jacques Derrida's idea of *différance* (a word he made up, which means both "to differ" and "to defer"). Derrida says there's no pure beginning or end. Things always refer to other things, words to other words. We can't get to some point beyond this. That leaves us with the problem of knowing where the one begins and the many ends. Which is the original and which is the copy? It's hard to tell. People like Andreu Ballús and Alba Torrents say that *Evangelion* as a whole is a "repetition without origin," by which they mean—following philosophers like Gilles Deleuze (1925–1995)—that there's no point at which we can reach back to a moment, an imagined beginning, where meaning is stable and complete. Things are always unstable, and things can never return or repeat themselves in exactly the same way.

Think of the very simple action of saying exactly the same thing twice. The very fact that you have said the same thing again changes things. If I say "Pen" and then say "Pen" again, I could just be stating a fact for emphasis, or talking about Misato's domesticated penguin. Repetition makes a difference. The Danish philosopher Søren Kierkegaard (1813–1855) in *Repetition* wrote about his attempt to repeat an experience he had had, only to discover that it was different the second time around. Things always repeat differently. It's the same with *Neon Genesis*.

Reality Effects

Reality is perceived differently by different people. We may look at the same thing, and come to different conclusions. Ryoji Kaji says as much in Episode 26 when he says that "There are as many truths as there are people." Diversity of perspectives is a fact. But this is one side of the story, for as T ji Suzuhara says, "A worldview that one person can hold in their head doesn't amount to much." Speaking about this tension, Dani Cavallaro says "people inhabit not one reality but rather multiple co-existing realities—or, more accurately, 'reality effects'. Any one narrative shape that one's life acquires is only a minute drop in an ocean of interplaying narratives." In other words, we're involved in creating "reality" as we go along, but these perspectives aren't the whole picture.

In the show, we're never quite sure whose perspective is real. Even we as the audience don't have a god's eye—or even an Angel's eye—view, for that matter. We're thrown into the mix, without much explanation, and have to try to piece things together—never mind the anime characters themselves! Chaos is always a possibility. But as T ji says, there's something about "truth" that can't be merely personal, something we merely patch-up and create for ourselves.

This is what the great (and very daunting) German philosopher Georg Hegel (1770–1831) believed. We come to an understanding of ourselves—or what Hegel calls "self-consciousness"—through making ourselves an object to ourselves. To reflect on ourselves, we must divide ourselves into both a sub-ject *and* an object, the knowing I and the known I. In this way, I become "conscious" of myself. But Hegel says that we aren't satisfied with this scenario until we encounter another object, a "self-consciousness" who stands over against us, and who we have to recognize and struggle with as someone like us (*Phenomenology of Spirit*, pp. 167–68). This is how we come to sense ourselves.

There's something similar going on in the final episode, where Shinji faces a rapid barrage of voices and characters from the series:

SHINJI: This . . . is an empty space. A world that's empty. A world that's empty of everything but me. I'm starting to become indistinct. I feel myself disappearing. The being that is me is fading away. WHY?

MISATO: That's because no one is here but you.

SHINJI: Because I'm alone.

MISATO: If nothing exists outside of yourself, you can't determine your own shape.

SHINJI: My own shape . . .
MY SELF IMAGE?

MISATO: Yes. You learn your own shape by observing the shapes of others.

ASUKA: You visualize your own shape by seeing the wall between 'self' and 'other'.

REI: You can't see yourself unless others are there with you.

SHINJI: But that means it's other people that let me be myself! If a person is alone, they're alone no matter where they go! The whole world is just me!

MISATO: You take shape through recognizing how you are different from others.

This is why in *The End of Evangelion* Shinji ultimately chooses a world of difference, rather than the single entity provided by Instrumentality. He prefers having human beings to being alone. He learns to love the One and the Many. This isn't easy. Life's not all fun, laughing, and Yebisu Beer.

As *Neon Genesis Evangelion* shows, living with others is dif-ficult. All of the main characters are continually dealing with their past traumas and relationships, often trying to escape them. Shinji is always trying (and failing) to run away. For as

Episode 16 ("The Sickness Unto Death, and then . . ."/"Splitting of the Breast") shows, Shinji might run but he can't escape "the other" in himself, "the other" revealed in the Sea of Dirac. Asuka also struggles to deal with the suicide of her mother and her own sense of self-worth. Misato is still processing her relationship with her dead father and her "It's Complicated" romance with Ryoji. Rei is trying to deal with her own murky history and transferred memories. None of these are resolved within the series.

As Episode 3 ("The Silent Phone"/"A Transfer") and Episode 4 ("Rain, After Running Away"/"Hedgehog's Dilemma") suggest: people are hedgehogs; the closer they get, the pricklier they become—here parroting Arthur Schopenhauer (1788–1860). Therefore, the moral seems to be that we have to live with other people, however prickly, because the alternative is being eviscerated into liquid consciousness, watching the sun's umbral glow as it sets on our failed apocalypse.

An Open Problem

The *Evangelion* series and the movies point toward an unresolved tension between unity and multiplicity. Much like Plato's so-called "unwritten" teaching, which says the highest principle is both the One and the Indefinite Dyad, *Neon Genesis* also keeps open the problem of the One and the Many. It doesn't solve it. This is its "terminal dogma."

May that give you some solace the next time you chance upon an avenging Angel.

IV

You Can
(Not) Exist

14
Living Questions or Dead Ends?

ZACHARY VEREB

What should I do? What can I know? What may I hope? What is a human being? Anyone who aims to think deeply, philosopher Immanuel Kant suggests, must reflect on these fundamental questions. Lucky for us, *Neon Genesis Evangelion* presses us through them. Let's dare to think!

Deep questions bubble to the surface even in *Evangelion*'s very second episode, where we glimpse Misato Katsuragi's inner thoughts: "On that day I saw Shinji as nothing more than a means to an end" (Episode 2, "Unfamiliar Ceilings" 16:40). First-time viewers begin to realize that this series will have much introspection. Philosophical reflection implodes, contrasted with bombastic, larger-than-life mecha battles.

Through the action, we get hooked. Then, the real trick happens: *Evangelion* draws us in and forces us to think deeply. And when we think deeply—philosophically—we gain a new appreciation for the complexity of the series as a whole. Great works of art, anime included, are defined by their ability to provoke us to ask the big questions.

Longtime fans know that *Evangelion* is pregnant with moral complexities. Seemingly good characters ruminate on whether they should exploit and manipulate others—even youth! Why do scenes like this disturb us? Obviously, the prospect of being treated by someone as a means to an end is horrifying. But why? What about this bothers us so? According to Kant, the key to the puzzle lies with the value of autonomy. It's that elusive part of the human condition that connects us back to our four philosophical questions.

In common use, autonomy is at the heart of politically charged discussions. We even fight over it at the family dinner table. Whether debating the rights of the dead, the ethics of harvesting organs, or the moral status of the unborn, autonomy inevitably confronts us with its penetrating gaze. In many ways, autonomy shapes the modern understanding of the self and the questions we ask. And yet, it remains difficult to pin down. *Evangelion* is captivating because it forces us to think through the limits of autonomy. This shakes us to our very core. It explains the existential dread some first-time viewers experience. Behind *Evangelion*'s nail-biting ethical dilemmas, its deep psychological frustrations, and its provocative political machinations, autonomy lurks in the dark.

Hindsight Is 20/20

Evangelion is fascinating for a variety of reasons, and it easily draws in anime, action, and gaming fans alike. Why are we so drawn in? Is it sheer entertainment? Giant humanoid mecha battles, explosions, and the end of the world: all these seem like Hollywood blockbuster gimmicks. They *are* entertaining. But as any true fan will tell you, this is just the outer shell, the armor. *Evangelion*'s action elements draw us in, exposing us to deeper themes in its womb. These philosophical themes taunt us, like traumatized souls occupying foreign bodies.

Due to the complexity of *Evangelion's* plot and the depth of its characters, many first-time viewers fail to grasp its unity, let alone its *meaning*. Yet, there's something about *Evangelion* that keeps hardcore fans coming back. What is this? Because the tensions and anxieties of autonomy are always in its background, *we see ourselves in the series*. We see ourselves in how Shinji struggles to become free despite his guilt and desire to be loved. We see ourselves in how Asuka desires to be understood and accepted for who she is. And we see ourselves in the attempts by characters like Gendo and Misato to manipulate their way to get what they want. What *do* they want? What do *we* want?

Thinking about autonomy can help us illuminate why the series is so compelling, and why we keep returning to it. Some claim that *Neon Genesis Evangelion* requires multiple views because its finale was hastily composed. Its replay value lies precisely in how it brings to life these living questions. *Evangelion* is no dead end, as it reminds us that philosophical reflection matters. And through it, we see *Evangelion* as a mirror to our very souls.

The Inhumaneness of Autonomy

What is autonomy, exactly? We should first consider what a *violation* of it looks like. *Evangelion* is particularly helpful for philosophizing about autonomy, since characters constantly treat others as tools. This is visible even in Episode 1!

Shinji Ikari's estranged father Gendo refers to his son as a "spare"—this suggests that he views Shinji as a tool for his own ends. Later, Gendo brings out a bleeding, injured Rei Ayanami in an attempt to guilt trip our hero Shinji to pilot the EVA mecha. Moments earlier, Shinji chooses against piloting the EVA. His own father, ever astute Gendo, knows that witnessing Rei in her debilitating physical condition will force him to give in. Gendo's coercion short-circuits the autonomy of our hero, and he simultaneously disrespects the autonomy of Rei in this power-move (Episode 1, "Angel Attack" 18:30).

Immanuel Kant, in his *Groundwork for the Metaphysics of Morals*, argues that autonomous humans ought to be treated as the sort of beings they are—as rational and free beings who have goals, hopes, dreams, and desires. We have moral obligations, Kant thinks, to treat autonomous beings with respect. Put differently, we should never use people as tools, resources, or *mere means*. And yet, in the very first episode Gendo treats his own son and Rei as mere means. By disrespecting the worth and dignity of our heroes, Gendo appears contemptuous to us. He inhumanely violates their autonomy to get what he wants!

Delicate Deception

Beautiful and brash, Misato is another character in the series who often violates Kant's moral imperative. We dislike Misato for her manipulative tendencies. Yet we grow to love her as she evolves through the series. Toward the end, she even takes on a motherly role. The ambiguous vacillation between care and coercion is best observed in *The End of Evangelion*. To save his life, Misato manipulates Shinji with moral guilt and sexual pressure. After urging him to continue, she hands him her cherished pendant. Misato then kisses him. "That's how grown-ups kiss . . . we'll do the rest when you get back, alright?" (*The End of Evangelion*, about thirty-two minutes in). After pushing Shinji into the elevator, she sacrifices her life to save him. Freudian Oedipal- and Death-drive themes are enticing interpretive lenses, but the clear moral problem here is the violation of autonomy. It's disturbing yet utterly human.

In another scene in the series, an inner dialogue between Ritsuko and Misato sets the stage for our ambiguous feelings for Misato. Before taking Shinji into her home, Misato recalls a confidential conversation with Ritsuko. "Making sure Shinji is operational is part of your job" (Episode 2, "Unfamiliar

Ceilings"). Misato continues to reflect on how she had only considered him as a means to an end. According to Kant, this attitude, tending to see individuals as mere means to be manipulated, reflects a deep moral failing. Autonomous beings are capable of free choice. Yet, when characters such as Gendo or Misato coerce and deceive our EVA pilots, they annihilate the possibility for them to make fully informed, rational choices. They reduce them to puppets, warns Kant.

As we know, only youth can pilot the EVAs to defend against the monstrous Angels attacking humanity. Hesitatingly, Misato and Ritsuko make the utilitarian decision that it's worth burdening fourteen-year-olds with irreversible psychological trauma to save humanity: "He's only fourteen. Burdening him with the fate of humanity is a bit much, isn't it?"—". . . We have no other choice" (Episode 4, "Rain, After Running Away" 8:20). They decide that the end justifies the means. The first moral problem is that they are being used as a mere means. The second problem is the question as to whether fourteen-year-olds can make autonomous decisions in the first place. At the very least, youth probably deserve extra protection against exploitation if their autonomy is still developing. You don't become legally 'autonomous' until age eighteen in most US states. Is it possible for these characters to make real, rational decisions? To answer this, let's start with Episode 4.

Land of the Depressed, Home of the Free?

A moping, self-isolating Shinji runs away. He cracks under the pressure of piloting the EVA. In the end, though, he makes a choice. Shinji chooses, freely, to stay. But wait a second—can youth make authentic choices? Can depressed people freely choose? What do autonomous choices look like anyway? Episode 4 helps us answer these questions.

In this episode, Shinji wanders for two days. He is zoned out, full of self-loathing. This makes sense since Shinji lacks an identity. He is estranged from his father and feels used. Listless at a movie, he even seems depressed. An apathetic Shinji doesn't care if he lives or dies in the EVA. Aware that Gendo and Misato are using him, Shinji feels as if his only ability to choose lies in rejecting his piloting role, even if this means abandoning humanity to the Angels. Shinji has no sense of duty. He feels hopeless and empty, like an automaton.

The episode then takes an interesting twist. We witness Shinji experience the value of friendship and the importance of community. Instead of leaving on the train, Shinji realizes his obligation to protect those around him. This duty is within his power. "Ought implies can" is how Kant would put it. Combining this sense of uncoerced belonging with moral duty, Shinji expresses his autonomous decision, "I'm home." For Kant, autonomy involves the rational capacity to act for the sake of community. This community is a reflection of oneself. This is why Kant thinks we have duties to others and to ourselves. Even amidst foglike tunnel-vision of depression, Shinji realizes his capacity to choose for both.

We might easily contrast Shinji's choice with that of Rei Ayanami. An anxious Shinji asks blue-haired Rei, "Ayanami, why do you pilot your EVA?" Toneless and detached, she replies, "Because it's my link . . . to everyone . . . I just have nothing else" (Episode 6, "Showdown in Tokyo-3" 16:20). Rei's decision to fight doesn't reflect a duty to humanity; she hasn't thought carefully about it. Rather, Rei's decision is *made for her*. Worse, she doesn't know who she is or what she wants. Rei pilots the EVA lacking identity. She lacks autonomy. She has nothing. Because she's a very dissociated character, it's hard to see how many of her choices, like these, could be autonomous. Recall that Rei, as a clone, lacks a soul of her own. Setting aside religion, Kant would simply say that autonomous choice must come from oneself. Otherwise, it is soulless, robotic even.

Killing in the Name of . . . Duty?

Do we have a *duty* to protect ourselves? Can we autonomously choose death? Since we have duties to ourselves, we must preserve our autonomy. It would be irrational to do otherwise, which is also why we can't rationally consent ourselves into slavery. Hence, "choosing" to be passive in a self-defense dilemma would be, for Kant, irrational and immoral. Two of the tensest moments in *Evangelion* involve self-defense at the cost of innocent life. We see this when Shinji must choose whether to kill the last Angel, the humanoid Kaworu, in the name of duty (Episode 24, "The Last Cometh"). Should he kill the first person who accepts and loves him as he is to save everyone from an apocalyptic Third Impact?

We again see the self-defense dilemma in *Evangelion*'s most brutal scene. Shinji decides he cannot kill another EVA pilot (who is, unbeknownst to him, his friend Toji Suzuhara!). "That's an Angel? That's my target . . . There's someone in there, and that could be the same age as me . . . probably a kid. What am I supposed to do? I cannot just murder someone!" Gendo replies, "you'll die if you don't!" to which Shinji fires back,

"Fine! That's better than murder!" Callous Gendo triggers the autopilot, "dummy mode" after Shinji's refusal, resulting in the gruesome mangling of Toji (Episode 18, "Life and Death Decisions").

Did Shinji do something wrong by not defending himself? The question is tricky. We might worry that innocent killing forfeits our own autonomy. In politics, this is how many people attempt to justify the death penalty. These are hardly easy questions. Should we use one person to save more people? Do depressed individuals have the capacity to make truly autonomous choices? Yet this is precisely why we return to *Evangelion* again and again. It pushes us to ask about what we can know in the first place.

The Horrifying Splendor of Instrumentality

Long-haired triple-agent Ryoji Kaji muses that we can't understand other people. Worse, we can't even understand ourselves! This question about what we can know is posed most strikingly in the Human Instrumentality Project. As we know, the elusive SEELE (German for soul, the mind pulling the strings of the United Nation's body) aims to bring about the Third Impact. As we also know, the Second Impact, discussed in Episode 7, nearly wiped out humanity in the year 2000. A Third Impact, then, would be a global, cataclysmic event. It would effectively kill everyone on Earth.

Why would SEELE want this? One motivation seems clear. Humanity is inherently destructive, selfish, and dominating. A Third Impact would be the erasure of all individual differences. Humanity would be as One. The ethical hope of perpetual peace is attained through a loophole. There can be no moral conflict if there are no people, after all. This is discussed early on, when Gendo reports to the Human Instrumentality Committee. "Indeed, that Project is the sole source of hope under the current desperate and destitute circumstances . . . humanity has little time to spare" (Episode 5, "Rei, Beyond the Heart" 5:50). The beautiful splendor of Instrumentality is contrasted with a view to its horror, the annihilation of autonomy. Ritsuko claims that the Evangelions exist solely to prevent a Third Impact (Episode 7, "The Works of Man" about halfway through). Our EVA pilots, by resisting the Angels and the Third Impact, are themselves fighting to preserve the autonomy of all.

Are we truly unique individuals, or are we better understood as part of a larger collective? In Kant's view, our properly human nature is our rationality. Rationality makes autonomy possible. To be autonomous is to be a self-creating lawgiver and a source of value. This involves being a rational legislator, as Kant puts it. When we follow our selfish inclinations, instincts, and urges, we let our bodies choose for us. They, in effect, enslave us. And when we are deceived by others, they decide for us as Shinji and Rei learn.

The problem that's expressed most horrifically in *Evangelion* is the question about knowing our true selves. If the true self is the rational bit, we're all ultimately the same! Your personality, her upbringing, his dreams. These are uniform ornaments on the single, glowing Christmas tree of Reason. The contradictory responses of *Evangelion* characters to the homogenizing Human Instrumentality Project, as a blissful nirvana or a living hell, is a key philosophical dimension worth exploring. Maybe Kant can assist us here, too.

What Makes Autonomy Possible?

If we're all truly unified through Reason, why not facilitate Instrumentality and make what is true in abstract theory become concrete in reality? According to Kant, as a rational species, we are united through Reason. However, though we are only autonomous insofar as we are rational, we also require individuality. Having an individuated body allows us to be rational legislators. Returning to the unformed lump of Reason via Instrumentality annihilates the possibility of moral autonomy. Shinji comes to this realization in the anxiety-inducing, existential Episode 26.

The series begins, we recall, with epic mecha battles. It ends with sustained introspection on knowledge of the self and limits of autonomy. Shinji has an introspective dialogue with other characters. These, however, are mere figments of his fragmented mind. This scene is *Evangelion*'s anti-climax, where Shinji confronts the world after Instrumentality as a world of nothingness:

SHINJI: What is this? A blank world? A world devoid of people?

SHINJI: A world of freedom!

SHINJI: Freedom?

SHINJI: Yes! A world of freedom where you are not tied down by anything.

SHINJI: This is freedom?

SHINJI: Yes! A totally free world!

REI: However, it is empty . . .

SHINJI: This is an empty space. An empty world, devoid of everything except me. I'm starting to become indistinct. I feel myself disappear. The being that is me is fading away.

MISATO: That's because you're the only thing here.

Instrumentality represents absolute freedom, devoid of autonomy. It's a world of pure nothingness. Autonomy is only possible, Shinji realizes, with constraints on freedom and the affirmation of individuality (Episode 26, "Sincerely Yours," halfway through).

Moving in a physical world requires being limited to three-dimensional space. Similarly, choosing in a moral world requires being limited by the constraints of other autonomous beings. Though these constraints limit our absolute freedom, they make human individuality possible. Instrumentality evades our responsibility to choose in a world of autonomous beings. It is, in effect, the easy way out.

MISATO: If nothing exists besides you, then you will not be able to understand your shape.

SHINJI: My shape?

MISATO: Yes. You learn your shape by looking and comparing to the shapes of others.

ASUKA: You envision yourself by looking at the walls that separate yourself from others.

REI: You cannot see yourself unless there are others with you.

SHINJI: I can only be me when others are with me . . .

MISATO: You understand your own shape through examining how different you are from others.

REI: The first is your mother.

ASUKA: Your mother is a different person than you are.

SHINJI: Of course, because I am me. But then at the same time, it's clear to me now that other people make up parts of my heart.

MISATO: That's correct, Ikari Shinji.

In the final scene of *Evangelion*, Shinji comes to accept his own self in all its imperfections. He affirms his autonomy, choosing to reject Human Instrumentality:

SHINJI: I hate who I am. But still, maybe I can change and like myself. Maybe it's really okay for me to be here after all. Yeah, I'm only who I am. I am me. I want to be myself. I want to be here. It's okay for me to be here in this world!

The ambiguous nature of humanity, that we are unified through Reason but separated through moral constraints of autonomy, is why the Human Instrumentality Project also appears so puzzling. Many characters in the series, like Gendo, see Instrumentality as divine. Others, like Shinji and Misato, see it as a fascistic horror, annihilating all meaning and value in the world. Both are right, and what *Evangelion* shows us, as does Kant, is that we must sustain the contradiction between our universal and individual natures. The human condition is paradoxical. This what makes autonomy possible, and life interesting.

Philosophy and the *Evangelion* Mirror Test

What is a human being? In the penultimate episode, Shinji has an epiphany about this. He can only exist as an individual human being alongside other humans. A human, Shinji understands, cannot meaningfully exist in a vacuum (Episode 25, "Air"). We can only realize ourselves in a social world. Our autonomy, though self-contained for ethical action, is only possible in an external world filled with other minds. Kant makes this precise point in a pivotal section of his *Critique of Pure Reason*, entitled "The Refutation of Idealism."

Shinji worries whether he could still exist in the world with only his mind (known as "solipsism" in philosophy). Kant argues that we could never even introspect internally, *in the first place*, unless we already lived in an external, intersubjective context. Shinji comes to understand this in the final epiphanic moments of *Evangelion*. He can only *be* a human being because he *chooses to live* in a shared world of meaning with others.

By reflecting on Shinji's own self-reflection, *Evangelion* puts a mirror to our very selves. We see this mirroring not only in Shinji, but in many other characters. For instance, consider when the sky Angel Arael beams a radiant light on Asuka (Episode 22, "Staying Human"). This light reflects deep into her inner psyche, shaking her to her very core. What we see in the mirror of *Evangelion*, as does Asuka in her inner-reflection, ultimately depends on how honest we are. Dare we look on?

As many *Evangelion* characters rationalize their own insecurities, we too are readily poised to dismiss its finale. *Boring! Rushed! Where are all the explosions, the mecha battles, the annihilation of humankind?* Isn't this the proper way to end a sci-fi anime series? No. Not all mirrors are made of glass, in need of shattering. Water is also a mirror, but it only reflects things in stillness. *Evangelion*'s anti-climax, revered and despised by fans alike, is a reflection on the nature of reflection. We must remain still, and ponder again: *What is a human being?* In truth, this question, as Kant realized, will never be easy. As autonomous beings, we are changing, evolving, and striving. Humans are dynamic, for better or worse.

Thus, we return to *Evangelion* and watch it again. Not simply to piece together the plot. We already know the plot! We watch it again because it is a mirror. Mirrors show change. This, my friends, is why *Evangelion* is so deep. It takes us to the depths to confront our demons, and it calls us back to choose how we want to live.

15
A Tale of Two Anti-Heroes

MARC CHEONG

In the world of *Evangelion*, Tokyo (and the rest of Earth) is constantly in flux—official narratives keep shifting, hidden machinations, war, collateral damage—you name it. In our own reality, however, we remember a not-too-distant time where war was inevitable (minus the Angels), where governments kept changing, and nothing was certain: World War II in the early 1940s.

An unlikely character in philosophical literature comes to mind: Meursault, from philosopher Albert Camus's 1942 novel *The Stranger*. Meursault (we never learn his first name) is a French Algerian man, described by critic Cyril Connolly as "citizen of France domiciled in North Africa, a man of the Mediterranean, an homme du Midi yet one who hardly partakes of the traditional Mediterranean culture."

Meursault is about twice the age of Shinji, yet despite living in different universes, they have much in common. Both share a reputation as existentialist anti-heroes, characters who are central to the story but lack conventional attributes of a hero while possessing traits valued by existentialist writers and philosophers.

From Our World to Shinji's

Why should we regard Shinji and Meursault as existentialists? Before delving into Shinji's angsty adolescence and Meursault's IDGAF lifestyle, let's understand what existentialism is. A popular definition, by existentialist philosopher Jean-Paul Sartre, is the claim that "Existence precedes essence." We humans come into existence without any pre-ordained meaning, purpose, or 'essence'. Consequently, our freedom and our choices in life take center stage. We aren't destined to be rebels, heroes, villains, or saviors. Our acts and words define who we are, and our lives are constantly a process of creating (and recreating), till the day we die.

Taking into consideration that we aren't destined for a specific, you know, 'whatever,' actually liberates us to take responsibility for our actions and to shape who we are by our thoughts, deeds and words. It's such a powerful philosophy that Simone de Beauvoir, another famous existentialist philosopher and contemporary of Camus and Sartre, used it as a foundation for her feminist theory: women are free and equal, and shouldn't be merely constrained to any preconceived female stereotypes or any inherent female essences dictated by society.

Shinji and Meursault—the Story so Far

Shinji Ikari is the first character we encounter in *Evangelion*. At the very beginning, it looks as if Shinji is just another teenager battling adolescence in a modern-day-looking Japan. We get a "Yeah you know, everything is useless, nothing matters" vibe. His meh-ness is summarized in this apt quote in the beginning of the manga series:

> I've never had any cherished dreams or ambitions. I don't aspire to any future profession or career. So far, in the first fourteen years of my life, things have always happened as they had to. And things will probably continue the same way. That's why I've never really cared whether I got into an accident or something had died. (*Evangelion* Manga, Volume 1)

We then realize that the world is in grave danger. Shinji is introduced to NERV by Misato, meets his estranged father (with whom he still has daddy issues), and before you know it, he has an awkward reunion with Gendo and learns about piloting EVAs. As we know, Gendo's plans (with a healthy dose of callousness within) force Shinji to be an EVA pilot, ostensibly to save the world. That's where Shinji's story begins.

Well, he'll make good mates with Meursault, Camus's antihero. This is how we first meet Meursault according to Camus:

> Mother died today. Or, maybe, yesterday; I can't be sure. . . . The Home for Aged Persons is at Marengo, some fifty miles from Algiers. With the two o'clock bus I should get there well before nightfall. Then I can spend the night there, keeping the usual vigil beside the body, and be back here by tomorrow evening. . . . For the present, it's almost as if Mother weren't really dead. The funeral will bring it home to me, put an official seal on it, so to speak. (*The Stranger*, pp. 1–2)

For Meursault, it's 'Okay, a close family member died, but, whatever, doesn't mean anything so guess what . . . I'll just kill somebody for no compelling reason'. Well, that escalated quickly!

Instead of showing emotion, Meursault behaves nonchalantly at his mother's funeral. Then, he goes back to work . . . and immediately hooks up with Marie, a former colleague of his. (Nothing seems to come of his mother's death!) The main event shaping the story is when Meursault hatches a plan with his neighbor Raymond who wants Meursault's help to frame his girlfriend for infidelity. Raymond's cruelty doesn't faze Meursault one bit. As a reward for bearing false witness in court, Meursault and Marie are invited to a weekend getaway with Raymond. Naturally, the framed girlfriend's brother (the story refers to him as an unnamed Arab man) wants to seek revenge, and Meursault manages to grab a revolver from Raymond to prevent him from acting rashly.

Now, all of this seems odd given that Meursault has just lost his mother. Yet, Meursault's actions to protect Raymond from harming the Arab man and his fellow avengers seem decent, almost praiseworthy. This is where the story gets weird. Meursault personally meets the unnamed Arab man, shoots him fatally with the commandeered gun, and continues pumping him full of lead . . . an extra four times! His ridiculous reason? "It was because of the sun." Damn!

He then goes into full anti-hero mode where he doesn't explain his actions (Did he do it in defense? For honor? For great justice? Nope!), expresses no remorse, and is so meh, he actually gets comfortable with his prison lifestyle. He doesn't bother about freedom, or clearing his name, or protesting vehemently about how he's innocent (or even crying "Fake news!").

How does Shinji even compare to this rogue, and why are they more alike than meets the eye?

Transcending the Mess They're In

We can say that Shinji is thrown into the deep end of the pool and forced to confront his new gig as an EVA pilot. The idea of 'thrownness', in the existentialist sense, is much richer than that. Martin Heidegger, a few years before Camus, came up with this idea. Charles Guignon, in his essay "Becoming a Self: The Role of Authenticity in *Being and Time*," explains it this way:

> We are always thrown into a world, already under way in realizing specific possibilities (roles, self-interpretations, etc.) that define our

place in the surrounding social world . . . What defines our being are the specific ways we are pressing forward into the possibilities of acting and being that are opened up by the cultural context into which we are thrown.

Shinji is thrown into this position where he's suddenly able to access actions, possibilities, roles, and responsibilities as an EVA pilot to the point where piloting an EVA shapes his entire identity and worldview. These possibilities wouldn't exist had certain events not occurred. Things would have been very different for Shinji had he not known Gendo at all.

Let's now fast-forward through a few events in *Evangelion*: consider Shinji deciding to stay in Tokyo-3 with Misato and Shinji's subsequent successful routine with Asuka to destroy the Angel Israfel. Each of the actions taken by Shinji sets the stage for new possibilities to choose from. When one door closes, another opens. This is where we discuss two elements shaping our past and future, according to existentialism. Rewind back to when Shinji decided to move to his uncle's place at the end of Volume 2 of the *Evangelion* manga.

The entire chain of events before him (from birth till his father's abandonment, their eventual reuniting at NERV, and his decision not to leave Misato), including the physical and causal characteristics of himself and the world around him (Angel attacks, him being the son of a scheming Gendo, and his innate high sync rate with EVA units) are known as his 'facticity'. Jean-Paul Sartre introduced this term to describe the current concrete situation we find ourselves in, as a combination of past choices, environment, constraints, and such. These things give him context and limit his freedom in the *Evangelion* universe. He can't sabotage the entire Human Instrumentality Project or become an Angel. He doesn't have the authority or power to do so, and can't defy physical and biological limitations. His facticity limits his freedom.

What can he do? Well, against the backdrop of any facticity he's in, he always has a choice, a fundamental freedom to choose his actions and shape his future, or what our friend Sartre terms 'transcendence'. In other words, what we are *transcends* the mere *facts* of our situation, and that surpassing constitutes our freedom.

Let's consider a point in *Evangelion* where Shinji is happy and high-spirited for a change. When we see Shinji at a party with his friends, Asuka, Rei, and Misato (*Evangelion* Manga Volume 5; Anime Episode 9) his transcendence offers him a few limited choices, but equally viable choices nonetheless. He could party the night away, or he could run away, or he could go to the shops. However, at each step of the way leading up to that moment of that party, his transcendence requires him to make a choice amongst the possibilities he's faced with, including doing absolutely nothing (which is a choice in itself!).

Making choices constantly from his limited transcendence is the only thing he can do at any given stage. After he's made a choice, he will be presented with another set of limited possibilities he must choose from. All of the other prior possibilities have become closed to him. His transcendence in the past becomes a facticity in the present. The party is only allowed to happen after he has decided to work with Asuka to fight Israfel.

Against this backdrop, Shinji is constantly forced to decide his next move, all while his environment, his self-perception, and the people he cares about are constantly changing (or destroyed). Shinji can be seen as a victim of circumstances, and yet as someone who has the ability to transcend whatever circumstances he gets thrown into. To paraphrase Sartre, Shinji is "condemned to be free!" Shinji faces turmoil in his life-world as an EVA pilot. He's torn between his given duty as an EVA pilot and denouncing the consequences, and his story doesn't fit into the archetypal hero found in, say, The Avengers!

Likewise, our anti-hero Meursault, like all of us, is bound to the same human condition. His previous choices contextualize who he is (his facticities), which include being in a state of apathy (possibly due to his choices to adopt such an outlook), and choosing to be in the company of unsavory characters, to name a few. However, other facticities aren't his own fault, instead they are circumstances against which he has had to constantly make decisions, including his mother's death, his background, and the conflicts and social tensions due to World War II.

Shinji and Meursault quickly realize one thing through the course of their literary lives: once their transcendence has led them to make a fundamental choice (spoiler alert: they committed murder), the menu of choices available to them is constantly revised, and they have to live with their new facticity, moving forward. To extend the menu analogy: imagine they've locked in choices for a three-course meal, and are currently about to finish their tiramisu dessert. They can't rewind time to try a different appetizer!

Responsibility, Bad Faith, and How (Not) to Take a Life

By now you might be thinking: how the heck are our strange bedfellows empowered by existentialist philosophy? Hold that for a sec: we now visit watershed moments where they both have had to take someone else's life. Shinji met Kaworu (Asuka's replacement) after Asuka couldn't mentally cope after an Angel attack (Manga Volume 9; Episode 24, "The Last Cometh"/"The Beginning and the End, or 'Knockin' on Heaven's Door'"). Kaworu became fast friends with Shinji (but is actually the Angel Tabris in disguise, seeking to ultimately merge with Adam/Lilith). Problem is, Kaworu is a dark and complex character who, among other things, nonchalantly kills a cat in the manga. When it's revealed that he's Tabris all along, Shinji is faced with the offer of killing him to save humanity. Though Shinji is deeply conflicted (and we can see the flurry of emotions, including guilt, sadness, and remorse conflict with his sense of duty), he has no choice but to terminate Tabris/Kaworu.

By doing so, he used his transcendence to close irrevocably any potential facticity involving Kaworu being his friend, or for him not to have taken any lives. In other words, he has to take responsibility for his actions and live with the consequences. Similarly, by killing the unnamed Arab man, Meursault has closed all possible past transcendences as an innocent non-killer, and instead locks it in as his facticity. This creates a new realm of possibilities for him. He can't change his appetizer when he's almost done with dessert, but he can definitely order more wine!

Well, to err is human, and to live in bad faith is all-too-human. Bad faith in the philosophical sense doesn't mean a certain maliciousness in humans. Without going into the technicalities, existentialist philosophers refer to bad faith as the denial of either (or both) our facticity or our transcendence as human beings. Writers such as Sartre have discussed various manifestations of bad faith, but we'll discuss two cases in terms of our anti-heroes.

The easier case of bad faith can be illustrated when Shinji or Meursault deny their transcendence and blame everything on their environments, circumstances, and so forth. Even though the consequences (of taking a life, of repercussions such as legal action for Meursault and internal turmoil for Shinji) are real, by refusing to accept that, they had a choice which they freely exercised. A limited choice is still a choice! Examples of how our anti-heroes can deny transcendence would be if Meursault blamed everything on his facticities, as if he didn't have a choice ("Mother's death caused me to do this" or "There was a gun that tempted me"). Or if Shinji kept attributing blame to his circumstances ("Gendo's coldness was why I had to do this" or "I didn't want to be an EVA pilot in the first place!").

Secondly, our anti-heroes can deny their facticity by denying the concrete situation they're in—their physical states and surrounding circumstances—and claiming they are pure transcendence and can wish for any outcome they want, For example, let's say after deciding to kill Kaworu/Tabris, Shinji starts wishing away what has happened, lives in denial, and refuses to believe that he killed Kaworu. In the case of Meursault, as the story goes, he illustrates how he avoids this second form of bad faith. While awaiting his fate in prison, he's offered religious guidance by the chaplain. But being the true existentialist anti-hero he is, Meursault actively refuses religious salvation. If he'd taken on the offer of religious guidance as a way to salvation, at face value, without truly believing in God, he would be anointed with . . . bad faith. Meursault would consider that a denial of his facticity, which would be to deny that deep down inside, he's the kind of guy with a core belief in "Whatever, man, IDGAF."

Our anti-heroes, as pitiful as their conditions are, manage to not succumb to bad faith. There's a glimmer of heroism in them! Shinji kept on doing the best he could, even against the backdrop of the Human Instrumentality Project. Meursault never denied his actions nor escaped his inevitable consequences, but went out with a bang!

Is Shinji Happy?

Meursault views human life as inherently absurd, which ties in with Shinji's revelations at times. The creator of Meursault, Albert Camus, introduced the idea of existential absurdity in his 1942 book, *The Myth of Sisyphus*. Here Camus claims that human life is inherently meaningless. In the ancient legend, Sisyphus was condemned to push a heavy rock up a hill, only to have it roll back down the hill again. He had to repeat this task eternally. According to Camus, "The workman of today works every day in his life at the same tasks, and this fate is no less absurd. But it is tragic only at the rare moments when it becomes conscious" (p. 97).

The consciousness of the absurdity is realized when Meursault is offered religious salvation before his impending execution. Lucky for his existentialist virtue (not so lucky for his mortality), Meursault chooses to embrace the absurdity of the human condition. Throughout the story, he observes that members of the general public are constantly "in an absurd hurry" and that it's so "absurd" to pay attention to the chaplain talking about God where he had more to worry about. For example, the "office was so stiflingly hot and big flies were buzzing round." Whoa! On what is potentially his last chance for salvation, Meursault finds that life, including his bouts of hedonistic pleasure, along with the contingent deaths of others, and ultimately people around him not taking responsibility for their own deeds, is inherently absurd. Doesn't this sound similar to the opening remarks by Shinji at the start of this chapter?

Shinji and Meursault both have a cold emotional distance with their families to start with; both try to find meaning in relationships but end up finding none; and both find themselves in surreal situations with no undo button. As we reach the conclusion of their stories, we're left with a question: How have they embraced the ultimate freedom of an existentialist and the absurdity of the human condition?

For Meursault, he rejects his world's purported notions of justice, religion, and salvation. As a murderer, he's now shunned by society, especially since he expresses no remorse for his murderous act. Through the closing chapters of *The Stranger*, we find that Meursault chooses to accept potential execution as a consequence, and not wish it away. He consciously and freely chooses to go out with a bang.

What about Shinji? Let's check out both the manga ending and the original anime ending. For the sake of space, I won't elaborate on *The End of Evangelion* alternate movie ending. Suffice to say that by rejecting Instrumentality and choosing an uncertain post-LCL world, in the darker movie ending, Shinji's decision is still congruent with his acceptance of existential absurdity. In Shinji's manga ending (Volume 14), we find that Shinji has rejected Instrumentality, despite Rei/Lilith's offer of the bliss and painlessness of LCL. Instead, he decides to find meaning in his own existence as a human, in spite of any pain he will encounter in his rebirth:

> their hands may hurt me again . . .
> and my hands may hurt other people . . .
> and joined hands may someday part . . .

This parallels Camus's allegory. If Sisyphus finally accepts the absurdity of his situation, it will set him on a path of freedom. Friedrich Nietzsche calls this the embracing of an eternal recurrence. If we're condemned to live the same life over and over again, and if everything happens the same way as before, what more meaningful life can we obtain but the path we choose freely?

Surreally, the manga concludes with a deus ex machina ending where Shinji, after being reborn from LCL, goes back to school with no knowledge of what happened, exclaiming: "I will do my best . . . I will find my own path . . . My future holds infinite possibilities" (Volume 14).

In the original anime ending, the storyline differs with the presence of an extended stream-of-consciousness and a different finale. In the original Episode 26 ("The Beast that Shouted 'I' at the Heart of the World"/"Take Care of Yourself"), Shinji again repeats his dictum that he does "not mean anything" to anyone and he "lacks value." Through the entire episode, we see his internal monologue on coping with an ever-changing thrownness. Shinji alternates from thoughts of unfettered freedom to having his facticity limiting his transcendence (as only being an EVA pilot confers meaning on him). The series concludes with Shinji exclaiming that "I'm only who I am . . . I want to be myself . . . it's okay to be here" with a surreal "congratulations" from other major characters.

In both endings, Shinji can be said to embrace existential absurdity, paralleling Meursault's calmness as he approaches his execution:

I laid my heart open to the benign indifference of the universe. To feel it so like myself, indeed, so brotherly, made me realize that I'd been happy, and that I was happy still. (*The Stranger*, p. 154)

What a rollercoaster ride, after all that! We've learnt that Shinji would make an excellent existentialist philosopher, and we've checked out how Shinji's story parallels Albert Camus's fictional character Meursault, despite their different universes. Through their stories, we've learnt that existentialist philosophy isn't pessimistic (although it might seem so on the surface), but rather, very empowering.

Hopefully, the empowering lessons of existentialism's values, in how they soldiered on, will help us find meaning in today's tumultuous (and absurd!) times. They remind us that we have the power to make the most of our situations, no matter how dire things can get! [1]

---

[1] This chapter is mainly based on my enjoyment of Gainax's manga version of *Evangelion*, though I did touch on the final fate of Shinji through the lens of the anime.

16
Plant a Tree, Build an AT Field, and Wait for the Apocalypse

Gionatan C. Pacheco

The epic battle in which the mass production model gang smashes Asuka and Unit 02 is a beautiful and bloody preamble to some very significant scenes. This battle—we're referring here especially to *The End of Evangelion*—occurs almost simultaneously with the "awakening" of Unit 01 with Shinji on board. But the really vital scenes take place *after* these two moments.

From a hodgepodge of guts and fury, we're transported to SEELE's cold, gray conference room. In this scene, there are a bunch of talking monolith stones. As soon as the Spear of Longinus returns to Earth, SEELE's members begin a kind of ritual prayer: *Bring forth the true form of the EVA series! The true form will evangelize humanity. Through indiscriminate death and through prayer, we will return to our original state.*

Immediately, Keel Lorenz, SEELE's leader, now solo, concludes: *And our souls will be at peace. Let the sacrament begin!*

The one to be "sacramented" is Shinji!

The awakened Unit 01 shows impressive power. He stands with AT field wings. But that's it. Shinji doesn't combat the gang. He doesn't even react when they mark him with the "sacred stigma." And then Keel announces: *Let us restore the Tree of Life!*

The figure of a *Tree of Life* is present in almost all religious mythologies. It is in this moment of *our* mythology—our *Neon Genesis Evangelion*—that the *Tree of Life* takes shape in the sky. It is a geometric figure composed of ten circles or spheres called *Sefirot*. In the movie, each sphere contains an EVA and Shinji occupies a central position there. The *Tree of Life* drawn there represents a Kabbalah's mystical doctrine. Now, if we don't count the drawing on the ceiling of Gendo Ikari's living room and a few moments from the opening vignettes of the TV Show, this is the only moment, until now, it shows up on the screen. So, what is it about this "tree" that can interest us? Answer: it intertwines the ethical theme with the metaphysical theme.

Whether on the TV Show or recounted in *The End of Evangelion*, episodes 25 and 26 are themselves full of intersections of ethical and metaphysical themes. You might say that in the TV Show, Shinji's reveries are mostly discursive, whereas in *End of Evangelion* these seem more illustrative—and perhaps the *Tree of Life* in the movie succeeds in doing that. It illustrates an idea in a similar way to how church decorations passed the Gospel's (*Evangelion* being the gospel in Christianity) message to the illiterate. In both versions, we've seen the *Third Impact* from Shinji's inner experience. Let's talk about it.

Would It Be Good to Be God?

Shinji's experience has a marked metaphysical character. The boy inside the EVA unit contemplates an existence without limitations. But it also implies a complete lack of determination. Thus, we could say nothing about something absolutely indeterminate, except that it exists. Now, is it possible for something to exist with no determination? Probably not. To exist is a determination, so it would be to say that something is, but that it is not what it is.

Kaworu's conclusion is more precise: "In truth, death may be the only absolute freedom there is." We will only be saved from this kind of paradox via a metaphysical distinction. It is necessary to distinguish between the existence (the *is*) and the essence (the *what is*). If we don't, we will be embarrassed about questions such as:

In that unity to which humanity would become, would it have any self-determination? That would be a big nothing.

We have to admit that there is no sense in this nothing. Now, if something is not, it cannot be big—bigness, in this case, is also a determination. In this sense, the Tree of Life is symptomatic. It is also worth remembering that this Tree soon becomes another figure, an Ark. Anyway, this whole ritual is not about non-being, but everything suggests that it is a reset.

Shinji's metaphysical experience is comparable to the experience of being a Spinozian substance. Baruch Spinoza (1632–1677) was the first modern philosopher to provide a metaphysical foundation for ethics without appealing to religious or social rules. He defined the substance as something absolutely infinite, something that is self-realized independent of everything capable of causing itself. In the Third Impact, when such a power is in Shinji's hands, we can see the wonders, confused with the miseries, of being an infinite God. It showed us that being an infinite, eternal, and formless Being—since every form implies limits—is not something we can envy. It's something that makes us love our ephemeral human finitude. Thus, Shinji's metaphysical experience is also a moral one. Whether it is good or bad to be a God, we can only judge from the affective field characteristic of a finite being.

When we think of what God's self-realization is, we must understand something other than the personality that our self produces in our self-realization. God's self-realization, according to Spinoza, can only convey with the self-realization of human beings because we use the same name: "They would not agree with one another any more than do the dog that is a heavenly constellation and the dog that is a barking animal" (*Ethics*, proposition 17). Thus, a perspective in which everything becomes one appears to us as a perspective in which everything becomes nothing.

We Are Our AT Field

Spinoza is the right guy to clarify some definitions for us here. Therefore, we begin with the very concept of definition. A Spinozian definition must "explain the intimate essence of the thing." Defining something is not merely pointing out characteristics and giving a name. To define something is to show how the defined thing is generated. Thus, it is not enough to define the circle analytically as the figure whose center is equidistant from all borders. It's necessary to point out the cause, to give a genetic definition. In the circle's case, it's a figure that is drawn on the extension, therefore, it exists because of the movement itself. So Spinoza defines the circle as: "It is the figure that is described by any line of which one end is fixed and the other movable. This definition clearly includes the proximate cause" (*Treatise on the Emendation of the Intellect*, p. 40).

It is necessary to conceive the essence as something positive. A circle is not the figure delimited in a drawing, because the figure itself doesn't say what the circle is, but, on the contrary, it says only what it isn't, its limit. In this sense, the figure is the opposite of the essence.

So, in the same way, no one defines himself as a human being because he has such a body mass and a particular mental capacity. The essence of the human being, according to Spinoza, is the effort to persevere in being. This includes the appetite, desire, will, and even intellect. Unlike the case of God, the human being has an essence that doesn't imply existence. This means that we are finite creatures, not only depending on the substance of which we are modifications (the universe), but we also depend on a finite cause, or a set of finite causes, which determines the beginning of our existence.

We must also understand the AT field in *Evangelion* as something positive, not just a determined figure from an indeterminate sea of LCL. The essence (or the AT field) allows something to maintain itself as one piece, even when it loses and gains parts. If we lose an arm, we don't lose our essence and disappear. We can understand the AT field, and the human essence, as a power. The AT field is the will. It was Shinji's will that allowed him to defeat the final Angel, Kaworu. About this Misato comments: "Only those who have the will to live get to survive. He wished to die. He abandoned his will to live, clinging instead to a false hope" (Episode 25, "A World that's Ending").

Our will is our power to assert our existence. It inhabits a world in which it maintains relations with an infinite number of other things. A multitude of these other things, it's easy to conclude, surpass us in power, subject us to countless interferences and make our will shift like a boat drifting in a stormy and infinite sea. Amid it all, the human essence clings as much as it can to its existence, trying to preserve and expand it. By the same effort, the mind seeks to understand itself and everything else because the will is more than the body. It is, we can say, our individual will that gives us a unique identity that, at the same time that it differs from other identities of other people, is also shaped by them. If we say that our social environment, or even family, defines what we are, then it means that the relationship between metaphysics and ethics is a two-way relationship. What we believe we should be and do also interferes with what we actually are.

A Geometric Tree and a Geometric Book

The concept of essence identified with that of will and power makes this close relationship between ethics and metaphysics possible. It is this concept that explains why the work where we find Spinoza's metaphysics have the title *Ethics*. This book has in common with the Tree of Life its geometric shape (*more geometricus*)—it presents definitions, axioms, and propositions linked like in Euclid's *Elements*. Alexandre Matheron (originally published in 1969) in his classic book on Spinoza even offers maps of the passages of the *Ethics* that form geometric figures similar to the cabbalistic Tree. But, besides, it is interesting to note also the correspondence of content pointed out by Matheron. The greatest correspondence of content between the doctrine of the Tree and Spinoza's *Ethics* is precisely the intersection between the question of being in general and the question of the condition of human beings in particular.

The Tree of Life represents a map in Kabbalah. This map, however, is at least twofold. We can see it as a path that goes from the creator to the creature, from the giver to the willing egoist. This map is also a map that shows how this piece of selfishness called humanity can be reconciled with the generous creator and thus achieve altruism. It forces us to agree that such duplicity of the same path has everything to do with Shinji's aforementioned experience. These three subjects so distinct from each other—an anime, a Jewish tradition, and a modern philosophy—come together by metaphysically presenting an Ethics, or ethically presenting a Metaphysics.

Halfway between the Womb and the Grave

So let's say that the AT field is the will. Only external forces can cancel our willpower or undo our AT field. This is clear because the will is defined as the internal force that can only be conceived as positive. It often appears that Shinji's willpower is completely subject to external causes. To lose your will is to have your AT field undone. And as we saw in the show, if our AT field vanishes, we explode like a water balloon, or in this case, an LCL balloon.

The Tree of Life also represents a path of human life that starts from pure egoism towards altruism. In the scene where this Tree forms at *The End of Evangelion* we see that Shinji and Unit 01 are in the center of the Tree, playing the role of the sixth sefirot. This sphere is Tiphereth, which means Grace or Beauty. By the way, a sefirot is each of the ten spheres that make up the Sefirotic Tree—another name for the Tree of Life.

Seen as a whole, we can take the figure of the Tree of Life as a path that goes from the pure energy that is God to his crudest creation, the physical world. The highest Kaether (Crown) sefirot is pure light. Kaether together with the spheres that represent wisdom (on the right) and understanding (on the left) represents the root of the tree. Kaether emits light that is filtered through the rest of the sefirot until it reaches the Malkuth (Kingdom) sefirot. Malkuth is the most obscure of all—our earthly world.

Shinji's central position in the design of the Tree of Life can have many meanings. Tipheret is in the center of the World of Formation, the part that corresponds to the branch of the tree. From top to bottom, it's the last sefirot that is part of the World of Creation, the trunk, and the first that is part of the World of Action, the fruit. Now, this almost exit from creation, which is also almost an entry into the world of action, seems to correspond very well to the teenager's condition—a condition of formation. The raised child must now become a social actor.

We're born fragile, wordless, toothless, and naked. We're a species that in our first years all we can count on is the good heart of the other. It is a long transition to adulthood. The age of fourteen for Eva's pilots isn't random, but chosen as a middle ground, in which you're no longer a child, but not yet an adult. According to Hideaki Anno, the franchise's creator, this age "symbolizes the problems of the heart."

We grow dependent and selfish. Suddenly, we have to deal with the prospect of independence and social insertion brought by adolescence. The new life outlook brings as a company a hormonal avalanche and, perhaps even more decisively, changes in the brain itself (and in the rest of the body). Favorable scenarios result in a self-centered and know-it-all teenager, such as Asuka. But, the years go by and we see, every year, that in previous years we were really stupid while considering ourselves smart. Gradually this impression passes, because we become wiser, or because we become less self-critical.

Now, leaving the condition of imaginative childishness to an ethical maturity is the long and lifelong path for all of us, no matter what life stage we're in. But on the way from the womb to the grave, adolescence is the crossroads.

The Eternal Puzzle of the Spotted Heart

If Anno says that this age symbolizes the problem of the heart, he also vehemently states that this problem will accompany us throughout our lives, or at least as long as we have a heart. As long as we're human, the problem will arise.

As we saw above, being a finite creature implies an incomplete condition. However, we also saw that it isn't this incompleteness, it isn't the existential voids that define us as human beings. What characterizes the human is her capacity to assert her being to the extent that her forces allow. We don't assert ourselves as human beings for ourselves and that's it. We assert ourselves as human beings in a world inhabited by forces that infinitely surpass ours, a world that we don't control, a world that, finally, we find other human beings engaged in the same affirmative effort.

The problem of the heart has no definitive solution. Each person, in each event of their daily lives, strives to solve it. The conditions of the problem change in each situation, either because the world keeps changing, or because we keep changing. The solution to the problem will never be an idea that we can resort to whenever it appears.

Our internal affective flow is constantly changing. Everything that happens to our body, reflects on our state of mind. Spinoza calls the interaction between us and the outside world *affection*. The affection is always simultaneously of the mind and the body. The mind always imagines what's going on in the body. But the ideas that the imagination generates, most of the time, says more about ourselves than about the outside world. If we abandon ourselves to a precarious image of the outside world, we will not see ourselves as an active part of the world's being. Result: We will be overwhelmed by the image that we build ourselves. This confused image of the world becomes a real structure—at least for us. A structure that surrounds us and that tries to impose goals and dreams on us. Anno himself comments, "Some extremely materialistic people do not bother to consider whether they make themselves disliked by others or not. I think we should live more essentially. In our current material security, the problem of the heart becomes a very current topic ."

How to get out of this imagined world and go towards the essentials of things?

Apocalyptical Confusion

Imagination is the cause of confused ideas. These, according to Spinoza, are responsible for every suffering that our mind can have. On the other hand, imagination is also the beginning of all our knowledge. This doesn't mean that we should embrace these images. If we go this way we believe that we remain immobile while the sun turns around us, that when a is placed half in a glass of water, the part that is submerged bends magically. Even so, it's true that we perceive it this way. But if we think that these perceptions correspond to the way that the world is, then even though we can say that we correctly perceive the world, we misjudge what we perceive. And this knowledge, that we perceive what we perceive, is an adequate idea that Spinoza would call an idea that is the product of reason.

Earlier we said that when imagining something, the idea formed is more about our nature than the nature of the imagined thing. On the other hand, Spinoza calls reason the product of all evident ideas, which are valid both for our subjectivity and for the outside world, "both for the whole and for the part." To know that I perceive what I perceive—or that *I think, therefore I am*—is to know a rational truth, but it is not to know the essence of anything. What concerns itself with the ideas of the essences of things is the third kind of knowledge: the *Intellect*.

An idea is much more than rules for applying a definition. An idea is a change in our mind in the same sense that we are a change in the world. Intellectual ideas have causal power, so there is no adequate idea that doesn't increase our power. Is it not a battle between Shinji's confused ideas against his adequate ones that decides the future of humanity in the face of the *Third Impact*?

Mother, Should I Build an EVA?

Everything around us, objects, our home, digital networks, political and economic institutions, the body we see when looking in the mirror, requires us to build an identity. So we built a shell around us, an *Evangelion*, supposedly to protect us, like a mother's womb. We build an identity based on what we *imagine* we are. It's an identity disguised as an AT field, as will. The whole human approach becomes toxic.

Ritsuko Akagi sums up this problem as the "Hedgehog's Dilemma" (Episode 3, "The Phone that Never Rings"). Schopenhauer's pessimism created this dilemma, Freud made him a figure of speech in psychology. To get rid of this dilemma, it's necessary to get rid of that shell and take responsibility for knowing what we are, knowing that others are like us, both in their strengths and their weaknesses. We have to accept ourselves and accept others.

Neon Genesis Evangelion is a manifesto against individualistic escapism. And this is present both in Spinoza's thought and in the doctrine of the *Tree of Life*. If God is sufficient for himself, we are not. Of course, we need to self-realize, even if we are a monk. That self-realization will necessarily depend on the world and the people around us. What Rei Ayanami said about herself, holds for all of us:

> I became who I am through the time I've spent and the connections I've made with others. I am formed by interaction with others. They create me just as I create them. These relationships and interactions

serve to shape the patterns of my heart and mind. (Episode 25, "A World That's Ending")

We will never know how *all* things relate to each other and the world. This exceeds our abilities. However, we must understand that they are *necessarily* related. Our capacity *to understand* things is as limited as our ability *to be*. On the other and tragic side, our sensitive or affective structure is capable of experiencing great suffering to the point of making us give up our self-realization. If our existence is unable to extend infinitely, on the other hand, it can be completely voided—and for that, it's not even necessary to die.

It looks as if we need a manual that teaches us how to avoid confusion. But, there is no such thing. Of course, in a way, there are too many manuals out there to choose from. If you internalize certain moral rules and act according to them, you will likely be more successful with them than without them. However, in an *Ethics* so connected with metaphysics, virtue cannot depend on rewards. According to Spinoza, virtue is the very affirmation of our essence in existence.

Whoever works with a system of rewards and punishments for actions is the imagination, which in this way becomes a maneuver for religions. Essentially, we aren't virtuous because we can resist doing such evil, but, on the contrary, it is because we are virtuous that we do not commit vileness. Our actions aren't processes to be judged by the court that says what is good and what is bad. Now, our actions either affirm or deny our *reality*. So, let's be real!

The two paths of the *Tree of Life* and the identity between Spinoza's *conatus* and Anno's AT field offered us more pieces or ways to put together the puzzle that is *Neon Genesis Evangelion*. But the solution to this puzzle is up to each person. Anno warns: "Don't expect to be catered to all the time. We all have to find our own answers."

What's the moral to this story? It's simple, first build your moral, then make your story in accordance. As if those phrases weren't clichés enough, it could end with a collage of the *Rebuild* titles: *You are not alone, you can advance, but you cannot redo.*

V

Tools to Rebuild After Impact

17
Hands Off My Show!

JEREMY CHRISTENSEN AND ERIC HOLMES

At the time of its release, *Neon Genesis Evangelion* was unlike any anime or anime series that had been seen in quite some time. Its production was superior to anything else available and its limited number of episodes made it feel even more special.

The show's initial airings were largely ignored by viewers but, like many pop culture phenomena, it began to build an audience based largely on word of mouth and by the end of its run, it was a real hit. It was a beacon of hope in an industry that had fallen on hard times and was running on autopilot.

Its production mirrored that of live action movies and its creator Hideaki Anno was allowed a much more *auteur* level of control of the show and its production. This combination of poor competition and a uniquely compelling and well-produced program enthralled audiences. However, it also became a victim of its own success, as its fans became invested in the show . . . a bit *too* invested.

Neon Genesis Evangelion's final two episodes were loathed by fans, many of whom took to the then-nascent Internet to express their displeasure and to even levy death threats against Anno. Accordingly, Anno produced two follow up movies, the second of which (*The End of Evangelion*) altered the originally broadcast conclusion to the story, providing a less-cerebral conclusion that assuaged fan concerns and made everything okay with the otaku universe.

Neon Genesis Evangelion is not the first show to develop a dedicated fan base that demanded alterations to the show (NBC's similarly high quality in a sea of low-quality sci-fi adventure series *Star Trek* was saved from a suspected cancellation in 1968 via a large-scale letter writing campaign

173

from viewers) and it certainly has not been the last. However, the vitriolic response from some members of its fan base toward the final two episodes of *Neon Genesis Evangelion* may be Patient Zero for the modern, digital effort to save cancelled shows and even to steer the direction of the narrative of shows not under the risk of cancellation. To better understand why this is, it's important to understand the continual tug of war that people feel toward fictitious movies and television programs.

The Value of Junk Television

At the core of this struggle is an essential question about the relations of production in economic systems: Who owns a product? Karl Marx argues in his "Economic and Philosophical Manuscripts of 1844" that capitalism relies upon alienation between the producer and consumer and commodity. The effect of that division is that producers retain power through the surplus value—the difference between the cost of the product and labor and the amount for which the product was sold (otherwise known as profit). According to Marx, in this system "the worker sinks to the level of commodity and becomes indeed the most wretched of commodities" (*The Marx-Engels Reader*, p. 70). As the rich get richer, workers become alienated from their own work, as they are forced to buy back their own value for the same products that they made with their own hands (pp. 71–72). Basically, it's like working at Wal-Mart stocking shelves and then spending your entire paycheck at the same Wal-Mart on the items that you put on those same shelves.

As capitalism evolved and grew, this situation got worse. Despite the invention of the forty-hour work week and other worker-friendly regulations, labor has continued to become more integral to people's lives and even identities. After all, when you meet a stranger, how quickly does the conversation devolve into, "So, what do you do for a living?" Careers or vocations have become the driving force behind most of life, including seeking a college degree.

Until the rise of the knowledge economy, most people worked in a production role either on a farm or in a factory. Human relations became embodied in the objects that people produced and consumed. As careers became the be-all and end-all of Western culture, production itself became an almost foreign concept to most people. Manufacturing was largely sent abroad and automation relegated a large number of laborers as obsolete. However, people still wanted to have a sense of production in their lives, thus the rise of "reality" television that is based on manual labor and production, be it gold-mining, blacksmithing, or commercial fishing among countless other examples. After all, would your great-grandfather who laid bricks, built houses, or worked in a machine shop want to watch television programs about laying bricks, building houses, or working in a machine shop? You only want what you don't have.

As people have grown more distant from the act of producing something and consumer goods became more abundant and affordable, the separation between the effort put into making something and its value became more distant. The efforts involved in producing a product, consuming a product, and owning a product have become utterly taken-for-granted. Because of this, according to Fredric Jameson, people have become more distant from the value of what they make (*Postmodernism*, pp. 313–14).

Television certainly played its part here. People moved from working in tobacco fields to peddling tobacco on the airwaves. Through its early phases, television has long followed a basic model: producers and broadcasters transmit a television program and pepper each broadcast with paid advertisements. The tacit expectation is that in exchange for the programming that you enjoy, you'll watch said advertisements for various products and services. This model has endured for decades despite technological advances (like cable television and streaming media) that have rendered broadcast television about as successful as Shinji Ikari's first time piloting Evangelion Unit-01.

Production of television remained centralized through much of the twentieth century and major film production houses held sway over the movies, mimicking the factory production models of Henry Ford. As an industry that was entirely driven by advertising dollars through much of the twentieth century, television viewers traditionally accepted show cancellations and underwhelming finales as par for the course. After all, historically most television programs were junk: poorly produced, poorly written, and poorly acted. Because of this, viewers tended to take them less seriously.

Seeing their favorite television show for the junk food that it is created a separation between themselves and the emotional investment that they otherwise felt toward other literature, which was presented in less commercialized ways, like a novel. Consumers consumed what producers produced for them to consume. The Marxist critic Fredric Jameson explains that in this position individuals felt as though their relations of production were blocked, when they no longer had the power over productive activity (p. 316). This powerlessness led to a certain kind of apathy toward production. Viewers may have been displeased with the last episode of 77 *Sunset Strip* but no one took to the streets or took out an ad making death threats to have it reinstated or revised. Instead, they merely changed the channel to see what else was on.

This was not the case with *Neon Genesis Evangelion*. Upon its conclusion, many fans were left confused and even angry that the show ended as it did and they let their thoughts on the subject be known. Accordingly, Anno and the show's producers rushed two follow up movies into production, including *The End of Evangelion*.

Unshackling the Digital Chains

In *The End of Evangelion,* Anno offers viewers a glimpse of some of the feedback that he received from fans of Neon Genesis Evangelion upon the airing of the final two episodes. In the form of letters, email, and even graffiti in Japan, Anno's labors resulted in messages of "die," "poop," and "Anno, I'll kill you!," which says a lot about the negative feelings that some viewers had toward the show's final two episodes.

Neon Genesis Evangelion was seemingly finished. There were no more episodes to air and yet some viewers took it upon themselves to protest, not in an effort to save the show but rather to exert some sort of control even in merely voicing their displeasure, which is a markedly different reaction to a television program's final episodes than the collective "meh" that nearly all other television programs have elicited from even the most dedicated viewers. Even a writer with one of Japan's largest newspapers, *The Mainichi Times*, weighed in and noted that the final two episodes felt like betrayal to the show's many fans across the nation.

This resistance, marked at the most extreme level by outright threats, marked a dramatic change in the relationship between consumer and producer that came about due to the overall changes in capitalism. Rising internationalism and changing technologies had erased some of the stark lines separating producer from consumer as "various modernist rituals were swept away and form production again became open to whoever cared to indulge in it" (Jameson, p. 317).

By the closing years of the lines separating, those who made things, those who oversaw their making, and those who consumed what was made became increasingly blurry. These changes, along with other shifts, spurred fans of *Neon Genesis Evangelion* to feel emboldened enough to question the way in which their product was made valuable. In fact, they not only questioned it, but to some degree, the consumer worked to take charge of the means of production of the program.

This change, while driven in part by larger systemic forces, also emerged from changing perceptions of value, in part stemming from dramatic improvements in technology. The junky quality of programming made television disposable almost from the beginning. Unlike the cinema, television doesn't require audience members to leave their homes or even to wear pants. The "no pants ever!" feature of television meant that consumer behaviors changed along with their roles. "Going to the theater" and the hoity-toityness of that expression, implied and demanded certain behaviors and manners of dress. It also led to a separation between consuming types: those deserving of the theater and those who weren't.

Nobody has ever said that they were, "Going to the television." Television was assumed to be for the lower classes, the theater for the upper-class, and television's form reflected that. Because of its utility, consistency, and historically low quality as entertainment, television has not been something that consumers wanted any sort of ownership of or to be connected with as an object at all, because it had no value. Before the rise of home video in the 1980s, successful films often lingered in theaters for months—even years in the case of hits like *Star Wars*. Successful television shows aired once and perhaps as a rerun in the summer. After that, they were gone. Despite initial fantasies of television being used as a medium for live performances of Shakespeare to be beamed into every home in America, it soon became a carnival of professional wrestling, quiz show fraud, and *My Mother the Car* . . . junk.

Glowing Values

Value shifted as technology improved, and then "going to the television" (which no one said) became a kind of mark. People didn't change their clothes to watch television, but they did change their behaviors. These changes, as Marx explains, happen in terms of how something becomes valuable. For Marx, it's not the financial cost of purchase that makes up value, rather it is that an object—whether it be a hammer or television program—has value based upon the "congealed state" of labor that goes into making that commodity (*Marx-Engels Reader*,

p. 316). Using the illustration of a coat, Marx writes that the linen used to make it and the process of tailoring to make a coat, as opposed to composing a uniform for example, becomes "accumulated in it" (p. 316). In this process, however, rather than simply having a coat to ward off the cold, something else happens that Marx writes creates a "mystical character of commodities," which emerges "only by means of the relations which the act of exchange establishes directly between the products, and indirectly, through them, between producers" (pp. 320–21). This "commodity fetishism" imbues value beyond the usefulness of the object and establishes social relationships.

Because of its high quality and juxtaposition with a seemingly endless stream of anime trash of the era like *Garzey's Wing* and *Eight Clouds Rising*, *Neon Genesis Evangelion* was treated by its fans as highbrow cinema and not merely as a cartoon series about teenagers wearing giant suits of armor to fight monsters. As a result, viewer expectations changed and, once those expectations were violated by the original finale being both ambiguous and revealed to be a dream sequence, the fans revolted.

However, this phenomenon does not stop at *Neon Genesis Evangelion*. As television has gotten progressively better in its production values, writing, and acting in the last thirty years, the same sort of expectations that consumers unfairly apply to movies have been applied to television. Because of this increase in quality and advances in how television is delivered to consumers, viewers have become more interested in television than ever. Whereas television used to be a way to pass the time between real moments in life, television in the latter years of the twentieth century became the real moments of life, as the emergence of destination television and the rise of special events like the Super Bowl made television the center of life in Western civilization.

As television technology has evolved, broadcasters have been able to draw incredible value from the data that they acquire by monitoring viewing habits, including what time of day, what day of the week, and how many episodes of the show that viewers watch in sequence. All of this data is aggregated by the producers and broadcasters of these programs. Aside from paying the monthly fee (or watching paid advertisements) that provides access to these television programs, viewers now are fully aware that their viewing habits produce data that is used (and sold) to better advertise to them and to produce other programming that they will watch, which produces even more valued data as they watch those programs.

This is where Marx's theory of labor has a fitting aspect for the digital age in which we live. Marx distinguishes what he refers to as "productive" and "unproductive" labor. Productive labor produces a tangible good that has value in and of itself, like a hat, tool, or piece of furniture. The produced item has value that can endure and last even beyond the life of its creator. At the same time, "unproductive" labor is service based—the value is fleeting. Marx uses the example of a singer—the song has value in the moment that it is sung but upon ending, its value also ends.

With television, the model mentioned earlier in this chapter (producers create a show and you watch it in exchange for your attention, which is directed toward advertisements) fell squarely into the unproductive model of labor. Attention, even if it is fully focused and not fleeting, only holds value in the time in which it exists. Once attention is shifted away, it's gone forever, never to be seen again, like Rei and Unit-00. However, the rise of streaming media has created an entirely new productive aspect to the traditional model. Instead of exchanging your fleeting attention (which is intended to be directed toward advertisements) for entertainment, viewers now exchange their attention and real-time data about that attention. Cable television providers and streaming networks are able to aggregate viewer data for the entire viewing experience, ranging from how many episodes of a show that you watch in sequence to how long and how often you pause a show as it plays.

That's My Show!

These changes in technology and relationships between consumers and producers created a shift in the expectation of the viewer of *Neon Genesis Evangelion*. To begin with, the non-productive labor of viewing a show was still labor and understood by the viewers as giving them ownership over the program. Consequently, when the program changed course from what they saw as their vision and their labor, the last two episodes were viewed as a kind of robbery. Partly, financial problems pressured Anno to change the project, which meant the story changed, particularly in the last two episodes. Eric Vilas-Boas explains in his comprehensive article on *Neon Genesis Evangelion* for *Vulture* that the plot took a "backseat to trippy, simplified animation." Imagine *Return of the Jedi* goes acid, and you would have a fair comparison.

Significantly, this change offered no resolution for the previous twenty-three episodes. Instead of a show that overtly invited the audience to interpret *Neon Genesis Evangelion* and build the narrative, Anno seized the means of production and forced it into the script. Instead of archetypal structures, he replaced it with psychoanalytic structures that dictated what the story meant. Labor's love was lost.

Marx explains a parallel to this in manufacturing and productive labor, arguing that "if the product of his labour . . . is for him an alien, hostile, powerful object independent of him, then his position towards it is such that someone else is the master of the object" (p.78). This loss of mastery, then, results in a violent backlash. The product is no longer *Neon Genesis Evangelion*; it is counterfeit. The director, rather than paying for their labor with a twenty-dollar bill, had instead paid them for their work with a bit of play money bought off a discount rack at the grocery store. This was not what they had worked for.

Further complicating matters is the role of what constitutes property. Can viewing an object give a person ownership over it? If I stand and look at the Prudential Building, does it become mine? Of course not. However, television and film are unique. The product relies upon meaning value and not use value. It's not a coat, or a building, or a hammer. It's a message that requires a receiver for it to have any value. A person's diary, for example, is an individual's property, because they use it and they view it. It is by definition private. A building, on the other hand, is complete whether or not someone uses it. It may not be practical, but it is fully there.

Television programs, on the other hand, are incomplete until someone watches them and until someone puts in the effort to view them, they are not finished products. The viewer is always part of the system of production and always has been, but the changing dynamics of technology made viewers understand their relationship to what has been made. By watching *Neon Genesis Evangelion,* the audience produces the value of each episode. Their fandom becomes the labor by which *Neon Genesis Evangelion* acquires worth.

Who Knew that Watching TV Was So Much Work?

English philosopher John Locke, in his *Second Treatise of Government,* writes a lot about property and what constitutes rightful ownership. Most of Locke's writing on property and ownership focuses on the state of nature and man's role in it (the right to pick wild fruit or dam a river). In describing how much of something that any one individual is entitled to take,

Locke offers a clear definition: "as much as anyone can make use of to any advantage of life before it spoils" (p. 14).

Locke's position is that products of the wild are free to be enjoyed and consumed so long as they are not wasted. If I take two apples from a tree, eat one and then let the other rot while you went to the same tree to find it picked bare, I'm a wasteful and glutinous jerk who, "offended against the common law of nature, and was liable to be punished" (p. 17). At the same time, in the state of nature, the key element of ownership is labor, the work needed to reap the harvest of nature's bounty. According to Locke, if you make the great effort of cutting down a tree and milling it into lumber in the state of nature, the lumber is rightfully yours, as your labor alone allowed the tree to go from a natural thing to a product.

While Locke's examples and central philosophy of property and ownership focuses on the wild, uncivilized areas of the world, it is fitting for understanding the fan rebellion that occurred with *Neon Genesis Evangelion* and continues to occur with many other television series. Like Marx, Locke is concerned with the virtue of work and what it represents; Marx focuses on its impact on the value of a good while Locke focuses on how labor leads to ownership of a good.

In the case of *Neon Genesis Evangelion*, as a television series that follows a clear consumer model, the fans felt a sense of ownership over the show, as it was a shockingly high-quality program in an era when such things were rare. Because of this, fans took the old "You provide it and we'll watch it and your commercials" model of laissez-faire viewing and realized that the show only has value *because they watch it*. Without their attention, the show is a failure. The viewers alone dictate its success and they had an epiphany not unlike Shinji in the show's much-reviled final episode.

Neon Genesis Evangelion, in their individual minds, was good enough to fight for; they always knew that they had the power to push back against a program that disappointed them but few things before *Neon Genesis Evangelion* were good enough to warrant that much effort.

Neon Genesis Evangelion was a watershed moment in fan-base response and other consumer and producer relations have followed suit. Fans of television programs have become more emboldened in their efforts and feel a much stronger sense of ownership over their favorite programs. From *Stranger Things'* #JusticeForBarb social media movement to the efforts to save Netflix's *The OA* (which included protests, a change.org campaign, and even a hunger strike), television viewers have more weight than ever to throw around due to the influence of social media. In the last five years alone, significant efforts have been made by fans to save NBC's *Timeless,* Fox's *Lucifer,* and SyFy's *The Expanse* (in which fans chartered aircraft to fly protest banners).

Neon Genesis Evangelion elicited the type of fandom that marketers and producers dream of: passionate, active, and quick to emerge. However, like Gendo Ikari, it can get out of control, especially when viewers feel a sense of ownership of the program.

18

Desperately Seeking Misato

DAVID BORDONABA-PLOU

Recently, I watched *Neon Genesis Evangelion* for the second time. The first time I watched it, I was a teenager, so I didn't understand the series's subtleties. On top of that, the last two chapters didn't exactly help me understand what was going on. I needed proper doses of caffeine and two or three brainwashes before I started to recover.

However, the second time I saw the series, I was an adult, and, as a philosopher, my trained eye saw a lot of new things. *Evangelion* is a series that can surprise you in many ways. There's its visionary nature, the in-depth psychological analysis of the characters, and the way it exposes the tension between faith and reason, to name just a few aspects. Nevertheless, what surprised me most this time was the fact that the EVA pilots, NERV staff, and, indeed, all of humanity hadn't perished in the first few chapters of the series.

Is It a Miracle?

Angel attacks are part of everyday life from the very beginning of the series. The first attack takes place in the Episode 1 ("Angel Attack") and, by Episode 14 ("SEELE, the Seat of the Soul"/"Weaving A Story")—the typical summary chapter that usually appears mid-season in many animes—there have been as many as nine attacks from different Angels, hardly a negligible number. On many occasions all seems lost, but NERV eventually triumphs. I remember thinking, "If they are still alive, it has to be a fucking miracle; otherwise, none of this makes any sense!"

A miracle is any event that can't be explained by the laws of nature. For example, if someone walks on water or turns water into wine, those are miracles for sure (especially the latter). No matter how many physicists or chemists you talk to, none will be able to explain such an event using our current physical and chemical laws. They may even take offense at the question, so be careful. However, although religion and faith are one of the central themes in Evangelion, one repeated idea made me realize that miracles had nothing to do with NERV's victories.

In *Evangelion*, if a plan succeeds, it's not a miracle; it's due to the knowledge and intuition of the people who work at NERV. As chief of operations, Katsuragi says, "Miracles are only worth a damn when you make them happen yourself" (Episode 12, "A Miracle's Worth"/"She said, 'Don't make others suffer for your personal hatred'"). In other words, the victories over the Angels aren't due to the intervention of a supreme being. Although sometimes NERV's victories may look like miracles, this is due to the people working to deal with the attack. One person stands out above all: Misato Katsuragi. She's the one who makes "miracles" happen.

Above all, Misato

Many people work at NERV: Gendo Ikari, the commander; Kozo Fuyutsuki, his right-hand man; Ritsuko Akagi, NERV's head scientist; and many others. They face the Angels together. However, Misato eclipses everyone when it comes to management and problem-solving. She's the head of operations at NERV. She's the one who always decides the course of action they should follow to defeat an Angel. The Three Magi—the supercomputers that run NERV and Neo Tokyo-3—provide her with a great deal of help. These supercomputers, created by Naoko Akagi, Ritsuko Akagi's mother, give the probabilities of success for any potential plan. So, Misato always has an accurate idea of the chance of success.

However, sometimes the help of the Three Magi isn't enough. In some cases, she has to make crucial decisions for the destiny of humanity using only her intuition. For example, in Episode 8 ("Asuka Arrives in Japan"/"Asuka Strikes!") Misato and the EVAs are on a ship at sea far away from NERV headquarters. Misato has to devise a plan to defeat the Angel Israfel, a giant jellyfish, taking into account that the EVAs aren't able to move through water. She decides to introduce two old warships in the mouth of the Angel and then fire all the weapons to make Israfel blow up.

The plan, although it may seem a little unsophisticated, is successful. Israfel literally ends up with lethal indigestion. On some occasions, Misato can meticulously draw up a plan and then evaluate it with the Three Magi's help. However, at other times, she has to come up with something on the spot. Besides the Three Magi's help, Misato's inventiveness and creativity in solving problems make NERV successful in dealing with all the Angels' attacks.

One of the most familiar images of philosophical practice finds the philosopher in her armchair, trying to disentangle philosophical puzzles with the help of her intuition alone. The use of intuition is the most common method in philosophy. However, for some years now some philosophers, including myself, have been doing philosophy using the power of machines. We may not have supercomputers as powerful as the Three Magi, but I can assure you that we can do fantastic things with a laptop and a couple of apps.

This doesn't mean that we need to forget about intuition entirely when doing philosophy, though. On the contrary, combining intuition and reason is the best way of solving philosophical problems. I hope to convince you of two things. First, an essential part of what makes NERV able to defeat the Angels is the way Misato uses both intuition and scientific methods to resolve the crises that arise. Second, philosophers can benefit significantly from following Katsuragi's example. Addressing problems requires respect for the findings of quantitative methods, but also trust in the intuition of the people working in the field.

Big Data Societies

I'm sure you've heard of machine learning, algorithms, and Big Data. These words define the societies we live in now. You will almost certainly have been impressed, or maybe even a little scared, of the way YouTube's algorithm can predict your preferences only by analyzing the history of the videos you've watched. Although it may be hard for us to admit, sometimes computers know what we like better than we do.

Today, we live in Big Data societies—highly technological communities where computational processing techniques are becoming more and more important for many different purposes and where the amount of data used is increasing exponentially. One of the best examples of the influence of this new paradigm is the Cambridge Analytica scandal. Cambridge Analytica was a research company that applied Big Data to electoral campaigns. It extracted vast amounts of data from many people—for instance, from their Facebook profiles—and then analyzed it to influence national elections. In short, if you had an obscene amount of money, they could probably get you elected. For example, they had a significant influence on the yes vote for Brexit in the UK and for Donald Trump's victory in the US. That's no small thing.

The institutional and political imagery of *Evangelion* resembles Big Data societies. As happens today, in Neo Tokyo-3 an essential part of the decision-making depends on computational analyses which use vast amounts of data. However, *Evangelion*'s society seems far more evolved than ours in that sense, as even NASA computers unraveling the origin of the universe can't achieve the power and the control of the Three Magi. Will our current society reach that level at some point, or is what we see in *Evangelion* pure science fiction? I would say that Neo Tokyo-3 represents a possible but distant future of our current society. I only hope that the fate of humanity doesn't depend on fourteen-year-old teenagers piloting gigantic mechas!

Neo Tokyo-3

In Neo Tokyo-3, the influence of Big Data reaches a new level. It isn't merely that the Three Magi help NERV by doing astronomical calculations that NERV otherwise couldn't; they run the government of the whole city. In Episode 11 ("In the Still Darkness"/"The Day Tokyo-3 Stood Still"), Deputy Commander Kozo Fuyutsuki says to Maya Ibuki, a secondary character in the anime, that "the city council is a charade. All city administration is effectively in the hands of the Magi." Imagine living in a city governed by computers: the sensation is somewhere between optimism and fear.

Just like Neo Tokyo-3, NERV depends on the computing power of the Three Magi. NERV's personnel rely on their analysis to cope with Angel attacks. The success of the plans to defeat the Angels is due, in large part, to the three supercomputers. Remember how close NERV is to collapse when, in Episode 13 ("Angel Infiltration"/"Lilliputian Hitcher"), the tenth Angel, Ireul, a collection of nano-machines, infects the Three Magi. The Angel infiltrates Melchior and reprograms it, then infiltrates and infects Balthazar as well. It's close to controlling the three supercomputers, but, in the end, thanks to Misato and Ritsuko, it doesn't infect Gaspar. They're able to reboot the entire system, which makes it possible to defeat the Angel.

NERV's dependence on the Three Magi is very high. However, when NERV can't rely on them, someone comes up with a plan. During Ireul's attack, Ritsuko's and Misato's ideas save humanity. Ritsuko knows the Three Magi perfectly as her mother, Naoko Akagi, built them. She tells Misato that a different part of her mother's personality (mother, scientist, and woman) has been transplanted into each of the three computers. Because of that conversation, her knowledge of how the three computers work, and her emotional bond with her mother, Ritsuko can design a firewall that stops the Angel's advance. She and Misato don't know if the plan will succeed. They believe or intuit that it will because of all they know and feel, but there's no way to prove this quantitatively since the Three Magi are down. In the end, it seems that they didn't need to either, as the plan succeeds. The lesson to be learned is that we sometimes don't need any computation or data to devise a successful plan, but only our intuition.

Misato Katsuragi, the Miracle Maker

In *Evangelion*, there are many remarkable characters, and many candidates for the title of hero. You may think that the heroes of *Evangelion* are Rei, Shinji, and Asuka. After all, they're the ones who defeat the Angels in their epic combats. Alternatively, maybe you think that the real heroine is Ritsuko Akagi because she's responsible for the EVAs' design. Without them, humanity couldn't fight the Angels. However, I believe that Misato Katsuragi is the real heroine of *Evangelion*. Why? Because she's the head of operations at NERV. She decides what to do, how to use the EVAs, and what the pilots' specific actions should be at all times. In short, she loves it when a plan comes together, and, in fact, she succeeds even in adverse situations. In situations where success doesn't seem possible, Misato Katsuragi, the miracle maker, comes out triumphant.

For instance, in Episode 12 ("A Miracle's Worth"/"She Said, 'Don't Make Others Suffer for Your Personal Hatred'"), the Angel Sahaquiel, a gigantic eye with two other smaller eyes, appears in Earth's orbit, far beyond the reach of the EVAs. Immediately, the Angel starts shooting pieces of itself onto the Earth's surface. Gradually, the explosions come closer to Neo Tokyo-3, which makes NERV think that, in the final blast, the entire body of the Angel could fall on the city. However, the Three Magi can't accurately determine the Angel's strike zone. The best they can do is say that the Angel will fall somewhere within a ten-thousand-meter radius. Thanks, folks! That's a big help. That's about one hundred football fields laid end to end and side by side. To get a feel for the scale, that's greater than the area of the Maldives or about the same area as Malta. The

Angel is "only" about fifty or sixty meters long, so the Three Magis' estimate is total bullshit.

So, what do you do when your supercomputers can't even come close to predicting where an attack will occur? What do you do when millions of calculations are effectively useless? You rely on the intuition of people who work in the field. To defeat Sahaquiel, Katsuragi devises a wonderful but risky plan. With their bare hands, the EVAs will catch the Angel, and, using their AT fields at maximum, they will stop it before it makes contact with the surface. If the Angel suddenly veers, game over. If any of the EVAs can't withstand the impact, game over. To many people at NERV, the plan sounds like complete madness. In fact, the Three Magi assign a probability of success of 0.00001%. However, against all these odds, the plan succeeds.

Not Just Once

Although it might be thought that the victory against the Angel Sahaquiel is a matter of sheer luck, in *Evangelion*, such "miracles" are more common than might be imagined, as many plans that sound crazy end in victory. There's another example where, against all the odds, Katsuragi's ideas resolve a situation that seemed doomed to failure.

In Episode 7 ("The Works of Man"/"A Human Work"), one of NERV's rival organizations is showing off its prototype giant robot, the Jet Alone. Unlike the EVAs, which require an external charging source because their battery power is very limited, the Jet Alone is a nuclear-powered mecha and can operate for a long time without any external charge. At a certain point, the Jet Alone's nuclear reactor collapses and it's in danger of meltdown. The leader of the Jet Alone team suggests waiting for the core of the reactor to shut down on its own. However, there's a very low probability of this happening. Besides, having an atomic bomb on legs with no control over it doesn't seem like the best idea. Misato prefers "desperate action over waiting for a miracle," so she decides to board the Jet Alone, risking her own life to deactivate it manually. Again, the plan is total madness. She's almost certain to die from the massive radioactive contamination inside the mecha. And yet, Misato manages to survive and stop the Jet Alone.

In short, "miracles" are *Evangelion*'s bread-and-butter, and it's Misato Katsuragi, the miracle maker, who makes them possible. She certainly takes good note of the Three Magis' predictions. When the Angel Sahaquiel attacks and, after assessing the situation, they recommend evacuating Neo Tokyo-3,

Katsuragi follows their advice with no hesitation. However, the Three Magi can only estimate the probabilities of success of a given strategy. They can't come up with plans. So, when things start to get ugly, when your supercomputers can't help you, you need a backup plan. You need imaginative and determined people who can deal with adverse situations. When traditionally reliable methods are unreliable, you need someone who uses her intuition in such a creative and imaginative way that she can make a plan even when nothing seems possible. In short, you need someone who makes miracles happen. You need someone like Misato Katsuragi.

Philosophical Wars

The battle between humanity and the Angels is a full-scale war, an all-or-nothing situation. The consequences of the Second Impact were tremendous. Antarctica was destroyed, thousands of coastal cities buried, the Earth's axis displaced, not to mention the fact that half the world's population perished in the incident. In the end, and despite all the damage done, the Katsuragi expedition, named after Misato's father, was able to return Adam to his embryonic state. However, that "victory" was only a temporary halt. The Angels, the sons of Adam, soon returned to Earth to destroy humans, Lilith's progeny. Thanks to NERV and, above all, Misato, humankind can continue fighting.

In philosophy, we also have wars. True, philosophers don't pilot gigantic mechas to fight Angels, but anyone who has attended a philosophy conference can confirm that philosophical discussions are sometimes more than passionate. Since the beginning of the twenty-first century, there has been a dispute within the discipline among those who uphold introspection, and appealing to intuition as a proper methodology, and those who distrust this method, instead championing the need to apply scientific techniques. Those who endorse the former think that philosophy doesn't need to look to any other discipline—introspection and appealing to intuition, the traditional ways of doing philosophy, are reliable methods. Let's call them autonomists. Those who endorse the latter believe philosophy has to be constrained by science. We'll call them naturalists. Introspection and appealing to intuition aren't reliable methods, so philosophical inquiry needs to apply more rigorous methods from scientific disciplines such as psychology, social sciences, or linguistics.

There are many characters in *Evangelion*. While some are convinced naturalists, others think in a way much closer to that advocated by autonomists. Ritsuko Akagi is the perfect example of a naturalist. As NERV's head scientist, she has full confidence in the Three Magi and immediately condemns any plan to which the three supercomputers have not given a high probability of success. Another prominent example of a naturalist is Gendo Ikari, NERV's commander. For example, in Episode 12 ("A Miracle's Worth"/"She Said, 'Don't Make Others Suffer for Your Personal Hatred'"), when talking with Kozo Fuyutsuki about the Second Impact, Gendo tells him that "science is the power of man."

On the other hand, Shinji Ikari, the Third Child, is much closer to the thinking and actions of the autonomists. Due to his introverted personality, he finds the solutions, very often in the middle of the combats, by letting himself be guided by his intuition. Another example of an autonomist is Ryoji Kaji, a triple agent working as a special inspector for NERV. In his philosophical conversations with Shinji, he always maintains that people only need personal reflection to understand social dynamics. Consider, for instance, when, in Episode 19 ("A Man's Battle"/"Introjection"), he's watering his watermelon garden and tells Shinji that people can learn a lot about human relationships by merely caring for and nurturing something.

A False Dilemma

The dispute between autonomists and naturalists seems to indicate that to solve a problem, whether it be a philosophical problem or how to defeat an Angel, there are two methods from which we have to choose only one: to trust our intuition, or to rely on the application of scientific methods. If Misato had thought this way, *Evangelion* would perhaps have ended in Episode 1, after the Angel Sachiel's attack. However, the way Misato resolves many of the Angels' attacks shows that having to decide between the two methods is a false dilemma. A false dilemma, or false dichotomy, is any statement that wrongly presents a situation where only two options are possible, whereas in fact, there's at least a third option. In this case, the third option is to use both methods. This is precisely what Misato does, which is why her plans are so successful even though, in the eyes of naturalists like Ritsuko Akagi, they may seem crazy.

In an article on "Naturalism and Intuitions," Hilary Kornblith defends a theory that brings together both the autonomists' and the naturalists' ideas. The way Kornblith sees it, intuitions aren't to be understood as natural, spontaneous, and lacking reflection, but as mediated by both our theoretical and empirical knowledge. I doubt that Misato read Kornblith, but her modus operandi perfectly illustrates the practice Kornblith describes as the best possible when doing philosophical research. When Misato faces a problem, she designs a plan using her intuition and, if the Three Magi evaluate the plan negatively, she often reworks it. As Kornblith points out in *Knowledge and Its Place in Nature*, if we trusted only our intuition, we'd be losing "the best available source of correctives for current mistakes" (p. 16). On the other hand, if we trusted only scientific or quantitative methods, we would be losing viable, imaginative solutions to specific problems. Misato doesn't have that difficulty. She uses both methods in a recursive and productive way.

For example, in Episode 6 ("Showdown in Tokyo-3"/"Rei II"), she devises a plan to defeat the Angel Ramiel, a giant blue polyhedron that's drilling into the Earth in an attempt to get to NERV headquarters. To beat Ramiel, Misato tries to breach the Angels' AT field by firing a focused high-energy beam from outside its range. The Three Magi assess Misato's plan as having a chance of success of eight percent. Ritsuko Akagi says that the plan is "loony" because, among other things, the EVAs' positron rifles can't handle such a burst of energy. What does Misato do? She thinks of a possible solution consisting of using a prototype rifle with enough firepower to disintegrate the Angel. However, someone observes that NERV can't provide the energy required to fire the rifle. Again, Misato thinks of a possible solution. She borrows power from the primary electric grid, leaving Neo Tokyo-3 in darkness for more than eight hours, but the Angel is destroyed.

Desperately seeking Misato

Is the plan to defeat the Angel Ramiel a loony plan, as Ritsuko Akagi suggests? Not at all. It certainly is a plan based on Misato's intuition, but what a naturalist like Ritsuko Akagi forgets is that, as Kornblith points out, Misato's plan doesn't rely on spontaneous and unreflective intuition. On the contrary, it's based on intuition grounded in empirical knowledge from her experience as chief of operations. The plan indeed needs reworking to be totally viable, but that's what successful planning is all about: designing a plan that appeals to our intuition, intuition based on our theoretical background and past empirical experience, and then using scientific methods to analyze it to find possible mistakes before correcting the plan in accordance with the results of the analysis.

How much analysis and reworking each plan needs will depend on the details of each situation, for example, the time available. Some of Misato's plans need a great deal of reworking, as in the case of Ramiel's attack. Others, however, need none, as in the case of the attack of the Angel Sahaquiel, where the imminence of the attack made it impossible to analyze the plan in detail. As Kornblith maintains, and as Misato shows, the best way to solve a problem is to think in a solution using our intuition, test it using quantitative methods, and correct it in light of the results if necessary.

Deciding between intuition or scientific methods to solve a problem is a false dilemma. We can follow Misato Katsuragi, the miracle maker, and choose the best of both worlds. To defeat an Angel, or to do philosophy, it's essential to have all weapons at our disposal. Therefore, whether you are a philosopher or not, if you need to solve a problem, and you have not yet found Misato Katsuragi, I urge you to follow her example.

19

From Kabbalah, Angels, and Apocalypse to Kaiju, Mecha, and Personal Growth

DENIZ YENIMAZMAN

> Just as in all spheres God opposes myth, mythical violence is confronted by the divine. And the latter constitutes its antithesis in all respects. If mythical violence is law-making, divine violence is law-destroying; if the former sets boundaries, the latter boundlessly destroys them . . . Mythical violence is bloody power over mere life for its own sake, divine violence pure power over all life for the sake of the living. The first demands sacrifice, the second accepts it.
>
> —WALTER BENJAMIN, *Critique of Violence*

Drawing on various tropes, themes, and notions of religion and myth, *Neon Genesis Evangelion* crafts an allegory on the fate of humans today.

In Judaism before the Middle Ages, the divine was sharply differentiated from myth. In a religious context, the notion of myth often serves as a counterpoint to the notion of religion. Whereas myth can describe a loose assortment of different cultic practices, religion is regarded as a more systematic spiritual approach with codified practices and beliefs.

It was considered one of the great achievements of monotheism that it could finally relegate mythical remnants of its origin outside of religious canonical doctrine. And yet, the myths never really went away. They were just relegated to a different place within our culture and our production of meaning. In the eyes of Walter Benjamin, the legitimation for violence by the state is always immanent, immediate, and self-sufficient; it doesn't need anything outside itself to justify any act necessary for its survival. Divine violence, on the other hand, is transcendental. It always refers to a cause or reason outside of the immediate here-and-now, to a kind of cosmic, timeless justice that transcends the mortal lives of humanity and therefore can legitimize anything in the service of the "greater good" or a divine world order.

This kind of dualism is present in *Neon Genesis Evangelion*, as it tells us tales of psychological and sociopolitical conflict and weaves them together into one great apocalyptic story arc. Can we decode the countless visual and narrative references of *Neon Genesis Evangelion* and relate them back to their historical origins, rooted in religion and mythology?

So, jump into your entry plugs, let the LCL flow and fire up the systems and engines; it's gonna be quite a ride!

Myth, Religion, and Violence

In a universe where the slightest dispute can lead to disaster, . . . the rites of sacrifice serve to polarize the community's aggressive impulses and redirect them toward victims that may be actual or figurative, animate or inanimate, but that are always incapable of propagating further vengeance. The sacrificial process furnishes an outlet for those violent impulses that cannot be mastered by self-restraint; a partial outlet, to be sure, but always renewable, and one whose efficacy has been attested by an impressive number of reliable witnesses.

—RENÉ GIRARD, *Violence and the Sacred*

As the anthropological philosopher René Girard has observed, the origin of religion is closely connected to an effort to replace *spontaneous* violence within a social grouping, such as tribal societies, with *sacrificial* violence, the latter occurring at a certain time and place and following certain rules in order to serve as a symbol and a control mechanism against the former. This, however, inevitably leads to what Girard calls a *sacrificial crisis*, as in the biblical case with Abraham and Isaac and in *Neon Genesis Evangelion* with the relationship between Gendo Ikari and his pilots, especially Rei Ayanami.

Rather than controlling violent impulses, a sacrificial crisis can lead to a runaway effect of self-perpetuating violence in the service of sacrifice while it becomes increasingly unclear what the aim of the sacrifice might be. The perpetuation of certain control practices has led to mythical, ritualistic, and religious narratives taking up this compensatory function.

The society we get to witness in the series after the Second Impact seems to be under constant martial law. The military enacting its monopoly on violence on its own soil, is legitimized via the state. In contrast to the world of humans, the kind of violence that the Angels in *Neon Genesis Evangelion* are able to exert can be considered sublime, in the sense of the sublimity of nature, not only because of the overwhelming power of their weapons in comparison to the arsenal of mankind (excluding the EVAs for now), but also in terms of the scope of their destruction and their obliviousness in regards to the loss of human life.

As for their personality traits, we can only speculate. It's not that the Angels are ignorant of human suffering. Rather, they seem to perceive mankind as alien, in a similar vein as they appear to humans, which can be observed during the first encounter with Sachiel during the first episode of the series. Humans and Angels can be considered equal insofar as they both show great resolve in sacrificing everything for their mission, whether that's enabling or preventing the apocalypse. The Angels only give up on their mission when they are killed by the EVAs, otherwise they continue relentlessly. The show also devotes considerable story time to Shinji's quest for motivation and self-belief, facilitated through the external conflict with the Angels and showing him gradually strengthen his resolve.

Kabbalah and *Neon Genesis Evangelion*

The Kabbalah deals with the idea of the individual, the Torah with that of the people. The Kabbalah is esotericism—it deals with the inner world, with the training of mental abilities, whereas the Torah is exotericism—it deals with the outer world. So the worldly goal of Kabbalah is: to unite all the male and female life forces that exist into one great harmony, into one *world person*. This is the hermaphrodite that unites man and woman. From this position of the Kabbalah come all the occidental theories of the "world soul" . . . The goal of Kabbalah can be realized by man, but the goal of Torah can only be realized by God alone.

—JACOB TAUBES, *KABBALAH*

Neon Genesis Evangelion employs a lot of Kabbalistic imagery and symbolism. For example, the *sefiroth*, different types of emanations (or virtues) by God, are featured multiple times in the show, in the opening credits as well as in the office of Gendo Ikari, located on the ceiling and floor in a geometrical arrangement that is known as the *Tree of Life*. Also, during *The End of Evangelion* (00h 50m 18s), we can see the ten Angels newly created by the SEELE organization lining up in the sky to form the Kabbalistic symbol.

Judaist scholar and philosopher Jacob Taubes (1923–1987), relates the difference between religion and myth to the difference between the world and the individual. In his interpretation,

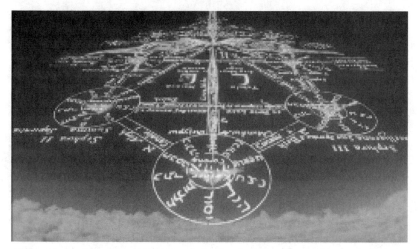

Figure 1: The appearance of the Sefiroth after Shinji's crucifixion during Third Impact

the Kabbalah filled the need for a guideline of religious personal conduct and meaning, since the Torah was predominantly occupied with the divine laws of the world. Generally speaking, the symbolism and imagery of monotheism employed in *Neon Genesis Evangelion* can be regarded as a form of exoticism, in a similar manner that *anime* and *donghua* were initially marketed as "exotic" (in the sense of unfamiliar and exciting) to Western audiences. Thus, there's a complicated relationship of cultural transposition and re-appropriation at work here. The aim of the undertaking, however, is obvious in both Kabbalah and *Neon Genesis Evangelion*. It's to be read as a giant allegory for personal individual growth. On closer observation, the use and merging of Kabbalistic symbols with Christian imagery in *Neon Genesis Evangelion* mirrors, in a way, the reception history of the Kabbalah in the European Middle Ages.

Originally of southern French origin and further developed by Sephardic scholars in Spain in the following centuries, the Jewish Kabbalah had a profound impact on the Christian Renaissance and Christian mysticism, most prominently starting in Italy around the late fourteenth century. In *Neon Genesis Evangelion*, the cross symbol is employed at various stages in the story.

Whenever EVAs or Angels use an AT Field to great effect, the discharge sometimes leaves a radiation field that looks like a Christian cross. Also, the huge anthropomorphic body that is to become Lilith towards the end of the series is kept in an underground facility, partially submerged in LCL liquid, which

Figure 2: Lilith surrounded by human souls during Third Impact

we later learn is her own blood. She is nailed to a giant cross, very much like Jesus Christ during crucifixion and it's safe to assume that the analogy was intended. During the apocalyptic finale, when the body of Lilith is rising above its constraints, losing her mask and assuming the face of Ayanami Rei, we see human souls all over the globe lighting up in a similar fashion to the afterglow of the AT field discharge, that is, in the shape of a cross (*The End of Evangelion*, 01h 18m 50s).

Angels in Religion and *Neon Genesis Evangelion*

Angels are made of a strange substance that has the properties of both a wave and a particle, just like light . . . Even though they're made of different material, their signal distribution and co-ordinates are strikingly similar to human DNA. 99.89 percent similar.

—RITSUKO AKAGI, *Neon Genesis Evangelion*

The pseudo-scientific commentary on the material properties of Angels by Ritsuko Akagi can serve as a metaphor for the ambiguities surrounding these enigmatic creatures across various cultures and religions. The account of their visual appearance varies greatly according to the respective source and individual Angel, but what they all have in common is that they appear to have wings and numerous, sometimes even thousands, of eyes. The latter feature seems to have lost prominence in Christian depictions of angels over the centuries, but we can find various historical images of angels

Figures 3 and 4: Historical angelic depiction by Adolphe Didron (left) and in the opening credits of *Neon Genesis Evangelion* (right)

having numerous eyes and multiple sets of wings. The opening credits of *Neon Genesis Evangelion* use historical images and illuminations from Christian texts as an inspiration for an Angel image where we can clearly see the mentioned characteristics.

Although the Angels appear to be different from men, they both share the same origin, a topic referred to in *Neon Genesis Evangelion* as well as in Christian mythology. According to the lore of the series, Angels were created by Adam before humans. However, all three do seem to share the majority of their genetic material and they all possess AT fields, which is a cipher for the soul. This origin story is consistent with most monotheistic creation myths as well as in *Neon Genesis Evangelion*.

In *Neon Genesis Evangelion*, the Angels are of the same material as God, but appear to be different in their shape and abilities and aren't considered deities themselves. They serve as messengers, depending on the individual interpretation either as messengers of God or as witnesses to His presence, since it could be argued that the body of Lilith is driving them towards Tokyo-3. They do possess a soul (their AT field), as does Adam, presumably, as well as the *lilin* (human beings).

It becomes clear, as the storyline of *Neon Genesis Evangelion* progresses, that it was in fact NERV that was trying to accelerate the global apocalypse in hopes of a new world order rising from its ashes. This is also a common eschatological motive found in various types of religious and political myths. The hubris of mankind in *Neon Genesis Evangelion*, playing God in more than one way by creating supernatural beings, waging war against the messengers of God and trying to bring about the end of the world on their own is, from a perspective of religious mysticism, presumably what makes the Angels appear on Earth during the time after Second Impact.

Apocalypse and Pharmakos

The concept of apocalypse is already present in the Old Testament, namely in the book of Daniel. It mainly portrays the advent of the reign of God on Earth and its implications for the history of mankind. Christian texts, such as the revelation of Jesus Christ to John, largely adhere to similar principles in the retelling of the end of the world, but shift the focus away from God himself onto the second coming of Christ, the son-of-God made flesh.

Again, *Neon Genesis Evangelion* skilfully manages to combine the tropes of Judaism and Christianity in the context of the apocalypse. The Third Impact is brought about by mere mortals, namely SEELE and its executive arm NERV. Having been responsible for unleashing the divine potential of Adam during Second Impact, these organisations have been engaging in certain activities in the context of Angels and EVAs, which can be described by the notion of *pharmakos*.

The origin of the term in Greek antiquity is connected to its sacrificial and religious function, a person destined for human sacrifice, endowed with special privileges within their society as well as a certain social standing. In return, it was expected that once the day of sacrifice arrived, the *pharmakos* would be ready to engage in it willingly and happily. Put in another way, through the public and ritualistic display of lethal violence, the ancient Greeks hoped to further control violent impulses in their societies with a form of religious spectacle. After the Middle Ages, however, the term also gained a medical connotation as well.

> Contrary to the Galenic assumption that 'contraria a contrariis curantur' that heat cures cold and vice versa, Paracelsus asserted the isopathic rule that 'like cures like'. . . If the cure against a poison is poison, then disease and health no longer lie along the axis of a frontal opposition,

but in a dialectical relationship that naturally makes one the opposite of the other, but also and above all, the instrument of the other. The pharmakon is both the evil and what opposes it, by bowing to its logic . . . *Disease and antidote, poison and cure, potion and counter-potion: the pharmakon is not a substance but rather a non-substance, a non-identity, a non-essence. But above all, it is something that relates to life from the ground of its reverse. More than affirming life, it negates its negation, and in the process ends up doubling it.*

   —ROBERTO ESPOSITO, *Immunitas*

In *Neon Genesis Evangelion*, the EVAs were supposedly created after the Second Impact out of the same material that Adam is made out of. Clearly, we can see the analogy to *pharmakos* here in its medical sense that Roberto Esposito, a political philosopher, alludes to in the quote above.

The EVAs were made from Adam's flesh precisely because they were designed to combat the power and influence of the angels, intending to fight fire with fire, as it were. The only way humans are capable of battling the angels is to confront them with an entity that is a variation of their self, albeit mostly under human control. The effect of this endeavor turns out to be something different than SEELE and NERV intended. Instead of the dawn of a new aeon under the auspices of the Human Instrumentality Project, that is, the almost totalitarian dissolution of all human subjectivity, we can witness the beginning of a new era in the last act of *The End of Evangelion* that is mostly characterized by an absence of purpose and of history. In other words, the apocalypse has been cancelled, but by the time the end credits roll, none of the protagonists really know what to make of it.

In the apocalyptic accounts of Christianity, the end of the world sets the stage for the Day of Judgment and the Second Coming of Christ. Therefore, and in contrast to its Jewish predecessor, the tone of the Christian narrative is an *eschatological* one. It entails a dimension of human salvation from the toils and suffering of the mundane world. In the narrative universe of *Neon Genesis Evangelion*, there's no final salvation by a monotheistic god, no ultimate forgiveness for our sins. As climactic as the Third Impact was, life after it simply seems to go on, albeit with a new existential quality of being without direction. Nothing will be like the way it was before. All categories have to be rewritten, all maps redrawn.

The overall moral of the storyline, however, stays intact. *Neon Genesis Evangelion* begins as a tale of alienation and despair, followed by self-exploration and acceptance and always accompanied by great personal suffering and human tragedy. In its finale, it provides hope by reinforcing the benefits of self-awareness and mindfulness towards the emotional needs of others, all while the world is coming to an end. Salvation from suffering is achieved at great cost, but ultimately, the overcoming of these obstacles is mostly immanent in nature, since large parts of the Third Impact play out in Shinji's mind while he is fused with his EVA, the soul of his mother (EVA-01's core), and Lilith. In the vein of ancient mystics, Brahmins, and Buddhist monks, the possibility for salvation or enlightenment is always situated within a person, not outside of it.

An alternative interpretation would be to view the story arc of Shinji Ikari in a messianic way. In the very beginning of the show, Shinji Ikari serves as the narrative anchor to the audience. Like us, this strange world he's been introduced to is as new to him as it is to us. He never knew his father, Gendo, and the fact that Gendo is now Shinji's boss opens the door to all kinds of oedipal problems. Traumatic experiences during childhood, emotional absence of his parents, a problematic relationship with authority, maintaining focus under increasing pressure, the loss of friends and family—all these conflicts make Shinji relatable to us. He experiences some of the things we ourselves might have experienced. Although the protagonist, he's far from perfect, and it's his frailty and vulnerability that make him so relatable as a character. In the same vein, Jesus Christ might have been born as a son of God, but he is mortal and human as well. Both Shinji and Christ seem to be gifted with divine knowledge, something that both only gain after their rites of passage and under great personal suffering.

And this is where the symbolism of Christ aligns with that of Shinji Ikari. They both commit the ultimate sacrifice to save the future of mankind. They both are *pharmakos*. The sacrificial death of the individual serves as an immunisation against the basic evil impulses of violence and revenge for the rest of society and is intended as a reminder towards our individual and collective virtues. But there's also a deeper analogy here in the sense that both Jesus Christ and Shinji Ikari possess a lineage of divine origin. In the case of Jesus Christ, that origin story is located at the beginning of the biblical accounts of his life. Whereas with Shinji, the allegory of his divine origin only becomes clear in the final acts of *Neon Genesis Evangelion*. During the fight with the new generation of mass-produced EVAs by SEELE, his body and mind fuse with his Eva-01 and its core. After his ritual crucifixion by the rival EVAs triggering the onset of Third Impact, he then is converted into the Tree of Life and fuses with the consciousness of the recently awakened Lilith via her third eye.

Neon Genesis Evangelion is a journey of personal development, both in relation to the inner psyche and the outer world. The most important message the show tries to convey in so many different shapes and forms is this: every person is responsible for their own destiny, even if all the other circumstances seem to be stacked against them.

Hope, kindness, mindfulness, even enlightenment will always start from within, moving towards the outside where we interact with others, all facing the same inner challenges. In the end, it won't be a deity or divine violence that will save us. Instead, the show reminds us that it will be each of us; we can save each other.

Bibliography

Arendt, Hannah. 1958. *The Human Condition*. University of Chicago Press.

———. 1979. *The Origins of Totalitarianism*. Harcourt, Brace.

Aristotle. 1985. *The Complete Works of Aristotle*. Volumes I and II. Edited by Jonathan Barnes. Oxford University Press.

Azuma, Hiroki. 2009. *Otaku: Japan's Database Animals*. Translated by Jonathan E. Abel and Shion Kono. University of Minnesota Press.

Azuma, Hiroki, and Akihiro Kitada. 2007. *Tokyo Kara Kangaeru (Thinking from Tokyo)*. NHK Books.

Ballús, Andreu, and Alba G. Torrents. 2014. Evangelion as Second Impact: Forever Changing That Which Never Was. *Mechademia* 9.

Barnes, Jonathan. 2001. *Early Greek Philosophy*. Penguin.

Benjamin, Walter. 2021. *Toward the Critique of Violence: A Critical Edition*. Stanford University Press.

Berque, Augustin. 2019. *Poetics of the Earth: Natural History and Human History*. Routledge.

———. 2014. *Thinking through Landscape*. Routledge.

———. 1993. *Toshi no Cosmology (Cosmology of the Cities)*. Kodansha.

———. 1986. *Le Sauvage et L'artifice: Les Japonais devant La Nature*. Gallimard.

Butler, Andrew M. 2003. Postmodernism and Science Fiction. In James and Mendlesohn 2003.

Campbell, Joseph. 2012 [1949]. *The Hero with a Thousand Faces*. New World Library.

Camus, Albert. 1955. *The Myth of Sisyphus*. Hamish Hamilton.

———. 1946. *The Stranger*. Editorial notes by Cyril Connolly. Knopf.

Cavallaro, Dani. 2009. *The Art of Studio Gainax*. McFarland.

Cavell, Stanley. 1990. *Conditions Handsome and Unhandsome: The Constitution of Emersonian Perfectionism*. University of Chicago Press.

Chroust, Anton-Hermann. 1961. The Origin of 'Metaphysics'. *Review of Metaphysics* 14:4.

Deleuze, Gilles. 1994. *Difference and Repetition*. Columbia University Press.

De Beauvoir, Simone. 1944. *Pyrrhus et Cinéas: A Cette Dame*. Translated by Marybeth Timmerman. Gallimard.

Derrida, Jacques. 1978. *Writing and Difference*. Routledge.

Eliade, Mircea. 2017. *Rites and Symbols of Initiation: The Mystery of Birth and Rebirth*. Spring.

Epictetus. 1916. *Epicteti Dissertationes ab Arriano Digestae*. Edited by H. Schenkl. Teubner.

Esposito, Roberto. 2011. *Immunitas: The Protection and Negation of Life*. Polity.

Frye, Northrop. 1957. *Anatomy of Criticism*. Princeton University Press.

Freud, Sigmund. 2016. *Civilization and Its Discontents*. Edited by Todd Dufresne. Broadview.

———. 1957a. *Beyond the Pleasure Principle*. Edited by John Rickman. Anchor.

———. 1957b. *The Ego and the Id: A General Selection from the Works of Sigmund Freud*. Edited by John Rickman. Anchor.

Girard, René. 1977 [1972]. *Violence and the Sacred*. Johns Hopkins University Press.

Grondin, Jean. 2012. *Introduction to Metaphysics: From Parmenides to Levinas*. Columbia University Press.

Guignon, Charles B. 2003a. *The Existentialists: Critical Essays on Kierkegaard, Nietzsche, Heidegger, and Sartre*. Rowman and Littlefield.

———. 2003b. Becoming a Self: The Role of Authenticity in *Being and Time* and Beyond. In Guignon 2003a.

Hart, David Bentley. 2013. *The Experience of God: Being, Consciousness, Bliss*. Yale University Press.

Hegel, G.W.F. 2018. *The Phenomenology of Spirit*. Cambridge University Press.

Heidegger, Martin. 2010. *Being and Time*. State University of New York Press.

Hermann, Erik. 2017. The Relevance of Remembering the Reformation. In *Concordia Journal* 43:1–2.

Howard, Christopher. 2014. The Ethics of Sekai-Kei: Reading Hiroki Azuma with Slavoj Žižek. *Science Fiction Film and Television* 7.

James, Edward, and Farah Mendlesohn, eds. 2003. *The Cambridge Companion to Science Fiction*. Cambridge University Press.

James, William. 2000. *Pragmatism and Other Writings*. Penguin.

Jameson, Fredric. 1991. *Postmodernism: Or, The Cultural Logic of Late Capitalism*. Duke University Press.

Kant, Immanuel. 1998. *The Cambridge Edition of the Works of Immanuel Kant: The Critique of Pure Reason*. Translated and Edited by Paul Guyer and Allen Wood. Cambridge University Press.

————. 2007. *Anthropology, History, and Education*. Translated and Edited by Günter Zöller and Robert B. Louden. Cambridge University Press.

————. 2012. *Groundwork of the Metaphysics of Morals*. Edited by Mary Gregor and Jens Timmermann. Cambridge University Press.

Kato, Mikiro. 2002. *Eiga no Ryobun (The Territory of Films)*. Filmartsha.

Kierkegaard, Søren. 1980. *The Sickness unto Death: A Christian Psychological Exposition for Upbuilding and Awakening*. Princeton University Press.

————. 1982. *Fear and Trembling / Repetition*. Edited and Translated by H.W. Hong and E.H. Hong. Princeton University Press.

Kornblith, Hilary. 2014. *A Naturalistic Epistemology: Selected Papers*. Oxford University Press.

————. 2002. *Knowledge and Its Place in Nature*. Oxford University Press.

Krämer, Hans-Joachim. 1990. *Plato and the Foundations of Metaphysics: A Work on the Theory of the Principles and Unwritten Doctrines of Plato with a Collection of the Fundamental Documents*. State University of New York Press.

Kuki, Shuzo. 1997. *Reflections on Japanese Taste: The Structure of Iki*. Power Publications.

————. 1991. *The Selected Essays of Shuzo Kuki*. Iwanamishoten.

Laitman, Michael. 2007. *Kabbalah for Beginners*. Laitman Kabbalah.

Laplanche, Jean. 1989. *New Foundations for Psychoanalysis*. Translated by David Macey. Blackwell.

Locke, John. 2002. *The Second Treatise of Government and A Letter Concerning Toleration*. Dover.

Lyotard, Jean-Francçois. 1984. *The Postmodern Condition: A Report on Knowledge*. University of Minnesota Press.

Maejima, Sotoshi. 2014. *What Is Sekai-Kei?* Seikasha-Bunko.

Marx, Karl H. 2008 [1867]. *Capital*. Oxford University Press.

Matheron, A. *Individu et Communauté chez Spinoza*. 1988. Paris: Les Édition de Minuit.

Mayeda, Graham. 2006. *Time, Space and Ethics in the Philosophy of Watsuji Tetsuro, Kuki Shuzo, and Martin Heidegger*. Routledge.

Merleau-Ponty, Maurice. 2010. *Child Psychology and Pedagogy: The Sorbonne Lectures 1949–1952*. Translated by Talia Welsh. Northwestern University Press.

Nietzsche, Friedrich. 1996. *Human, All Too Human*. Cambridge University Press.

Nishida, Kitaro. 1990. *An Inquiry into the Good*. Yale University Press.

Origen. 2017. *On First Principles*. Edited and translated by John Behr. Oxford University Press.

Paul, L.A. 2016. *Transformative Experiences*. Oxford University Press.

Pickstock, Catherine. 2013. *Repetition and Identity*. Oxford University Press.

Plato. 1997. *Complete Works*. Edited by John Cooper. Hackett.

Plotinus. 2018. *The Enneads*. Edited by Lloyd Gerson, Translated by George Boys-Stones. Cambridge University Press.

Reiner, Hans. 1990. The Emergence and Original Meaning of the Name 'Metaphysics'. *Graduate Faculty Philosophy Journal* 13:2.

Rilke, Rainer.1939. *Duino Elegies*. Translated by J.B. Leishman and Stephen Spender. Norton.

Sadamoto, Yoshiyuki. 2012. *Neon Genesis Evangelion*. English edition of the manga. Studio Gainax. VIZ Media.

Saito, Tamaki. 2011. *Beautiful Fighting Girl*. Translated by J. Keith Vincent and Dawn Lawson. University of Minnesota Press.

Sakuta, Kei'ichi. 1993. *Seisei no Shakaigaku wo Mezashite: Kachikan to Seikaku (Toward the Generative Sociology: On Valuing and Characters)*. Yuhikaku.

Sartre, Jean-Paul. 1976. *No Exit and Three Other Plays*. Translated by S. Gilbert and M.M.A. Gilbert. Vintage.

———. 1948 [1943]. *Being and Nothingness: A Phenomenological Essay on Ontology*. Translated by Hazel Barnes. Philosophical Library.

Sassen, Saskia. 2001. *The Global City: New York, London, Tokyo*. Second edition. Princeton University Press.

Schopenhauer, Arthur. 2016. *Parerga and Paralipomena: Short Philosophical Essays*. Two volumes. Oxford University Press.

Spinoza, Baruch. 1985.*The Collected Works of Spinoza Volume I*. Edited by E. Curley. Princeton University Press.

———. 2002. *Spinoza: Complete Works*. Hackett.

———. 2015. *Ética*. São Paulo: EDUSP.

Stevens, Wallace. 1984. The Idea of Order in Key West. In *Collected Poems*. Faber and Faber.

Thomas, Flynn. 2013. Jean-Paul Sartre. *The Stanford Encyclopedia of Philosophy*. Fall 2013 Edition. <https://plato.stanford.edu/archives/fall2013/entries/sartre/>.

Tsunehiro, Uno. 2011. *The Imagination of the Millennial Generation*. Hayakawa-Bunko.

Tsurumi, Yoshiyuki. 1993. *Namako no Me* [Eyes of a Sea Cucumber]. Tokyo: Chikuma Shobo.

Tucker, R.C., ed. 1978. *The Marx-Engels Reader*. Norton.

Valéry, Paul. 2001. *Notebooks Vol. 1*. Edited by Brain Stimpson. Peter Lang GmbH.

———. 2003. *Notebooks Vol. 2*. Edited by Paul Gifford. Peter Lang GmbH.

Vilas-Boas, Eric. 2019. Anime Classic Neon Genesis Evangelion Is Finally on Netflix. So Why Are Some Fans So Upset? Vulture. <www.vulture.com/2019/06/neon-genesis-evaNeon genesis evangelionlion-netflix-controversy-explained-guide.html>.

Walton, Kendall L. 1970. Categories of Art. *Philosophical Review*

79:3.

Washida, Kiyokazu. 2013. *Kyoto no Heinetsu (On the Normal Temperature of Kyoto: A Philosopher's Guide to the City)*. Kodansha.

Watsuji, Tetsuro. 1961. *Climate and Culture: A Philosophical Study*. Yusodo.

Whitman, Walt. 2009 [1855]. *Leaves of Grass*. Oxford University Press.

Williams, Rowan. 2014. *The Edge of Words: God and the Habits of Language*. Bloomsbury.

Yeats, W.B. 1989. *The Collected Poems of W.B. Yeats*. Edited by Richard. J. Finneran. Collier.

Pilots

DAVID BORDONABA-PLOU holds a PhD in Philosophy from the Universidad de Granada, Spain. He enjoys a postdoc scholarship awarded by the Fondo Nacional de Desarrollo Científico y Tecnológico (FONDECYT) at the Universidad de Valparaíso, Chile, with the project *A Computational Dynamic Analysis of Public Debates on Politics, Aesthetics and Taste*. He's an associate researcher at the Centro de Estudios en Filosofía, Lógica y Epistemología (CeFiLoE) of the Universidad de Valparaíso, Chile, and a member of the research group Filosofía y Análisis and the Unidad de Excelencia FiloLab from the Universidad de Granada, Spain.

ADAM BARKMAN holds a PhD from the Free University of Amsterdam and is Professor of Philosophy at Redeemer University College, Canada. He is the author or editor of thirteen books, including *Manga and Philosophy*. Among other things, Barkman teaches Kabbala in his Medieval Philosophy class, but when he does so, he's always got Shinji in the back of his mind.

HEATHER BROWNING is a zookeeper turned philosopher who currently works as a research officer in animal sentience and welfare at the London School of Economics. She holds a PhD from the Australian National University in Canberra, which looks at some philosophical issues in the measurement of animal welfare. Her primary research areas are animal welfare, ethics, and consciousness with occasional forays into pop culture and other topics.

LUCA CABASSA is a PhD student in Philosophy at the Philosophy PhD joint Program (University of Pisa / University of Florence, Italy). The project focuses on the historical-critical analysis of some fundamental notions in the construction of contemporary biological knowledge. In particular, the focus is on the phenomena of conceptual crossing-over performed by some metaphors derived from mathematical contexts or programming theory and the epistemological assumptions underlying such application. He cyclically sinks into the world of *Neon Genesis Evangelion*.

MATTEO CAPARRINI is a graduate student in Philosophy at the University of Padua, Italy. His PhD project deals with different grammars of law and legal pluralism. In particular, he's busy trying to imagine what kind of future there is for law in a political organization that goes well beyond traditional States. To surpass traditional ways of organizing the body politic also means studying the attempts at radical change that have been tried throughout our recent history. For him, *Neon Genesis Evangelion* is a reminder that this kind of radical change is possible.

MARC CHEONG is a digital ethicist at the Centre for AI and Digital Ethics, University of Melbourne, Australia. He has a high sync rate with both disciplines of computer science and philosophy, and his ongoing research explores the possibility of existential authenticity on social media (in our world, not Shinji's). Given a choice, his idea of 'instrument-ality' is to play his harmonica and drink cheap whiskey in an eternal recurrence, rather than the one proposed in the TV version of *Evangelion*.

JEREMY CHRISTENSEN has served as a communication and English professor, as well as debate coach, at institutions across the US for the past twenty years. Currently, his academic focus is irritating his two children with forced puns and tours of roadside kitsch and his fiancé with references to obscure Eighties movies.

JONAS FARIA COSTA is a third-year PhD candidate in Philosophy at the University of Manchester. His main research interest is philosophy of action and social ontology. In his research, he takes an interdisciplinary approach encompassing social psychology, game theory, and philosophy. The focus of his research is analyzing the difference between individual and collective agency and the difference between private and public spaces.

CHRISTIAN COTTON is an independent scholar and freelance author. He has taught philosophy at Piedmont College and the University of Georgia. He remains unsure exactly what Shinji's deal is.

KHEGAN M. DELPORT is a Research Fellow in the Department of Systematic Theology and Ecclesiology at the University of Stellenbosch and Technical Editor of the *Stellenbosch Theological Journal*.

HANS-GEORG EILENBERGER is a doctoral researcher at the Department of Culture Studies at Tilburg University (the Netherlands). He is interested in how people make sense of the passage of time and is currently running a project on the lived experiences of aging and old age. Apart from his soft spot for twentieth-century French philosophy, Hans-Georg is enthusiastic about Buddhist ontology and growing plants. He has yet to try his hand at watermelons.

DAVID FAJARDO-CHICA is a bipedal biological entity who holds a PhD in philosophy and is enrolled as a postdoctoral researcher in the Mental Health and Psychiatry Department at Universidad Nacional Autónoma de México. He does research on pain and sufferings from a philosophical approach informed by psychology and health sciences. David enjoys sci-fi anime dramas, role-playing games, and skirmish-level war games as temporary and therapeutical dy-synchronization from his body.

ERIC HOLMES is an instructor at Purdue University Global and is pursuing his PhD at the University of South Florida. His primary academic interest is horror and he has published critical works on *Dexter, Stranger Things*, and EC Comics. He's proud of the fact that his student evaluations are usually better than the public response to *Neon Genesis Evangelion*'s final episode.

YUUKI NAMBA is an independent research and holds an MA in Art Theory from Kobe University at Hyogo, Japan. He writes in the areas of aesthetics and philosophy of popular culture, especially science fiction. He is currently researching on science-fiction prototyping. He hopes children will find a truth in the end.

GIONATAN C. PACHECO is a PhD candidate in the Universidade Federal de Santa Maria. His greater interest is to think of his homeland, the underdeveloped pre-adamic paradise that is Brazil. He is proudly both a gaucho admirer of the Guarani culture and, at the same time, an otaku interested in the high-tech-post-apocalyptical hell that is Eva's universe.

LUKA PERUŠIĆ is currently a PhD student at the Faculty of Humanities and Social Sciences of the University of Zagreb, where he researches the bioethical aspects of contemporary science. He co-founded the Croatian Association for Scientific Communication and serves as its vice-president.

JAKE POTTER is the student ministries pastor at Christ Fellowship in McKinney, Texas, where he serves middle school and high school students in the only youth group that he is aware of where kids feel comfortable coming to church in full cosplay. He received his ThM from Dallas Theological Seminary, with an emphasis in Intercultural Ministry. He has a strong passion for mission work in Japan, and using pop-culture as a way to talk about Jesus. He even wrote his thesis on *Neon Genesis Evangelion*! He moderates one of the largest Evangelion discussion groups on Facebook, evangelion seriousposting. Jake has had his work published in many magazines and papers, but most of his published work is in music. He is the lead vocalist and song writer for metalcore band Crucify the Flesh, which has released two full length records and several singles. He is married to his best friend Katie, whom he loves more than anything in the whole world.

YOSHIHIRO TANIGAWA is a Specially Appointed Lecturer in the Department of Design (Product Design) at the Kyoto City University of Arts. He works in the areas of philosophy, pedagogy, and cultural sociology.

WALTER VEIT is a naturalist philosopher with interdisciplinary interests ranging through philosophy, economics, biology, and cognitive science. Having studied in the UK, the US, Germany, and Finland, and even working for a while in the European Parliament, he is currently pursuing a PhD in Australia in the History and Philosophy of Science, looking into the evolution of consciousness.

ZACHARY VEREB is a Visiting Assistant Professor in the Public Policy Leadership Department at the University of Mississippi, where he teaches courses in applied ethics, the philosophy of leadership, critical thinking, and public policy. He completed his doctorate in philosophy at the University of South Florida. His research focuses on the relevance and application of Kant's philosophy for environmental ethics and climate change, including its political and ethical dimensions. He is also interested in modern and post-Kantian philosophy.

NATHAN VISSER is interested in the intersection between philosophy and psychology, particularly issues of free will and responsibility. When not thinking deeply about popular culture and anime, he thinks about Plato.

ANDREW M. WINTERS teaches philosophy and religious studies at Yavapai College in Prescott, Arizona. He wonders whether we're experiencing the Third Impact or whether humanity is going through its own adolescence.

DENIZ YENIMAZMAN holds a Master's Degree in Interactive Media: Critical Theory and Practice from Goldsmiths College, London, and a PhD in Philosophy and Aesthetics from the University of Arts and Design in Karlsruhe. He teaches media studies at the University of Bayreuth. Deniz is currently working on the topic of power, violence, and secrecy from a theological and technological perspective.

SANO YASUYUKI is an Assistant Professor in the Graduate School of Human and Environmental Studies at Kyoto University. He specializes in phenomenology, existential philosophy, and French philosophy. He is a reviewer of Japanese popular culture (manga, anime, light novels, and science fiction) with experience as an initial screener of a prize for new writers of light novels and a writer for *S-F Magazine*.

Index